THE SPIRIT OF OPEN ADOPTION

The Spirit of Open Adoption

James L. Gritter

CWLA Press • Washington, DC

CWLA Press is an imprint of the
Child Welfare League of America, Inc.

© 1997 Child Welfare League of America, Inc.

CHILD WELFARE LEAGUE OF AMERICA, INC.
440 First Street, NW, Third Floor, Washington, DC 20001-2085
Email: books@cwla.org

CURRENT PRINTING (last digit)
10 9 8 7 6 5 4 3 2 1

Cover and text design by Sarah Knipschild

Printed in the United States of America
ISBN # 0–87868–637-1

Gritter, James L., 1950-
        The spirit of open adoption / James L. Gritter.
        p.   cm.
        Includes bibliographical references.
        ISBN 0-87868-637-1 (pbk.)
        1. Open adoption--United States.   I. Title.
HV875.55.G75   1997
362.73′4′0973--dc21

To my father, Richard Gritter,
a wise and gentle man of great faith.

All who are guided by the Spirit of God are sons [and daughters] of God: for what you received was not the spirit of slavery to bring you back into fear; you have received the spirit of adoption....

Romans 8:14–5 *(New Jerusalem Bible)*

Contents

Acknowledgments

Gratitude is the heart of this book. It is an important dynamic in adoption, and it is an important aspect of writing about adoption as well. I am deeply thankful for the support and inspiration of many people who helped *The Spirit of Open Adoption* come to life.

My gratitude begins with people I've never met but who have affected my thinking enormously. Do writers like Henri Nouwen, Lewis Smedes, David Steindl-Rast, and Frederick Buechner ever wonder if their efforts are in vain? I imagine they do, but I hope they and many others like them will press ahead with their explorations of the Spirit. I presume their honesty, grace, and gentleness is relevant to every field, but I am certain their message of hope is important in the realm of adoption. Their insights open us to many possibilities.

I am thankful to Marcy Axeness, journalist, thinker, and adoptee, who offered a number of very useful ideas that helped organize the flow of ideas. And of course, I appreciate the willingness of the Child Welfare League of America to enter the fray and publish *The Spirit of Open Adoption*. It is written in a tone that is a little different than most of their books, and I am glad for their willingness to stretch. Special thanks to CWLA editor Steve Boehm, who caught the tone of the book and graciously smoothed off its rough edges.

I am grateful to a number of leading people in the field—Pat Dorner, Reuben Pannor, Joyce Pavao, Sharon Roszia, and Randy Severson—who reviewed the manuscript and offered encouragement along the way. Sincere affirmation from the best minds and hearts in open adoption is, to say the least, extremely gratifying. Everyone should have such friends. I am particularly thankful to Reuben, Sharon, and Randy for following the book's progress chapter by chapter and offering speedy commentary. As *The Spirit of Open Adoption* took shape, friendships were nourished with frequent communication.

I am thankful for bright, committed, and spiritually sensitive colleagues through the years at Catholic Human Services: Tim Uhlmann, Mike Hardy, Sister Pat Ace, Ellen Campbell, Audrey Juola, John Feys, my longtime goofy sidekick Abbie Nelson, and secretaries who took sincere interest in this amazing journey. Together we thought, fought, prayed, and dared our way into new territory. I am thankful for the trust of administrators and board members like Dick Beachnau, Chuck Veeser, Dave Martin, and Don Miles. Progress requires vulnerability, and vulnerability is never a comfortable place for those in charge. We would not have gone far without their trust.

As I travel to share our open adoption experience with professionals in different parts of the country, I have met many outstanding practitioners. They are inquisitive, thoughtful, and good-hearted. They are gifts to their communities, and they give me great hope for the future of adoption. Several of them—Sister Karen Yesh from Catholic Social Services in Anchorage, Alaska; Dave Zimmerman from Catholic Social Services in Houghton, Michigan; Christine Grey from Christian Family Care in Phoenix, Arizona; Susan Massa from Catholic Community Services in Colorado Springs, Colorado; and Terri Winterberg, Mary Fleishman, and Monica Kuhlman from Catholic Service Bureau in Covington, Kentucky—kindly reviewed the manuscript with an eye toward relevance. I was pleased when they reported that it squared with their experience in open adoption.

Obviously I owe the most to the many incredible participants who bet their happiness on our program. To them, open adoption is not just something interesting; it is their life story. They continue to share generously. I have learned from close friends like the Vander Haagens, who allow me to enter the reality of open adoption on a daily basis. I also have had the advantage of learning from astonishingly articulate participants like Michael Spry, Brenda Romanchik, Dan Wolf, and many others like them. It seems there is something about the fresh air of Northern Michigan that enables them to describe their thoughts and feelings with exceptional warmth and clarity.

Finally, I am thankful for an understanding wife and patient children. A dad parked at the computer every night isn't much fun. Good news, though. With the book finished, maybe I can fix the door that's been driving us nuts. Of course, there are a few new ideas I should take a little time to explore....

Introduction

One Worker's Journey

Thinking without roots will bear flowers, but no fruit.

Abraham Heschel, *I Asked for Wonder**

I would like to achieve a state of inner spiritual grace from which I could function and give as I was meant to in the eye of God.

Anne Morrow Lindberg, *A Gift from the Sea*

In the introduction to my book, *Adoption Without Fear*, I shared a brief account of my professional journey through the world of adoption. I was surprised how many members of the adoption triad reacted with interest to that information. It is almost as though they were surprised to discover that the adoption experience affects the professionals who organize and carry it out. It most surely does.

I believe the experiences of the participants and the professional are intertwined; we are in it together. Recently, a family called wanting to enter our program at Catholic Human Services. They indicated that they had already adopted a child through open adoption, and they were eager to impress me with their experience. I asked what program they had worked with, and they responded enthusiastically about the marvelous virtues

---

* *Most references to specific works will be found in the bibliography at the end of this book. When a work cited in the text does not appear in the bibliography, the source is footnoted.*

of open adoption. Two more questions about the professionals they had worked with netted similarly evasive responses. Finally, it occurred to me that they did not intend to tell me with whom they had worked because they were ashamed of the service provider. His poor reputation loomed over their experience detracting from the pride and satisfaction they found in their adoption. Clearly, for better or worse, the worker affects and is affected by the process.

The professional has an indisputable obligation to be objective. Often, this obligation is interpreted as a mandate to stay disengaged and maintain emotional distance. There is some wisdom in that view. It is, after all, easy to lose one's bearings in a sea of emotions and lose one's usefulness, but it does not seem reasonable to conclude that any form of emotional investment will be fatal to objectivity. It is hardly a simple matter, but I believe it is possible to be emotionally invested while maintaining intellectual objectivity. As writer Madeleine L'Engle puts it in *A Circle of Quite*, "Detachment and involvement: The artist must have both. The link between them is compassion." Things seem to go better when I feel the freedom to become personally invested in the challenges of the moment, when I put what highly respected business writer Max DePree calls "emotional labor" into the process. I am convinced it is possible to fully experience the intense emotions of adoption and still objectively keep one's feet on the ground.

An effective worker is one with the message. If the message is courage and candor, that is what the role requires of the worker. If the goal is friendship between birthfamilies and adoptive families, then the worker, if he or she is to carry the message with integrity, must be a friend. If the participants are immersed in pain, the professional is as well. If, on the other hand, the participants are celebrating their shared accomplishments, the worker joins in the revelry—all the while, of course, keeping an eye on the big picture.

NECESSARY FOR WHO?

Scenes and sensations from the days preceding open adoption are seared into my memory forever. In those days, it was routine for a birthparent to put her total trust in me, an act of phenomenal faith that terrified both of us.* To find peace of mind and justify this massive trust, she told herself that this was a reasonable thing to do. She reasoned: "You're a nice person, and it's clear that you care about me and my baby. I think you might even be halfway on the ball. I know you'll put my baby with a wonderful, loving family, won't you? Won't you??" That logic may have relieved some of her anxiety, but it added significantly to mine. She needed more reassurance than I could realistically offer. I especially remember the unnerving comment of one birthmother who looked me in the eye and declared, "I don't worry about the adoptive parents at all because I'm sure they are just like you." In the absence of real information, I, of all people, represented the fantasy parents.

The moments of separation were especially daunting. I recall many occasions when I would peer into a hospital room to make sure I was in the right place. The young lady I had come to know and respect from weeks of planning would be there resting, her face radiating the contentment and fulfillment unique to a fresh mother. My arrival never failed to affect the atmosphere dramatically. In an instant, the tranquillity drained from her face, replaced by four-alarm panic. I was the social work equivalent of the Grim Reaper, on site to claim her baby. The necessary work accomplished, I would hustle back to the office to debrief with my kindred-spirit colleague, Abbie Nelson. Together we would commiserate, weep, and decide to resign from this wrenching undertaking. I knew I was not cut out for life as an adoption worker; I knew that, over time, this work would dull the parts of me I liked the best. There was only so much of the wilting pain of permanent separation that I could tolerate. A few weeks later, though, the withering drama would resume as I accompanied the wide-eyed birthmother to court, where the judge would ask whether it was her intention to "execute" a release of parental rights. Her rights would be "terminated," and her life as a ghost would begin.

You see, what the introduction to the first book did not reveal is that open adoption was not necessary just for the benefit of the birthparents, adoptive parents, and adoptees—it was also necessary for me.

---

* *References to birthparents will be feminine, reflecting the sad fact that birthfathers, for various reasons, usually are not as involved in the adoption drama as birthmothers. Birthfathers are discussed in Chapter 9.*

When we shifted from closed to open adoption, we knew that all of us—birthparents, adoptive parents, adoptees, and professionals—were heading into a wilderness of unscouted possibilities where all things were possible. We probably should have been consumed with fear, but, oddly, we were not. Although there was no way at that point to predict the effectiveness of the open approach to adoption, we looked to the future with confidence. We were convinced that there had to be a better way. Our confidence was based on the simple belief that an approach based on candor and transparency would not lead to disaster. From a less positive perspective, we were sufficiently disenamored with the closed system to conclude that we did not have much to lose.

It was immediately clear to us that the open approach to adoption felt better. We were encouraged and excited, but the change to full open adoption did not occur overnight. We learned that clients ask for the amount of openness that we as workers were comfortable in offering. Since we had a substantial amount of consolidating and growing to do as professionals, client requests for open adoption started slowly and grew gradually. Looking back, I feel sad for those who failed to take advantage of the innovations available during our transition, but the gradual pace of change kept us from feeling overwhelmed.

Keys to Growth

There was much to learn, and the avenues for learning were—and, of course, continue to be—endless. The initial key to growth was a commitment to listening. At the outset, we knew more about what we wanted to avoid in adoption than what we wanted to accomplish through the process. Negative information was readily available to anyone willing to listen to the excruciating accounts from the accelerating numbers of birthparents and adoptees who resented the closed system of adoption. It was not easy listening though, for the adoption professional was invariably painted with villainous colors. The angry tone of the commentary led many professionals to discount this invaluable feedback. Ironically, trained listeners often have difficulty hearing the message. Where some heard the voice of misfits and extremists, we heard the voice of prophets. Those who carry the most pain often possess the most crucial information.

We also listened intently to other professionals who, like ourselves, were searching for more effective procedures. In the early days of open adoption, I had the impression that a handful of social workers around the country were in their basements quietly brewing new ideas. Many stayed in the basement because they felt they could get more done with a low profile. Others were too modest to draw attention to themselves. Whatever the reasons, open adoption programs labored for years in isolation. At Catholic Human Services, we were fortunate to find a few kindred spirits early, and those connections added to our courage.* Open adoption proponents, few in number and often facing vitriolic opposition, felt great loyalty to each other. Sadly, the single-mindedness of purpose that once characterized open adoption advocates has diminished in direct proportion to the general acceptance of open adoption. These days we can afford, apparently, the unhappy luxury of dissension.

A second crucial source of growth was imagination, a powerful tool that is frequently underestimated. To prepare for the unknowns of open adoption, we pondered the issues from every vantage we could generate. Because we had given so much consideration to the potential problems of open adoption, it sometimes occurred to me that I could have been a formidable opponent of open adoption. It was an amusing thought. Actually, responsible opposition would have been welcome because it would have helped to clarify and sharpen the issues. Unfortunately, the opposition that did emerge preferred to muddy the waters and defend their point of view on the basis of emotions. At any rate, our exercises in imagination were worth the effort, because we have anticipated most of the situations we have encountered over the years.

The third and most valuable source of instruction and growth was experience. In the early days, every open adoption was a novel foray into exotic territory, and every adoption constituted an obvious opportunity to learn. Operating without the benefit of experience, we had no protocol; every decision required fresh thinking. Lacking precedent, we had no idea what was "normal" in open adoption and what was not. Happily, with the passage of time, the territory feels less exotic and less anxious.

---

* *The agency originally was called Community, Family, and Children Services, later changed to CFCS–Catholic Charities, and presently Catholic Human Services. Although the name has changed through the years, the philosophy of the adoption program has endured.*

Our trepidation has been replaced with pleasant anticipation as we wonder what we will learn from each new arrangement that comes together.

The most crucial experience was surviving our first "catastrophe," otherwise known as a birthmother changing her mind about adoption after the prospective adoptive family had taken the baby into their home and hearts on an "at risk" basis. Because of our system's lingering overidentification with adoptive parents, we dreaded this possibility more than any other. There were many sins that could be overlooked in adoption, but we doubted that anyone could forgive the disappointing of a prospective adoptive family. They were, after all, victims of severe biological disappointment, card-carrying members of the middle class, paying customers, and most likely future board members. Lurking in the unconscious somewhere was the impression that it would be a simple matter for a disappointed couple to make a social worker's life miserable.

Our first "disaster" started in typically promising fashion. The birthmother selected the Thomases, a particularly likable family with a laid back lifestyle. The families were obviously compatible, and plans moved forward. The baby was born healthy and adorable. The prospective adoptive mother's mother flew from a distant state to lend an experienced hand to the awesome project of baby care. Shortly after arrival, grandma bought church raffle tickets in the names of each of her grandchildren. In story book fashion, the new baby was a hundred-dollar raffle winner; the omens were all positive.

Two weeks later, the scene shifted dramatically. The birthfather decided to pursue custody, a prospect that the birthmother found abhorrent. Panicked by that possibility, she decided to summarily resolve the matter by resuming custody of the baby herself. An unprecedented moment of truth was upon us.

We called the Thomases with the news and listened to their stunned silence over the phone. The plan called for them to return the baby the next day. We had failed our unofficial social work mandate to engineer a happily-ever-after outcome, and our fears had 24 hours to multiply exponentially as we awaited the devastation of "the worst that could happen."

The next day, the Thomases carried the flag of all would-be adoptive families with magnificence. Through their tears, they shared with absolute sincerity, "This is a beautiful baby. She is relaxed, easy to take care of, and completely lovable. What's more, she's a prizewinning baby, and we want to share this"—the envelope with the raffle winnings—"so everybody gets off to a good start. We are thankful for the opportunity to be part of her life story. God bless this new family."

A bitter family might have stalled our progress indefinitely, but the Thomases blessed our program with extraordinary grace and dignity under unimaginable pressure. They moved the program forward by demonstrating that we could survive the worst that could happen. They taught us that prospective adoptive parents are stronger and more loving than we had ever recognized in the days of our patronizing overprotection. And, as fate would have it, during the two weeks the Thomases had the baby, they conceived miraculously and truly did live happily ever after.

Over the years, our language for these situations has shifted from *catastrophe* to *disaster* to *reversal* to *turnabout* to *change of heart*. Michael Spry, one of the most insightful adoptive parents to go through our program, and an outspoken advocate for ethical standards in the field, noted that there is a certain justice in the change-of-heart circumstance. Prospective adoptive parents are asked to do what they have asked birthparents to consider; namely, placing a treasured child into someone else's arms. Just or unjust, these situations test the characters of everyone involved; and in an odd way, they constitute some of the most beautiful moments for our program. We marvel at the strength of character demonstrated by prospective parents in the face of devastated hope. Open adoption hinges on their integrity.

For all the risks associated with open adoption, it was quickly apparent that our adoptive parents enjoyed it. They liked the candor. They liked the greater control over the experience that open adoption gave them. They liked the improved information they received. They liked the chance to be involved with the baby in the hospital. They liked being able to express gratitude to the people who deserved it. They just plain liked it.

"Always Tragic"

I became a better-than-average adoption worker on April 15, 1982. Our agency was holding the first national conference to center exclusively on open adoption, and the first day was over. The presentations had gone very well, and I was filled with the excitement of the conference. I strolled out of the meeting room with Lee Campbell, the bright and gutsy founder of Concerned United Birthparents and a key presenter at the conference. "Lee," I said as we exited the room side by side, "this open adoption thing is really neat." I kept babbling and moved a few steps further before I noticed she was no longer at my side. I turned to see that my comment had literally stopped her in her tracks. "Neat? *Neat? Adoption neat??*" Apparently, she had not put the two words together before. "Jim," she said with an unusual mixture of intensity and kindness, "adoption is always tragic." And that stopped me in my tracks. It was easily the most important lesson I have learned in the course of my work in adoption.

The extent of the denial of pain associated with adoption is almost conspiratorial. Everyone seems in such a hurry to get to the good news of adoption that the issue of pain is overlooked and short-suited. The joy of adoption is amazingly seductive, and it is an extremely rare program that honors the pain that exists at the core of the experience. Most descriptions of adoption feature the gains but are interestingly silent about the losses. I believe this pain-cleansed version of adoption creates credibility problems for the institution. Can there really be all this gain without loss? A sugarcoated perspective on adoption is offensive because it trivializes the life experience of everyone involved. To me, adoption without pain feels like adoption without love.

Noticing that adoption programs handle the issue of pain in various ways, it occurred to me that there are actually many variations on the open adoption theme, and they are not equally effective. Another of our outstanding adoptive parents, Dan Wolf, taught us to differentiate our form of open adoption. His advice led us to label our style of adoption to distinguish it from other variations on the theme. There were many appropriate qualifying words to put on our approach to adoption— covenantal, consensus, child-centered, integrity—but we settled on *values-based open adoption*. Values had provided our original foundation, and now, as we matured in our understanding, we learned that they could also supply the vision. By projecting our values into the realm of outcomes, we developed a clear sense of direction. With this breakthrough, we not only knew why we were doing what we were doing, but also what it was that we were trying to do.

Differentiation leads naturally to considerations of quality. If there truly are variations on the open adoption theme, it is sensible to try to determine which forms are most promising. A major purpose of this book is to explore the meaning of quality in adoption. As open adoption diversifies, and as standards of quality emerge, it is increasingly difficult to generalize about open adoption. I am not interested in furthering open adoption in every form. In some forms, open adoption generates predictable frustration. Only the most mature manifestations of open adoption deserve continuing consideration; and even then, we do well to stay alert for problems. We must recognize that even the most promising variations on the theme are imperfect and filled with pain.

Relationships, Leadership, and Spirituality

Our agency's journey toward open adoption began with concern for birthparents. As mentioned earlier, it quickly found unexpected favor with adoptive parents. I am ashamed to admit that it took several years for the most crucial reason to move ahead with open adoption—the meaning it has for adopted children—to truly sink in. From the beginning, we expected open adoption would benefit the children, but that prediction was incidental to our purposes. Mostly, we did open adoption because it met the needs of the adults involved.

Experience has completely altered our thinking. Although much remains to be learned about the meaning of open adoption for children, our observations so far are very encouraging. Children raised from infancy in the open system of adoption view it as normal, and they are very secure in their relationships. We believe open adoption offers vital opportunities for the important people in the life of the child to affirm him, opportunities that the closed system was unable to provide. Based on our observations regarding the positive effect of open adoption on children, we now believe the foremost reason to do open adoption is to benefit the children.

This realization has completely revitalized our commitment to open adoption and interestingly has lessened our tolerance for those who dabble with open adoption. Many service providers cheerfully offer a smorgasbord of adoption alternatives. Pleasing as that sounds, it leaves me wondering about the sort of host that smiles while offering guests, among other possibilities, poison apples.

Our understanding of open adoption is continually maturing. Many growth spurts have followed the discovery of certain gateway words—words rich in meaning that capture crucial ideas especially well. The simple word *relationship*, for example, completely altered our understanding of open adoption. Once it registered that open adoption is at heart a relationship, it made obvious sense to reorganize our process of preparing our clients to reflect that realization.

Another breakthrough word is *leadership*. This word emerged when an experienced open adoption agency asked for training because they were confused about the professional's role in the process. It seemed to them that they had turned everything over to their clients, and now there was nothing left for them to do. Although open adoption professionals are far less controlling than their counterparts in the closed system, the role remains formidable. In fact, I believe open adoption makes workers more indispensable than ever before. The role of the professional is best summarized as leader. Effective professionals will study the leadership role and learn to function comfortably in it.

Spirituality is another gateway word. In his fascinating book, *Adoption: Charms and Rituals for Healing*, Randolph Severson— a psychologist with a poet's heart—notes that adoption is "essentially a spiritual relationship." There is great truth and great promise in that observation, promise that we should not underestimate. Although adoption in some form or another has been around forever, our understanding of it is almost primitive; neither its science nor its art is well-developed. Research interest in adoption is growing, and hopefully the social science of adoption will move forward as a result. I wish these researchers well—their efforts will be helpful; but insofar as adoption is ultimately a matter of the heart and spirit, I am convinced the mysteries of adoption will persevere. At heart, adoption truly is a spiritual relationship, and this book is a conscious effort to begin to understand the implications of that truth.

SECRECY AND SHAME

The adoption scene was dominated for decades by secrecy. For years, I understood secrecy from three perspectives: historic, functional, and problematic. From the vantage point of history, clearly secrecy was well intended. It developed as a means to protect adoptees and birthparents from the censure of their communities. The goal of secrecy was to spare them the stigma of devastating labels like "bastard" and "fallen woman" at a time in history when such diminished status was disastrous. In positive terms, secrecy sought to preserve the opportunity for adoptees and birthparents to participate in their communities as full-status members. It is crucial to note, however, that the protection offered birthparents and adoptees was from the censure of the community, not from each other.

The historical perspective is useful to explain the origin of secrecy; but in the face of dramatically altered social conditions, it does not explain its continuation. With the stigma of illegitimacy fading rapidly, the need for protection has dwindled. What, then, sustains the secret-based system? If it does not meet the needs of most adoptees and birthparents, why keep it? The obvious answer is that it meets someone else's needs. Two major groups have lobbied for the retention of secrecy: adoptive parents and adoption professionals. Many adoptive parents fear openness because they are afraid they will somehow lose their children. Secrecy gives them the power of exclusivity, but sadly, power is an unpromising foundation for enduring family life. Secrecy also made adoption practitioners powerful. As the only fully informed players in the drama, adoption workers were in total control of the process. Their control was cemented by the privilege of confidentiality, which insulated them from any form of accountability. I am convinced, to the extent it perseveres, the current function of secrecy is more control than protection.

Most of the time, I simply viewed secrecy as a problem. It was the enemy and, as such, was a factor to contend with and overcome. A disheartening amount of my time was and is spent attending to the aftermath of secrecy, as searching birthparents and adoptees ask assistance in their search efforts. Let there be no confusion about this: Secrecy is a tremendous problem for adoptees. The institution claims that, more than anything, it seeks to serve the adoptee; but judging by performance, the institution has obviously lied.

More recently, I have come to understand secrecy from a fourth perspective: as a symptom. Secrecy is symptomatic of a much deeper issue—namely, shame. Adoption founders as an institution because it is built on a foundation of shame. For decades, adoption has functioned essentially as a two-step process of disowning and owning. In that form, it is an almost perfect script for shame, for there is great shame in disowning and owning; and, obviously, there is great shame in being disowned and in being owned. Shame is a matter of defect, powerlessness, and rejection—all familiar themes in adoption. Very familiar.

This simple observation has completely altered my thinking about adoption. It is so easy to get tangled in the endless symptoms of shame—denial, avoidance, haste, manipulation, rage, secrecy—that one never gets to the root issue. The symptoms will not disappear until their source withers and loses vitality. Secrecy and the other symptoms will linger as factors in adoption in proportion to the shame that remains undetected and unrelieved.

I believe shame is at the heart of adoption as we have known it in our lifetime. It is the DNA of closed adoption. If that is an accurate appraisal, it raises an immediate question: How do we explain the great variety of people we all know who came through that experience in good condition? Their health does not testify to the effectiveness of that system of adoption; they shine in spite of the system, not because of it. For the most part, I believe the historic shortcomings of adoption are in the design of the institution, not in the people who live it out. If birthfamilies, adoptive families, and adoptees are sufficiently ingenious to make a seriously flawed system work, it is exciting to consider what they will accomplish within the structure of a healthier system.

Unaddressed shame is incredibly resilient. As long as adoption is built on a foundation of shame, its capacity for wholesome outcomes will be significantly limited. On the other hand, if we transform adoption from a shaming process into an honoring process, we will experience dramatically different results. It will not be easy to redeem adoption from the burden of shame—the ultimate remedy is to transform adoption into a truly healthy institution, and good health does not seem second nature for adoption.

The effort to redeem adoption is sure to be a struggle. As we gain on the problem of secrecy, we are rapidly losing ground to commercialism. Although few recognize it, adoption is shifting from a professional service to a business. This shift is significant and worrisome. In a professional model of service delivery, participants reasonably assume that the practitioner's self-interest is under control. In a business climate, however, the assumption is "consumer beware." Furthermore, in the professional model, fees are usually linked directly to services rendered. The commercial approach views fees as a matter of whatever the market will bear. Given the unbalanced nature of supply and demand in the realm of infant adoption, the commercial approach to adoption has tremendous potential for financial abuse. Money has always loomed as a worrisome element in adoption, and a commercial approach to adoption is certain to exacerbate the problem.

The institution's vital signs are mixed. While commercial adoption grows, healthy programs generate increasingly wholesome adoptions. One of our wisest birthparents, Brenda Romanchik, declared at a recent conference: "No matter what the circumstance, I have always acknowledged my son Matthew. I have never denied his existence and never will." She affirms him publicly, privately, and at times when he does not even know about it. Is it any surprise that Matthew has a wholesome attitude toward his adoption? Brenda reminds us that adoption is capable of health.

The purpose of this book is to stimulate thought about ways to transform adoption into a healthy institution. The future is very uncertain. As currently practiced, adoption ranges from repulsive to magnificent; it encompasses the shameful and the transcendent.

Some in this field see nothing but pain, while others deny the pain and see nothing but beauty. I see them both. Pain and beauty are not antithetical dynamics. To the contrary, they are closely related. Pain does not always lead to beauty, but it often presents the potential for beauty. I am convinced that most of the beauty in the realm of adoption is integrally linked to its pain.

Sometimes people interested in adoption are pigeonholed into one of two camps. There are those who are for adoption, and those who are against it. I find that a pitiful simplification of the issues. Adoption is not a singular phenomena. Am I in favor of a shame-perpetuating form of adoption? Absolutely not. Am I in favor of an honor-based approach to adoption? Certainly. An honoring form of adoption will never eliminate the pain, but it can without question generate beauty. I have seen situations where adoption returned the sparkle of life to the eyes of everyone involved. When a 3-month-old child's eyes change from vacant to inquisitive in two day's time, something undeniably important is going on.

REPLACING SHAME WITH HONOR

The time has come for us to revisit and rework our most basic understandings. How do we justify this life-altering experience called adoption? It is a frightening question, because our answers will surely reverberate through all of our subsequent actions. With international adoption, we point to socioeconomic issues and note that abject poverty is often fatal. In special-needs adoption, social surgery is justified by the documented shortcomings of the original family. In that context, adoption seeks to remedy significant life threatening or life diminishing dynamics. But how do we justify infant adoption? In years past, the rationale was primarily a mixture of socioeconomic and moral necessity. Can this rationale sustain the practice of adoption in an era in which single parents enjoy at least some measure of economic and moral support? Vestiges of social and moral pressures remain, but it appears that infant adoption has largely evolved from a "yielding to pressure" or have-to process to an elective one. This makes an enormous difference. Whereas in the past the most crucial issues driving adoption were connected to the birthparent reality, these days the fundamental question of adoption is, "How can we most effectively meet the emotional needs of children?" The contemporary basis for infant adoption might be referred to as "psychological upward mobility."

Needless to say, this view of adoption is debatable. It immediately generates several crucial questions: Can a plan that begins with a profound loss offer more promise than a course of action that features continuity of parental care? How crucial is the continuity of care offered by the birthfamily? Will it really be continuous; or will it, in practical terms, involve greater discontinuity? What toll is extracted by this loss? What does *readiness* for parenting mean, and how important is it? What is the impact of poverty? How important are fathers?

If psychological upward mobility truly is the contemporary rationale for adoption, we must get serious about learning what this means. We must face the fact that if we do not quickly become very skilled at meeting the emotional needs of those who are adopted, infant adoption becomes very difficult to justify. It becomes, in fact, a farce.

The shame that has dominated adoption for so many years must be replaced with honor. Yes, honor. Some will no doubt scoff at this idea. They live in a mercenary world of calculation and expediency and have concluded that honor is an archaic, perhaps even silly, idea. They have given up on honor. They operate in an value-drained world where cynicism prevails. Instead of making a case against honor, I believe they document the need for it.

We need honor, but it frightens us because it calls us to personal responsibility. All of us long for honor, and each of us, as a private act of moral courage, is fully capable of producing it. Furthermore, if anything can motivate us to seek honor, I believe it is the innocence of children. If we cannot hazard the vulnerability of honor for the sake of children, the cynicism is deserved.

In *The Gift of Honor*, family experts Gary Smalley and John Trent offer an impressive and helpful definition:

> Honor is a decision we make to place high value, worth, and importance on another person by viewing him or her as a priceless gift and granting him or her a position in our lives worthy of great respect; and Love involves putting that decision into action.

Honor—profound respect for others—is crucial to the institution of adoption. Without it, adoption quickly degenerates into exploitation.

Can honor truly function as the foundation for adoption? The field's foremost expert, Sharon Kaplan-Roszia, wisely describes the experience of open adoption as "life." Given that insight, the question becomes, how will life play in this arena, which, because it is premised on upward psychological mobility, is somehow supposed to be better than life? A local reporter put the issue in sharp focus with an insightful question. "Would you, if you could," he asked, choosing his words carefully, "undo the openness of any of the adoptions you have arranged?" That one made me think. Certainly not all of our adoptions have been wonderful. Some people were admitted to our program who should have been screened out. Some initially promising participants ultimately proved disappointing. If we could, we would surely change some players, but would we change the openness? The answer, after careful deliberation, is a firm "No." To my knowledge, after watching more than 400 open adoptions come together through our program, the privileges of openness have been handled responsibly. We would not undo the openness of any of them.

THE SPIRIT OF HOPE

Open adoption really does work—not every time and not with equally satisfying results each time—but it does work. The breadth and depth of satisfaction that participants feel is impressive. When open adoption is based on genuine candor, unpressured choice, and enduring respect, it reliably produces remarkable results. When we first tried this style of adoption, there was no way we could know the creative forms it would take. Now, with the benefit of extensive experience, we are better informed. Our conclusion? The variety and depth of the open adoption relationships that our families enjoy surpass anything we imagined in our most optimistic moments.

To the chagrin of the cynics, the open adoption highlight film continues to lengthen. As I reflect on the years, a collage of pictures comes to mind. I remember the first time I saw a birthmother exit the courtroom with a genuine smile on her face after releasing her parental rights. Her smile proclaimed, "I made a good decision, and I feel good about it." After years of watching birthparents slink out of court, sobbing and consumed with shame, it had not occurred to me that this was possible. I recall a minister baptizing three children as the study group of which he was a part gathered to celebrate the arrival of a baby for the final family in the group. Champagne, baptismal water, and tears of joy flowed in equal parts that day. I see adoptive parents cheering in the crowd as the birthmother they have come to love receives her diploma, and birthparents getting married with birthchildren standing at their sides.

The years have brought equally poignant moments of a somber variety. In my memory, I see a birthmother weeping at the adoptive mother's funeral, wondering how fate could be so cruel. I see adoptive parents in the second car of a birthmother's enormous funeral procession, counted as vital members of the birthfamily at a time of intense sorrow. I will never forget the pathos of two mothers desperately clinging to each other as they grieved the death of their fragile daughter.

Try telling any of these families, celebratory or sorrowful, that open adoption is an idea that cannot work.

In addition to images, words and phrases are pressed upon my memory. The caller from downstate begins his conversation with the observation, "I hear miracles are going on up there." A conference-goer shakes her head and muses, "Your families don't act like other adoptive families." An especially gregarious birthmother declares, "I have lots of friends, but my best friend is my son's adoptive mother. She's closer than a sister to me." I also think of the sweetest words in adoption: "See you later." At the awful moment of separation, those mundane words are ineffably beautiful. And then there is the common but puzzling birthparent comment, "I never could have done this without open adoption." I must admit that I never know how to react to that statement. Might she have found a creative way to stay with her child if our program was not available?

It is fun to watch participants find braver and more generous versions of themselves. Routinely, we see people coming out of the experience healthier than when they went in. They are transformed. They like the way they have handled things, and they are fanatical about the people they have met along the way. It is a privilege to observe as participants rediscover the joy of courage, cooperation, and commitment.

The nurturing culture of a healthy open adoption system brings out the honor in people. This is most clear in moments when plans change. We have witnessed tremendous courage, grace, and dignity under wilting pressure. We have seen friendships persevere even when there was no placement. We have observed reversals of fortune and role in which birthparents have ministered to adoptive parents going through difficulties.

We have learned at Catholic Human Services how to do open adoption well. We have seen so many remarkable outcomes that we have come to expect them. As unbelievable as it may sound, they are routine. That is encouraging news. It is also true that our efforts sometimes fall short. There are times when we are not able affirm our way beyond the fear. There are times when we are not able to calm the urgency and call people beyond the lure of short-ranged thinking. Sometimes we cannot transform selfish agendas into meaningful covenants. We are forever humbled by our painful failures. We are also humbled by successes. When arrangements between families transcend our most shimmering hopes, we are reminded that more happens in adoption than we can humanly account for.

Although the basic "Can it work?" question is settled, it is not time to relax. The freedom of open adoption permits—perhaps even invites—distortion and excess. As open adoptions become more common, exotic and unpleasant cases will surely arise. These unfortunate situations will not disprove the potential of open adoption. They will remind us that there are many variations on the theme and that they are not equally promising.

Others will tackle the science and technology of adoption. This book wrestles with the art and spirit of adoption. It is obviously subjective and will not be the last word on the subject. Hopefully, the simplicity of this narrative will not create an impression that it is easy to create adoptions of honor. That is far from the case. The values underlying this approach to adoption have obvious merit and are relatively simple to describe. Their application, however, is a very different matter. Bringing the values to life is hard work. It is an art form requiring sensitivity and sacrifice. It is in the application of the values that the real challenge and creativity of an honoring form of adoption come into play.

This book explores the spirit—the essence, vitality, and power—of open adoption. Springing from respect and commitment, it is a spirit of creativity and freedom. Putting it in those terms, it is clear that we are dealing with the spirit of children. It is a spirit of hope. If we can overcome our fears and trust our better instincts, we can replace the debilitation of shame with the promise of honor. As we grow in our ability to honor each other, we breathe new life into a weary institution. As we sincerely honor children, we kindle the amazing, affirming spirit of open adoption.

Chapter 1

Understanding Open Adoption

Open adoption is the opening of the spirit and the heart to the realities of the flesh and history.

In an open adoption, there is the assumption that there will be as much [communication and contact] as possible within the limits of courage, compassion, and common sense.

Randolph Severson, *Adoption: Charms and Rituals for Healing.*

It sometimes appears that open adoption is destined to be forever misunderstood. In part, the confusion is connected to the word *open,* an obviously pivotal word which, unfortunately, is poorly suited to communicate precise meaning. The foot-thick *Random House Dictionary,* for example, assigns over 80 definitions to the word. If these scores of denotations were not sufficient to create genuine bewilderment, the word also generates a wide range of connotations that stir emotions that frequently cloud and confound clarity. For many, the word *open* is political. It is a word that seems to invite immediate judgment, independent from its application to any particular subject, and the responses it evokes are often cast in terms of good and bad.

Complicating the matter further, many people in the field handle the language of open adoption carelessly. Sometimes, the carelessness is the inadvertent result of inadequate information, but often the imprecise language is partially or fully intended. Confusion serves a purpose. It allows adoption promoters, for instance, to capitalize on the appeal that open adoption holds for potential birthparents while evading the responsibilities attendant to genuine open adoption. There is little accountability in an atmosphere of confusion. Still others, scrambling to preserve the closed system of adoption, foster confusion in a conscious effort to discredit the movement and thwart prospects for change.

Despite the ambiguous nature of the adjective, the emotions that swirl around the word, and intentional efforts to confuse the issue, it is possible to clearly define open adoption. True open adoption has four observable ingredients:

- the birthfamily selects the adoptive family,
- the families meet each other face to face,
- they exchange full identifying information, and
- they establish a significant ongoing relationship.

These factors can be summarized as choice, connection, candor and trust, and commitment. Of the variables, the ongoing relationship is the most crucial and largely presupposes the other factors. It constitutes the sternest test. To be considered open, an adoption must involve a significant ongoing relationship. If there is no ongoing face-to-face relationship, an adoption should be considered semiclosed.

Fleshing out the definition, pioneering social workers Kathleen Silber and Patricia Martinez Dorner note that there is a distinctive quality to the open adoption relationship. They point out that the relationship is familial, that it has the feel of kinship. "In open adoption, the birthfamily is extended family, like other relatives within the adoptive family." Their insight moves open adoption from the abstract to the concrete. Birthparent Brenda Romanchik extends our understanding with an incisive observation about this remarkable relationship. Capturing the heart of open adoption in a single idea, she states, "Genuine open adoption features a relationship between the adoptee and his or her birthfamily." She reminds us that respect for children is always at the core of open adoption.

Although open adoption is defined in observable terms, it is probably best understood as a set of attitudes. It comes fully alive when it is founded on sincere care and mutual respect. In *Adoption: Charms and Rituals for Healing*, psychologist Randolph Severson wisely puts open adoption in a context of "courage, compassion, and common sense." It takes courage to face uncertainty, compassion to consider the experience from the perspective of others, and common sense to iron out the details of an emerging relationship. When birthfamilies and adoptive families work cooperatively and sacrificially to benefit children, the results are extraordinary. On the other hand, an arrangement that meets the technical definition of open adoption but lacks heart does not satisfy. It is a sham and serves no one well.

COMMON MISUNDERSTANDINGS

Since there is so much confusion surrounding open adoption, it is as useful to clarify what it is not as to describe what it is. Topping the list of the many peculiar ideas associated with open adoption is the notion that it is unstable, insecure, and subject to endless legal challenges. This errant impression appears to have its origin in media-celebrated custody cases. Closer examination of those sad situations make it very obvious that they have nothing to do with open adoption, but public perception often has little to do with the facts. The legal security of an adoption is a matter of process, not style. It is an important issue for adoptions of every kind. Legal security in adoption, open or closed, is built on a careful, legally sound termination of parental rights.

The odd thought that open adoption generates insecurity is especially off base in the area of emotional security. In the most comprehensive study of open adoption to date, the research team of Harold Grotevant and Ruth McRoy discovered a very clear pattern:

> The strong general pattern is that parents in fully disclosed adoptions demonstrate higher degrees of empathy about adoption, talk about it more openly with their children, and are less fearful that the birthmother might try to reclaim her child than are parents in confidential adoptions.[*]

---

[*] *Harold Grotevant, Ruth McRoy, Carol Elde, and Deborah Lewis Fravel. "Adoptive Family System Dynamics: Variations by Level of Openness in the Adoption."* Family Process 33 *(June 1994): 141–142.*

Their findings are consistent with the longstanding impressions of open adoption practitioners and should go a long way toward putting this completely unfounded misperception to rest.

Another idea sometimes confused with open adoption is coparenting. Most people holding this misunderstanding believe that coparenting is a totally ineffective model of family structure and are inclined to reach the same conclusion about open adoption. This misreading of the situation results from confusion about the boundaries and roles in open adoption. In coparenting, the parent figures have equal authority, roles, and access. In open adoption, there is no equivalency in authority, roles, or access. Let's take a closer look.

From the perspective of authority, birthparents in most forms of open adoption have no legal standing. The involvement of birthparents is based on good will and cooperation, not authority. The clarity that open adoption enjoys with respect to authority significantly reduces the likelihood of unsavory power struggles that are sometimes associated with coparenting.

Confusion between the roles of mother and open adoption birthmother is unlikely because the roles are very distinct. Although each role carries the title of mother, they have little in common. The adoptive mother carries out the boundless role of the near-deity called "Mom," while the birthmother's role resembles that of aunt or special adult friend.

Finally, there is the matter of access. Detractors like to portray a birthmother lurking in the attic, monitoring every conversation through the heat ducts, and waiting for the most inopportune time to make a dramatic and disapproving appearance. Against such a fantastic backdrop, the mundane reality—likely featuring a scheduled monthly dinner and a stroll through the park—seems rather tame. Critics routinely overlook the fact that birthfamilies, just like adoptive families, want a measure of emotional distance. Many of them set aside the prospect of adoption in their extended family because it struck them as a little too much and a little too close.

Some people suggest that open adoption is nothing more than glorified baby-sitting. They complain, "You do all the hard work, pay all the bills for 21 years, and then they leave you." That sounds like parenting to me. Without realizing it, they offer tribute to the importance of biology. They are suggesting that the siren call of the biological connection is so powerful that it can easily cancel two decades of daily interaction. If biology is that powerful, it is wiser to work with it than to try to thwart it. Furthermore, if an enduring relationship with the adoptee cannot be forged during 20 intimate years of family life, something is seriously awry.

An especially frightening misunderstanding is the notion that there is no room for privacy in open adoption, that it requires total exposure of those who participate in it. Critics insinuate that it is akin to standing naked for all the world to inspect. This is where the common sense to which Severson refers makes a splendid entrance. Certainly open adoption features a spirit of candor and transparency, but the sharing is purposeful and kept within the limits of common courtesy and decency. There is much that each family needs to know about the other if they are to enter a relationship intelligently and if they are to serve the adoptee well over time. On the other hand, there is much that does not need to be known. Healthy open adoption relationships feature reasonable and mutually respected boundaries.

The misunderstandings we have considered so far are typically associated with people who are wary of open adoption. There is another misperception, less common than the others, held by some proponents of open adoption. It is the idea that open adoption is an almost perfect solution to the problems of untimely pregnancy and infertility. This is hardly the case. Open adoption does not solve or fix either circumstance. Furthermore, some people simply are not cut out to participate in open adoption. Prospective adoptive parents, for instance, with pronounced needs for predictability, control, or privacy will not find open adoption attractive. Quite to the contrary, they experience open adoption as unrelenting terror, and it is better for everyone that they not become involved.

Open adoption should not be oversold. It can work beautifully, but it does not erase the original pain. If people get the idea that open adoption relieves all the pain, they are certain to be disappointed. Open adoption is thoroughly painful and imperfect. It does not provide happy endings for every predicament. In many circumstances there may be better alternatives. It is fair to say, however, that at least some of the time for some of the people, open adoption offers a warm and positive alternative.

EVOLVING BEYOND THE CLOSED SYSTEM

Another way to grow in understanding of open adoption is to consider its relationship to the closed system of adoption. Open adoption originally emerged as an effort to correct many shortcomings intrinsic to the philosophy of closed adoption. Judgment of the closed system ranges widely; some live within its confines very comfortably and sing its praises, while many others vociferously decry its liabilities. However generous or critical the appraisal, the existence of hundreds of adoption search and support groups around the country testifies powerfully to the fact that the closed system generated an unacceptable number of profoundly discomforted participants.

The closed approach has many drawbacks. Most of its liabilities are linked to its affection for secrecy, a deleterious devotion examined in Chapter 4. It limits access to information so thoroughly that everyone involved—birthparents, adoptive parents, and adoptees—lack the basic data needed to work through the unique issues they confront. In the absence of information, fantasy abounds. The closed system is an assembly line that stifles personal initiative and fosters total dependence on the system. In this style of adoption, the professional is all-powerful. The closed system leaves many birthparents feeling like they have a loved one missing in action. Adoptees often feel a haunting sense of incompleteness, sometimes called *genealogical bewilderment.* The closed system ties the hands of adoptive parents by depriving them of the information they need to meet the needs of their children effectively.

Open adoption emerged in the United States in the late 1970s as an alternative to and a remedy for the deficiencies of the closed system. It originated as an effort to correct the longstanding emphasis on secrecy by giving participants the information they needed to find peace of mind. It recognized the uniqueness of each adoptive arrangement and worked to put control of the experience into the hands of those who lived it.

Initially, open adoption met with resistance and skepticism, but years of mostly satisfying results have established it as the most promising contemporary approach to adoption. The evolution of open adoption continues, and new variations on the theme surface continually. Unfortunately, many adaptations fall far short of the idealism that characterized the open adoption movement in its early years. Since the variations produce very different outcomes, they merit careful consideration. Presently, there are at least eight recognizable styles of "open adoption." They are mostly distinguished by the importance they assign to the continuing availability and involvement of birthparents. In discussing the styles of open adoption, we must remember that the theoretical distinctions we draw clearly in abstraction are often less obvious in practice.

Partially Open Adoption

The first variation, *partionally open adoption,* is mislabeled and not a true form of open adoption. This type of adoption typically has some features of open adoption—perhaps some involvement of the birthfamily in the selection process, or a meeting on first-name basis—but lacks the more crucial ingredients of exchanged identifying information and ongoing personal interaction. It is actually semiclosed adoption with the term *open* tacked on in error. Practitioners in this mode often use the phrase *openness in adoption* because it is so fluid that it is virtually undefinable.

Partially open adoption constitutes significant progress over a totally closed system and is a typical phase as a program evolves from closed to open. Partially open adoption can work well in circumstances in which the birthfamily has some exceptional liabilities that make continuing contact between the families hazardous. It is not, however, a good place for the transition to stall, for this halfway measure falls far short of the optimal adoptive experience. The shortcomings of partially open adoption will become more obvious as the eight qualitative values are developed in this book.

At first glance, it may appear that partially open adoption is an attractive means to glean the advantages of both systems: the protection of the closed system and the detailed information of the open approach. Unfortunately, it is not that simple. Because the two systems are ultimately mutually exclusive, a valid compromise is not easily accomplished. It is not possible to be candid and secretive simultaneously. It is not possible to trust and distrust simultaneously. It is not possible to embrace birthparents while keeping them at arm's length.

The partially open system is more likely to bring the disadvantages of each system into play. It communicates the distrust of the closed system while generating the uncertainty that plagues ill-conceived versions of open adoption. Furthermore, the injudicious use of the word *open* can generate expectations in birthparents that are unlikely to be met. In *A Letter to Adoptive Parents on Open Adoption,* Severson speaks to this frustration in wrenchingly practical terms: "That's when you check the mail daily. That's when your heart is in your throat every time the phone rings. In the end, you feel even more rejected, even more abandoned, even more alone." In this fashion, partially open adoption may unintentionally accentuate the rejection theme. And even if letters arrive regularly, they are only letters. Does one really know a pen pal?

The partially open form of adoption offers the birthfamily a measure of hope, but the hope is mostly false. It is odd for adoptive parents to inflict this on birthparents, for most adoptive parents are well-acquainted with the torments of false hope. With a little prompting, they vividly recall their days of fervently pursuing fertility. They remember the headlines proclaiming new medical breakthroughs and the monthly teasing of biology. Better than most, they know the cruelty of hope that leads one on, always glimmering just out of reach.

As is true of the closed system, an 8-year-old adopted child can demolish the partially open approach to adoption with two simple questions. "Mom, was my birthmother a good person?" Obviously, there is only one satisfactory answer to such a question: "Of course your birthmom's a great person. She's a big part of the reason you're such a great person." Any other answer runs the obvious risk of undermining the child's self-esteem. Reassured, it makes sense to the youngster to follow up with another question: "If my birthmom is a good person, why don't we go to visit her?" Chances are the child's question will be deflected, because a candid answer would be awkward and painful. The truth is, few parents are inclined to admit their fears to their children.

The biggest drawback of the partially open system, then, is that it denies the adoptee the satisfaction of continuing tangible affirmation from her birthfamily. The birthparents are known to others but are not available to the child. What is she to make of their unavailability? Their absence puzzles her, and she is likely to conclude that either they are bad people who must be kept away or that they do not really care. Either interpretation seriously detracts from her self-concept. On these terms, she is either "from bad stock" or she is unlovable. Reassuring words are unconvincing and bring little comfort. Ultimately, the only relief for the child's discomfort is positive personal contact with the birthfamily.

De Facto Open Adoption

Many adoption situations are fully disclosed, even though the parties involved did not consciously set it up that way. Hundreds of children are adopted each year by foster parents, and most of them are familiar with their birthparents. Interestingly, most states heavily promote the involvement of birthparents in foster care situations but grow skittish about it when adoption emerges as a possibility. Additionally, many more adoptions occur annually within extended families, and still other adoptions seem to spring up spontaneously among friends, neighbors, and general acquaintances.

Although these families typically know a great deal about each other, the missing piece usually is the relationship between them. They have, of course, some sort of relationship, but it is commonly left in vague, undefined terms. As a result, the connection between the families—even though there is frequently much good will between them—often feels awkward and even embarrassing. In some of these situations, thankfully, sensible participants take things into their own hands and say, "Hey, you know what? We are somebody to each other. We need to spend a little time together and work things out." Too often, though, the connection between the families is left unattended, flapping in the wind. It is vital that professionals who help organize these adoptions assist the participants to understand the extremely meaningful and consequential relationships they are entering.

Pragmatic Nontherapeutic Open Adoption

A third variation is *pragmatic nontherapeutic open adoption.* This system holds that open adoption is essentially the only form that contemporary birthparents will choose. It is, therefore, a necessary inconvenience for prospective adoptive parents to endure. The connection to the birthfamily is an unavoidable price to pay for the privilege of parenting.

Much like a business deal, this model of adoption is simply a legal transaction moving the child from one set of custodians to another. The more dispassionate the process, the better. No one is expected to grow from the encounter or to particularly enjoy the connection to the other family. It is simply a matter of doing what needs to be done. In its lowest form, prospective adoptive parents are coached to string the birthfamily along until the adoption is legally consummated: "Tell them what they want to hear. Nothing is binding. Once the adoption is legal, you can shut them out."

There is nothing positive about this approach. It initially meets the technical requirements of open adoption but completely misses the spirit. It usually diminishes the lives of those involved. The best we can hope for is that the participants may find each other interesting and choose, in spite of the advice they have received, to stay involved with each other. Any good accomplished through this form of adoption is accidental.

The pragmatic nontherapeutic approach to adoption is tantamount to planned betrayal and is a script for disaster. Its premise—that adoption is a simple legal transaction and nothing more—completely misses the reality of adoption. Like the closed system, it ignores the emotion and lifelong consequences of adoption. The only constraints on the method are those listed very explicitly in the law, and it easily degenerates into exploitation. This style of adoption has vast potential to generate disillusionment, tension, and conflict. Reuben Pannor, an early advocate of honesty in adoption, succinctly describes the usual sequence: "Until an adoption is finalized, the birthmother is treated royally and seductively. Then the contract is abruptly broken off."[*] Betrayal of this magnitude can create righteous fury in the birthparents, a rage that makes the long-term outcome very tenuous. The pragmatic nontherapeutic approach is a script for a lifetime of misunderstanding and exasperation. Its short-term expediency creates long-term anxiety. Even if the birthparents somehow rein in their desperation and contain their frustration, a day of reckoning awaits the scheming family. Eventually, the adoptee will learn the cruel and fraudulent details of his adoption, a discovery that will likely demolish any trust and respect he felt for his adoptive parents.

---

[*] *Quoted by Nancy Gibbs in "The Baby Chase." Time. October 9, 1989.*

Autonomous Open Adoption

Autonomous open adoption could be known also as do-it-your-self adoption. This approach is closely related to the pragmatic nontherapeutic model but is more positive and less calculating. It retains a pragmatic perspective but is receptive to the possibility that a relationship with the birthfamily could be satisfying. This perspective rests on the worrisome premise that adoption is a simple matter that any reasonable group of adults can work out. It holds an implied corollary that it is wise to avoid professionals as much as possible because they unnecessarily complicate the procedure with their tiresome questions.

This approach to adoption is typically energized by prospective adoptive parents trying to find children to adopt. It is predictable, then, that the emphasis is on helping these families find the most effective methods for discovering potential birthparents. If professionals are involved, it is in the role of marketing consultant. The major service they offer is to advise couples about the best ways to market themselves to potential birthparents. In some situations, professionals are left out of the marketing process and are only brought in as an afterthought to tidy up and give things the appearance of being proper and in good order. It concedes that certain procedural requirements related to adoption are handled most easily by professionals with unchallenged access to the health care and legal systems.

At first glance, the autonomous approach is open adoption in its ultimate form. It offers maximum flexibility as participants work together to create a workable process. In the process, it generates a strong sense of client ownership. There is also something undeniably attractive about dispensing with the adoption middle man; few are quick to rise to the defense of yesterday's unbending bureaucrats.

A longer look, though, brings significant liabilities to view. The premier advantage of the autonomous system—flexibility— is also its chief drawback. This approach is so flexible that it offers virtually no direction. Unable to benefit from the prior experiences of others, participants invent the wheel for themselves and find it difficult to anticipate future circumstances. The autonomous system does not deal with the fear and desperation that many adoptive parents feel as they enter the adoption arena. In fact, this approach, with its competitive perspective and resultant isolation, may even feed and reinforce that desperation. It is naive to expect unprepared and unsupported prospective adoptive parents—accountable to no one—to exercise self-restraint. Often, the autonomous approach prematurely narrows the range of options available to birthfamilies. Instead of choosing from a field of many suitable candidates, birthparents have a choice of one. Finally, because the autonomous experience is completely idiosyncratic, it contributes nothing to the cause of improving the larger institution.

Streamlining the process and bypassing the adoption professional may seem attractive, but, as is true in many life circumstances, shortcuts often prove shortsighted. Complications in a proposed adoption are difficult to handle in the best of circumstances; in an unsupported circumstance, they are excruciating. Unfortunately, we are acquainted with these situations from many desperate phone calls through the years: "What do we do? We've had the baby for over a year now, and the birthmother is withdrawing the power of attorney!" Usually, the only thing to do is prepare to gracefully return the youngster and start working on the regrets and second-guessing that surely follows. Tragically, the greatest victim of the shortcut is the child. The truth is, tempting as shortcuts may be, the overwhelming majority of successful adoptions are the result of hard work and substantial preparation.

Contractual Open Adoption

Contractual open adoption strives to protect the interests of the birthfamily and adoptive family by putting the agreement between them into contractual form. The contract clarifies the expectations and spells out the mechanics of the relationship. Jeanne Etter, an adoptive parent through the open system and a strong advocate of the open approach, has championed a form of this approach called *mediated open adoption*. In their *Adoption Mediation Training Manual*, she and coauthor John Chally state,

> Mediated open adoption is planned communication between birth and adoptive parents while the child is growing up, spelled out in a written agreement. The agreement is mediated by someone who understands the range of possibilities and is sensitive to the issues of both sides. It is pre-conflict mediation designed to avoid future problems.

This approach is a substantial step forward, offering two very important features. It is genuinely concerned with the rights of birthparents. This is crucial, since birthparents usually are the most vulnerable participants in the process. Second, the contractual approach has the significant advantage of clarity. Clarity is extremely valuable because it reduces the prospects for misunderstanding in the open adoption relationship. Even in the best of circumstances, where people are working together comfortably, clarity is elusive. Because everyone is excited and eager to get on with it, the tendency is to overlook distant details. Furthermore, there is usually some active resistance to clarity because everyone involved, birthparents included, wants some wiggle room. The ultimate impediment to working out a well-defined arrangement, of course, is that no one can predict the future. The tendency is to give up too quickly and declare, "We'll figure that out when we get to it." Experienced open adoption practitioners know it is wise to work out as many details as possible in advance.

Unfortunately, there are major drawbacks associated with the contractual approach to open adoption. To begin with, the unambiguous clarity that is the primary strength of contractual thinking can also be its chief demerit. It is difficult to build into contracts the flexibility required to meet the rapid changes of daily life. Contracts are usually oriented to the adults who enter them, and there is a tendency to overlook the voice of the adopted child that emerges as she grows older. Another problem is the false impression of security that contracts may generate. As one of our adoptive fathers cynically observed, "There has not yet been a contract written that a little more expensive attorney couldn't get you out of." A related problem is the question of sanctions. If contractual obligations are not met, what leverage is there to apply? Will the adoptee be a pawn in the adults' struggle for control?

Finally, and most crucially, contracts have the potential to alter the attitudes of the parties in open adoptions. Contracts suggest distrust. If participants talk about the need for a contract, it is a clear signal that more preparatory work is needed. It suggests that one or both of the families are withholding their trust. Contractual thinking can easily rob an open adoption relationship of its warmth and intimacy. It can change the dynamic from a "want to" to a "have to," an attitude shift of tremendous importance. In have-to situations, our creativity

naturally searches for avenues to escape our onerous obligations—quite a contrast to want-to circumstances, in which we
use our ingenuity to enhance the plan. When continuing contact occurs willingly, it is joyful and comfortable. If it occurs in
a spirit of obligation, it can become mechanical and degenerate into a source of resentment. The youngster is sure to detect
any stilted interaction between the adults and react negatively.

Guardianship Open Adoption

Annette Baran and Reuben Pannor, indefatigable advocates of
adoption reform, have suggested another approach to the long-
term care of children called *guardianship open adoption.** This
style of adoption uses permanent guardianship as the legal foundation for the arrangement. This legal mechanism offers some
important advantages, chief of which is that it does not require
termination of parental rights. For many birthparents, the experience of relinquishing rights and having their rights
terminated is harsh and demoralizing. Many take exception to
the wording of documents, which baldly state or otherwise
imply that they are uninterested in their children. Since
birthparent rights are not terminated in the guardianship system, they retain a measure of legal standing. This gives them
some leverage in the event they are betrayed. Additionally, permanent guardianship does not require a name change or
revision of the birth certificate and does not alter the child's
opportunity to inherit from his birthfamily.

Guardianship open adoption features a nonpossessive view
of children. It believes that a child is not an entity to take title
of but rather is a unique person to be nurtured in an environment that recognizes and respects her individuality. In
guardianship open adoption, the family unit is not fully established psychologically until the adoptee lends her informed voice
of assent.

This approach has more merit than is generally recognized
but suffers from a significant language problem. The idea of
guardianship does not appear to comfortably mesh with the
idea of adoption. For most people, guardianship expresses less

---

* *Baran and Pannor introduced this concept at Catholic Human Services' 1991 conference, Open Adoption as Standard Practice,
Traverse City, Michigan.*

commitment and less finality than adoption. Critics of this style of adoption are concerned that the protection gained for the birthfamily is gained at the expense of the security and stability of the larger plan. The preservation of birthparents' rights may inadvertently create a confusing legal foundation for the arrangement. The relatively weak legal underpinnings may invite litigious problem solving resembling the power struggles commonly associated with acrimonious divorce settlements. Critics worry that adoptive parents who feel insecure in their roles will transmit their anxiety to the children. Although it is undesirable for adoptive parents to own or possess the children entrusted to their care, it is crucial that they claim them, identify with them, and emotionally invest in them. In the bleakest scenarios, the insecurity of the arrangement interferes with the willingness of parents and children to fully commit themselves to each other. Adoption in any form produces substantial anxiety for adoptive parents. Since the guardianship system shifts even more anxiety from the birthfamily to the adoptive family, it may be very difficult to find adoptive parents who are willing to make a lifelong commitments on this basis.

Cooperative Adoption

Sharon Kaplan-Roszia, open adoption's most articulate advocate, and Mary Jo Rillera, a champion in the adoption reform movement, have outlined a system called *cooperative adoption*. They define cooperative adoption as a legal transfer of responsibility for the child during his minority years, in which

> the child is continuously considered a primary participatory partner even when still unable to speak for his/her self, so that as the child grows, (s)he will become an increasingly involved participant in the decisions that affect his/her life. The birth and adoptive families continue interaction and personal communication about their concerns.

This approach emphasizes three important values. To begin with, it has the great virtue of child-centeredness. Whereas most styles of adoption gravitate toward meeting the needs of the adults involved, the cooperative approach truly prioritizes the adopted child. Second, it recognizes the child as a developing person who will change dramatically through the years. To genuinely meet the shifting needs of the adoptee as he matures, the cooperative system stresses the importance of flexibility. Third, it suggests an effective basis for the open adoption relationship—namely, cooperation. It assumes that the goal of serving the needs of the adoptee will unify the birthfamily and adoptive family. If the adults involved are serious about their resolve to meet the needs of the child, it is clear they will have to cooperate.

These three primary values—centering on the child, flexibility, and cooperation—move our understanding of open adoption forward significantly. These values bring fresh vitality to the institution. The primary difficulty with cooperative adoption is that it is not fully developed as a system. After Rillera and Kaplan-Roszia established the core concepts of cooperative adoption, they turned their energy in other directions. Kaplan-Roszia went on to coauthor *The Open Adoption Experience,* easily the most comprehensive book in the literature of open adoption. That book thoroughly examines the issues of open adoption in general but does not expand on the particular ideas of cooperative adoption. As a result, the cooperative model of open adoption is not fully developed.

The cooperative approach to adoption is positive, promising, and incomplete. Like other responsible systems of open adoption, it is vitally concerned with preventing the betrayal of birthparents by adoptive families. Cooperative open adoption seeks to prevent this betrayal by highlighting the important advantages that cooperation offers to everyone involved, most especially the youngster. The benefits of cooperation are substantial, but are they sufficient? The gravity of self-interest pulls vigorously, and it is not unheard of for people to set cooperation aside once it has served their selfish purposes. The concern with cooperative adoption, then, is whether the appeal of cooperation is strong enough to keep participants involved with each other through the decades that await them.

Values-Based Open Adoption

At Catholic Human Services, we offer *values-based open adoption,* an approach that builds on and expands the cooperative system of open adoption. It includes the explicit values of cooperative adoption—child-centeredness, flexibility, and cooperation—and adds several more. As the title suggests, values are at the core of this approach to open adoption. Values are the basic assumptions we have about the nature of life. We gather them from a variety of sources, and we incorporate them into our being so thoroughly that often we are not entirely conscious of them. Values are our "givens." They are concepts we hold true without having to take the time to prove them each time they are brought to bear. That makes them very useful for sorting through the complexities of morally challenging circumstances.

Values must be handled intelligently. The fact that we frequently draw on them without taking time to justify them makes them efficient, but it also makes them frightening. If our givens are inappropriate, it follows that the decisions based on them will likely be flawed. If values are to serve us well, we must take the time periodically to examine them and make sure that they merit continuing endorsement. If basic values are not occasionally reconsidered, they can become a source of stagnation and close-mindedness.

At Catholic Human Services, our first application of values was to use them as a foundation for the practice of open adoption. Our program's early movement toward open adoption, for example, was largely based on our singular commitment to the value of candor. We reasoned that if we could somehow be true to it, things would work out well. That elementary conviction has produced phenomenal results for us through the years.

As our experience and sophistication with open adoption grew, we came to realize that values could also supply a vision for our program. Through a process of imagining outcomes based on the assumption that the central values of this approach to adoption could be faithfully applied over time, we were able for the first time to gain a clear grasp of what we were trying to achieve. With a clear sense of foundation and vision for our program, we have a vivid and invigorating sense of purpose and direction.

Values enrich our program in other significant ways. Our value system serves as a measuring stick that enables us to monitor the quality of our work. Since most efforts to evaluate adoption are quantitative, it is exciting to approach the delivery of services from a qualitative perspective. Because we believe the quality of our work is directly linked to how well we operationalize our values, we pay close attention to this portion of our practice. Outcomes can be evaluated in terms of how well they approximate our values-based vision. Chapter 2 addresses the issue of quality in detail.

The values-based open adoption system challenges participants to search their hearts and identify their most fundamental beliefs. It strives to make their values explicit and relevant. Ideally, these personal values lead participants to a clear vision of what they wish to accomplish and what they wish to avoid as they move through their adoption experience. A values-based approach brings depth and soul to the decision-making process.

An understanding of our values helps us understand our relationships better. We usually get along well with people who share our values, but we often struggle with people who hold different values. Values are, therefore, an indispensable consideration as birthfamilies and adoptive families get to know each other and make initial decisions about whether to join in adoption. A clash of values can quickly undermine compatibility. Similarity of values, on the other hand, can galvanize the relationship.

As participants grow in awareness of personal values, the likelihood that they will choose truly compatible partners for their adoption journey improves dramatically. Based on shared values, participants place the experience in an ethical framework and together fashion and commit themselves to a plan to cooperatively honor the child through the years. The values-based system engenders a covenantal connection between birthfamilies and adoptive families. It is a sacred commitment, a matter of heart, integrity, and honor.

Since the twists and turns that surface during the normal course of open adoption defy prediction and therefore also defy concrete planning, open adoption must be based on a foundation capable of great flexibility. The foundation must also be very enduring, because the open adoption arrangement will be in effect for decades. It is not easy to find a foundation that is both flexible and enduring, but a values approach appears to fit both requirements. We are not aware of a better way to keep the link between the families simultaneously stable and dynamic.

Experience has taught us that there are at least eight values that are crucial to satisfying experiences with open adoption. Each is distinct, yet related to the others. The eight values can be understood as variations on the overarching value of respect. Because the values are closely related, it is unusual for them to conflict with each other.

We believe that every adoption plan must

- **Honor the adoptee.** Every child deserves to be honored as a unique gift from God. The needs of the adoptee are paramount.

- **Be based on candor.** Accurate information equips people for effective living. Candor produces the best results when it is coupled with a spirit of kindness.

- **Be based on choices.** People take responsibility for decisions when they freely choose them from real alternatives. Conversely, people tend to resent outcomes that result from coercion.

- **Honor the pain.** Adoption has a tragic element that cannot be ignored.

- **Be covenantal.** The quality of an adoption will depend on the integrity the participants bring to their commitments.

- **Transform.** Adoption is a life-altering experience for each person involved.

- **Be adaptable.** Adoptive relationships are dynamic, never stagnant.

- **Build community.** Adoption is best understood as a system. Each participant affects and is affected by the others in the extended adoptive clan.

Like every other style of open adoption, the values-based approach has noteworthy drawbacks. This approach relies heavily on personal integrity and honor and works well when the participants carry out those values. Realistically, though, we know that there will be times when honor is set aside in favor of expediency. Painfully, if people abuse the honor system, there is no recourse for those who have been taken advantage of. To protect against the prospect of dishonorable behavior, the values-based system requires a great deal from the professionals involved in terms of screening, preparation, and inspiration.

The values-based approach to open adoption can generate a pedestal effect. We expect exceptional results from our participants, and these expectations are routinely met or exceeded.

Participants are complimented and affirmed by our expectations and usually respond positively. Eventually, though, it is human to fall short of expectations, and it is especially painful to admit our shortcomings to people who believe in us. It is possible that pride can prevent participants from reaching out for assistance at moments of particular need. Hopefully, the burden of great expectation is lessened by two major themes: forgiveness and the discovery that we can still be lovable despite—or because of—our imperfections. Open adoption works best with people who are at peace with their imperfections.

OVERCOMING FRUSTRATIONS

So we see that open adoption is not monolithic; there are many variations on the theme. Potential participants in open adoption do well to exercise great caution in selecting a system of adoption. Some styles are far more promising than others, but none are free from problems. Even the most promising of the variations will generate some difficulties. As noted, quality adoption requires courage, compassion, and common sense. It also requires continuing effort.

Most frustrations associated with open adoption are best understood as relationship problems. These problems take many forms. The most serious concern for birthparents is the possibility of being double-crossed by adoptive parents who fail to follow through on their promises. Responsible systems of adoption do their best to curb this prospect, but it always lurks as a devastating possibility.

The chief concerns of adoptive parents are the possibility of a birthparent change of heart and the prospect of birthparent "intrusion." Carefully crafted open adoption provides birthfamilies with ample opportunities to change course in the early going so there is less potential for that trauma latter on. Most birthparents find that their sense of quiet desperation is calmed by the availability of continuing contact with the adoptive family, and they are impressed with the tenderness they see between the new parents and the baby. As a result, they are less likely to challenge the arrangement. Clearly, there is a subjective quality to the issue of intrusion—it is a combined matter of birthparent behavior and adoptive-parent perception. In adoptive arrangements that fully empower birthparents in the selection process and clearly define the boundaries of the relationship from the beginning, the sensation of intrusion seldom arises.

The foremost worry regarding the children is that they will somehow find the experience of open adoption confusing. Our experience so far indicates that well-designed open adoptions do not confuse the children. Is it our usual experience that good information confuses us? Obviously not. Accurate information—firsthand and continually updated—helps children make sense of and understand their life stories.

Values-based open adoption has great potential. Like most items of exquisite merit, it is not accomplished simply; it requires extensive preparation. Birthparents and adoptive parents must reach deep to find the strength to overcome their fears. They must come to terms with their losses and commit themselves to the high road of integrity. Those who succeed bring extraordinary blessings to their children—and to themselves.

Chapter 2

Exquisite Adoptions

> When we talk about quality....we are also talking about
> the quality of our relationships and the quality of our
> communications and the quality of our promises to
> each other. And so, it is reasonable to think about qual-
> ity in terms of truth and integrity.
>
> Max DePree, *Leadership Is an Art*

> Quality is about people.
>
> Tom Peters and Nancy Austin, *A Passion for Excellence*

Recently I had a brief, familiar, and rather mundane hallway
conversation with my administrator, an amiable fellow with
an honest appreciation for our program. It was the season for
preparing budgets, and he asked quite simply, "How's it going?" I responded, "Good." He brightened at that answer.
"Good," he said. "That's good." Information exchanged, we
went different directions. It was high-level, meaningful corridor conversation, and I expect to struggle with the implications
of those few words the rest of my career.

Back at my desk, as I reflected on this routine conversation,
it struck me that we had defined *good* in distinctly different
ways. His question was actually administrative code for, "How
are the numbers holding up?" My answer, on the other hand,
was clinical and based on my impression that the last several

placements had come together in particularly wholesome fashion. The question was quantitative and the answer was qualitative. It is so easy to confuse the two.

Not all adoptions are alike; some are qualitative and others are not. That observation does not seem especially profound, but it took me almost two decades of practice to figure it out. Those of us who live or work in the world of adoptions know they are experienced very differently. There are times when I go home with an extra measure of contentment because I was part of something truly extraordinary, a quality adoption. There are other days when my work seems depleting. Perhaps that signals that I have been part of an adoption that did not shine, an adoption that fell short of its potential. Parents who have adopted several children report that the adoptions feel very different. Although they aspire to equality and fairness for their children, there is no way around the fact that some adoptions are more satisfying than others.

I think adoption may be the last institution on the planet to discover the idea of quality. Given the extraordinarily consequential nature of adoption, that is a most surprising observation. Hopefully we can grow in understanding of quality as it pertains to adoption by considering five questions:

- Why have we thought so little about quality in adoption?
- What does quality mean in general terms?
- How do the various participants perceive quality?
- What is the professional perspective on quality in adoption?
- How can quality become a central focus in adoption?

Thinking About Quality

The first puzzle is our disregard for the issue of excellence in adoption. In a culture that measures the quality of everything from pizzas to schools of engineering to slam dunks, it is amazing that we have ignored the quality of the adoption experience. There is some hazard in making this observation. I am not suggesting we trivialize adoption with some superficial rating system. We do not need the participants of adoption wandering around saying, "I was a 9.7 on the Quality of Adoption Scale. How about you?" The hope is to generate greater consciousness of quality in the practice of adoption. An important step in that direction is to consider the reasons that the issue of quality has been overlooked so long.

The answer is found mostly in two areas: an undynamic nonprofit culture and the oppressive legacy of secrecy. Let's consider these factors one at a time.

I am convinced that there is no better system for delivering adoption services than a lively, creative nonprofit agency. Featuring accountability, generations of experience, community ownership, follow-up, appropriate leveling of socioeconomic issues, and a robust thirst for research and development, the dynamic nonprofit agency has peerless potential to provide services of distinction. Sadly, however, the nonprofit system of service delivery in uncreative form is a script for lackluster performance. It seems that the goal of many nonprofit organizations is just to get by. They are often fascinated with the challenge of accomplishing things inexpensively. That is to say, they are cheap. Without intending it, their enthusiasm for frugality sends a devaluing message to consumers. It tells them that they do not merit the expenditures associated with excellence.

Many nonprofit organizations create a culture of mediocrity. There is a pack mentality that says, "We are all in this together and none of us is any better than the others." Services are presumed to be equivalent and interchangeable. Competition is actively discouraged. I remember being criticized in an annual evaluation because "other agencies are saying that you make them feel like they aren't measuring up." An ideal nonprofit worker, it appears, does not stir discomfort among colleagues, or there will be talk.

The rest of the answer lies embedded in the old secretive system of adoption, whose legacy lingers in ways that are easy to overlook. Its effects will reverberate for years to come. The secrecy of closed adoption generates an atmosphere of isolation in which there is no opportunity for feedback or comparison. Where there is no opportunity for comparison, there is no awareness of quality.

Furthermore, the closed system functions as an assembly line. In the closed system, all adoptions really are alike. By design, each adoption resembles the one that precedes and follows it. There is a sameness to adoption that suppresses creativity and individuality. What sense does it make to search for exceptional quality in something engineered to be identical to other outcomes? In a system that takes pleasure in generic outcomes, the concept of quality is not important.

Perhaps the greatest impediment to a qualitative examination of adoption is the simpleminded assumption that all adoptions are good. Without exception, the thinking goes, adoption is a very good thing. It spares children the pitiful fate of life with their no doubt marginal birthfamilies and makes deserving families happy in the process. In a world starved for happy stories, adoption is well-regarded. Anytime an adoption is arranged, a very fine thing has been accomplished.

Really? Is anything good all the time? This is an amazing, perhaps even dangerous, assumption. If we accept the assumption that each adoption is good, it follows that 10 adoptions are better and 100 are even better. So there it is again—the confusion between quantity and quality.

Each adoption must be considered on its own merits. It is neither automatically good nor bad. The goal is not to do two million adoptions, but rather to do each adoption deemed necessary in the eyes of the participants as beautifully as we know how. That is a goal worth striving for.

DEFINING QUALITY

Let us move on to the second major question. If we intend to grow in our understanding of quality as it relates to adoption, we do well to start with some basic consideration of the concept of quality. In general terms, what is quality? There are several angles that merit at least brief attention.

Consider first that quality is associated with things beautiful, elegant, fragrant, tasteful, and harmonious. It has inherent unity, clarity, and coherence. In some forms, quality is redemptive; it is able to rework disaster into beauty. Delighting us with freshness, creativity, and truth, quality hits us like a personal revelation. It startles us and grips our imagination. An item of quality has a way of haunting one's memory. Or note that, sometimes, quality is linked to efficiency. It is something productive, a good value, a good return on an expenditure of energy. It features a beautiful simplicity. Yet another perspective holds that quality is solid and enduring. It holds up over time, maybe even improves with age. It is endearingly and delightfully dependable.

Quality can be understood as something exceptional, extraordinary, or transcendent. Something distinctive that hits the spot in indisputable fashion. I know my youngest daughter has spotted quality when she jumps into the air with her arm thrust high and hollers, "Yes!" In *Leadership Is an Art,* business writer Max DePree uses a wonderful expression to describe exquisite acts of quality. He calls them "gifts to the spirit."

Finally, there is the Olympic model of quality, which adds two insights to this discussion. Some of my early thinking about quality occurred against the backdrop of the 1994 Winter Olympics. Like all the world, I was fascinated by the dedication, skill, and concentration of the athletes; but I have to admit to a measure of disappointment when the leading figure skaters played it safe at the end of the competition and deleted the triple jumps. If the goal is simply to succeed, playing it safe will do quite nicely. If, on the other hand, the goal is unsurpassed beauty, we have to keep the triple jumps in the program. In the arena of human relationships, it is better to aspire to the extraordinary and come up a little short than to not even try.

The Olympic world also contributes the idea of *degree of difficulty.* It is obvious to anyone involved in adoption that the various circumstances present very different degrees of challenge. Sometimes, the birthfamily and adoptive family are such effective people that a sterling outcome is inevitable. Other times, though, the raw material we are working with is, in fact, quite raw. Those are surely the occasions of greatest challenge. If we tackle an unpromising circumstance, and through our coaxing, educating, leading, affirming, finessing, and reframing are able to transform it into a relationship that shines, then we can be sure we have done work of substantial quality. This is a good place for those of us who work in the realm of infant adoption to salute those who labor in the world of special-needs adoption. Those professionals who find inventive ways to preserve the birth heritage in a context of unimaginably perplexing circumstances are surely the unrecognized heroes of adoption.

QUALITY THROUGH THE EYES OF THE BEHOLDER

We have moved from abstract consideration of quality to application, so we are ready for the third question: Exactly what does quality mean as it pertains to adoption?

A few preliminary considerations are in order. First, we must recognize that our understanding of quality is certain to evolve over time. It is dynamic; we will never "arrive" at a final understanding of quality in adoption. That means we do well to stay open to new standards in the years ahead. Equally important, we must be careful not to apply current concepts to adoptions from 40 years ago. Second, there is no way around the fact that a focus on quality is also by contrast a focus on "unquality." Resistance can be expected. Third, any discussion of quality must take place in a context of grace and forgiveness. Without a gracious spirit, a consideration of quality is depressing. The clearer our vision of what should be, the worse we feel about our shortcomings. Finally, we must highlight the fact that this is very subjective territory.

Since quality is in the eye of the beholder, let's try on the spectacles of the various beholders. We must keep in mind in this exercise that it is always hazardous to generalize about diverse groups of people.

How do prospective adoptive parents understand quality? They may answer this question in different ways, depending on how far into the process they are. Their usual initial priority is that a program is fast; their second priority is that it is swift, and their third is that it is speedy. The desire for immediate relief is so strong that it prompts many prospective parents to set aside their usual caution. For some, the longing is so great that nothing else matters. Those who successfully contain their panic realize that the really crucial factor is that their adoption has a solid legal platform. As a result, they look for a program that operates within strict ethical standards. For many, thankfully, that is a preeminent consideration.

A factor that appeals to prospective adoptive families is a nonjudgmental and nonintrusive style. In other words, they appreciate a program that in no manner disturbs their perceptions of reality. After all, they reason, parents whose children are born to them do not have to prove themselves to anyone.

Another ingredient to a quality program is that it understands and appreciates their needs for children and prioritizes their needs as paying customers. If there are conflicts at some point in the process, they assume their agents will promote their interests. It is frosting on the quality cake if a program also happens to be economical.

Prospective birthparents enthusiastically share the adoptive-parent longing for nonjudgmental treatment. They want a streamlined program—low on bureaucracy and rigmarole and long on simplicity. They want a program that accepts their coping strategies without challenging them. Birthparents typically want a program that leaves the decision making in their hands, although some are tempted by a course of total passivity. And, of course, the ultimate factor for birthparents is a program that produces outstanding adoptive families. Birthparents will define *outstanding* in many different ways, but mostly it means adoptive parents who will treasure the youngster and accept her as a full member of the family. For most birthparents, *outstanding* means a family that will honor the commitments it made during the adoption planning.

What about adoptees? What do they think constitutes a quality adoption program? In the past, this was a totally irrelevant question; adoptees got what they got. Sadly, few people have been genuinely interested in what adoptees think because it takes them too long to grow up and formulate their opinions. Those who take the time to listen, however, will find that they have some clear ideas about quality. Adoptees want a form of adoption that supplies them with thorough, accurate information so they can make sense of their life stories; and they want this information as a matter of right. They want a system that is consistent and follows through on the promises it makes. Adoptees want a system that promotes respect between birthfamilies and adoptive families. They do not want to be in the cross fire of an adversarial system that generates loyalty dilemmas for them. Above all, in the eyes of adoptees, quality means control. An exquisite adoption allows them to take charge of their lives appropriately.

How do our communities evaluate adoption? What is their impression of quality? For the most part, they are not losing much sleep about the subject. I believe there has been a shift in public sympathy from a concern for children to a concern for infertile families. The public wants someone to do something about all those nice but sorrowful families who deserve children. The only other expectation our communities have of the institution is that it should be trouble free; they do not want the courts cluttered with contentious adoption cases. The public wants adoption cheerful and simple.

THE PROFESSIONAL PERSPECTIVE

The final beholders are the adoption practitioners, and that brings us to our fourth major question: What is the professional perspective on quality in adoption?

As is true of each group of beholders, there is a range of opinion on the subject. To our discredit as professionals, there has not been much discussion about quality. There has been crude debate whether open is better than closed, but that is the extent of it. Until there is more discussion in the field, this commentary should be considered preliminary thoughts on quality in adoption.

In the earlier description of values-based open adoption, I suggested that the eight values that compose its foundation can also provide a vision for desired outcomes. They constitute a helpful framework for us to approach the issue of quality. It is possible that a values perspective can move the adoption community toward some needed consensus about the definition of quality. We will briefly consider the eight values for the moment and take a longer look at each of them individually in subsequent chapters.

Quality adoption will genuinely focus on the needs of the child.

Every form of adoption claims to serve the best interests of the child; but, often, the claim is empty and without meaning. Quality adoption is deeply committed to understanding the needs of the adoptee, and it recognizes that these needs and perceptions change as he moves through the many phases of life. Quality adoption dignifies the child through its carefully designed process; it is the antithesis of a haphazard or accidental process. Quality adoption honors the child by recognizing his individuality, and it equips him to handle challenging circumstances by keeping him fully informed. In an exquisite adoption, the adults bless the adoptee through their willingness to cooperate and sacrifice, a spirit that enables the child to be affirmed by all the crucial people in his life. In genuinely child-centered adoption, the voice of the adoptee in the arrangement grows over the years in proportion to his maturity.

Indisputably, children deserve a system that honors their questions and provides accurate answers. They need to know why and how adoption decisions were made. Over the course of their lives, they benefit from accurate and updated medical information. Most delightfully, they benefit from the active love of the important people in their lives.

Quality adoption will shine with candor.

The first rule of open adoption is candor. Candor exceeds honesty. It is a transparency that volunteers information that is not even asked for. People of candor are eager to share information and to be known. They exude confidence and health and good will. A beautiful adoption will positively shine with information. The information will be direct, comprehensive, relevant, and updatable. An adoption that lacks quality will be characterized by deceit, secrecy, and manipulation.

Candor is a liberating platform for interaction. People who interact with candor do not paint themselves into corners, and they do not carry the burdens of maintaining secrets. They tend to live and love robustly. Candid people can admit to their imperfections, and this quality makes them easy to relate to. Candor creates an atmosphere in which trust can grow and flourish.

Quality adoption features a genuine choosing process and as a result is fully endorsed by its participants.

A system of adoption that places the major decisions in the hands of the participants has the desirable effect of putting people in charge of their lives. This decision making enables participants to gain comfort with outcomes and to mature as individuals. A qualitative adoption is "owned" by the participants. The relationship is affirmed and endorsed; it is a "want to," not a "have to." Adoptions stand a better chance of meeting needs if they are designed by the participants. In the warmest of adoptions, the endorsement generates a sense of mutual gratitude.

Adoptions that lack quality invariably restrict choices. The narrowing of choices can take many forms. Sometimes it is outright coercion or threat, but more often it emerges as pressure and obligation. Undue haste is often a factor in the premature narrowing of alternatives.

Quality adoption acknowledges the pain.

This is a critical value that is difficult to embrace. Given the magnitude of the losses associated with adoption, most of us flinch long before we draw near to its core. Sometimes, we quickly settle for denial or lip service; other times, we minimize the losses and magnify the gains. We settle for superficiality. Quality adoption charts a very different course; it faces the pain head on. In adoptions of substance, the pain is shared. The participants work through it together, and the shared pain feeds their appreciation, commitment, and loyalty. Pain is often an expression of love and in a mysterious way is frequently linked to beauty. Adoption that denies the pain also denies the love of adoption. Those who hang in and wrestle with the pain stand on the threshold of extraordinary possibilities.

Quality adoption is covenantal.

An adoption of distinction is very conscious of the other persons involved. It takes the Golden Rule seriously. It is deeply respectful and treats the commitments made as matters of sacred honor. If the choosing has been done carefully and the pain of adoption has been weathered jointly, the open adoption relationship becomes genuinely satisfying. An inferior adoption operates from the premise that the ends justify the means. It views the others involved in the adoption as tools to be used.

Quality adoption transforms the participants.

A quality adoption affirms and activates the best in people. Perhaps this is the real *open* of open adoption. It works best with people who are receptive to growth. I know an adoption has worked when I see togetherness and community rather than doleful isolation. Quality adoption moves participants closer to the living edge. It is the liberation of transparency and candor. A quality experience seems to waken values that had slipped into dormancy. Participants often apply the principles and values they used in their open adoption experience to other circumstances in their lives.

An adoption short on quality produces dramatically different outcomes. If participants have not been at their best, if they have cut some corners, if they have been selfish, if they have sold their counterparts short and built unnecessary walls, if they have sacrificed their youngster's access to answers for the sake of personal convenience, they are sadly diminished. They live with perpetual anxiety, and they live with shame.

Quality adoption is adaptable.

The adoption that has a future is amendable. It is possible to do what needs to be done to keep the arrangement relevant and satisfying. Since the adoptee's needs will vary greatly as she grows through the years, many adaptations may be necessary to truly meet her needs. An adoption that lacks quality is set in concrete. It is not adjustable; it is all or nothing. It is not alive. It has a fragile future.

Quality adoption recognizes the open adoption clan as an interdependent system.

Every adoption brings families together for a lifetime. There is really no way around this fact. In a constricted adoption, the faceless "other" members of the system lurk around every corner. They are not active members of the system, but they are, nevertheless, powerful members of it. Participants in a quality adoption recognize that everyone is in it together. Each member of the system affects the others. From the vantage of qualitative adoption, attending to the well-being of the others is a matter of self-interest.

One of the greatest benefits of values-based open adoption is the sense of community it creates. Whereas the closed system, by design, generates separation and isolation, effective open adoption invariably builds togetherness and community. Life's greatest delights are found in the realm of go-for-broke relationships.

Recently, I sat in a living room sipping champagne and celebrating new life and new relationships with an adoptive mother and father and a birthmother and father. We were celebrating this painful, beautiful thing called open adoption. I asked myself a few questions. Did the arrangement honor the youngster? Did it feature candor? Was it thoughtfully chosen and fully endorsed? Did it acknowledge the pain? Were the participants committed to the plan as a matter of honor? Was it transforming? Was it adaptable? Did it recognize interdependence? YES! In that sacred moment, there was no room for shame.

MAKING QUALITY THE FOCUS

What will it take for us to get serious about quality in adoption? This is a larger question than we realize. We must search our hearts and decide whether we just want to do adoptions or whether we want to do quality adoptions. Rephrasing the question more pointedly, we need to ask ourselves whether we are willing to do adoptions that lack quality. Our answers have fantastic implications for the amount of energy and courage we will need to summon, for there is no such thing as cheap quality. Quality will require leadership from everyone who cares deeply about the institution of adoption.

I believe we must become fully conscious of and fully committed to quality in adoption. It needs to be on our minds relentlessly. We must end the confusion between quantity and quality. We must not settle for mediocrity. No doubt the worst words in adoption are *settle for.* In the service of children, "good enough" is not good enough. Perhaps we will approach quality through the back door of indignation with unacceptable practices. As we become more clear about what is not acceptable, we become more clear about what is desirable.

I am convinced that our joy and fruitfulness as professionals is directly linked to our commitment to quality. Dedication to quality will make an enormous difference in our everyday practice, because it provides a sense of direction. A commitment to quality enlivens and exhilarates. This commitment can defend us from every professional's nightmare—a lingering, vitality-sapping plateau. If we pursue quality, we are slated for growth.

Our challenge is this: We must do the next adoption beautifully. We must keep all the triple jumps in the program and hit the landings cleanly. And maybe, with a bit of good fortune, people will notice and say, "Hey, look at those guys. They're different. They are a gift to the spirit."

Chapter 3

Honoring the Child

> Bringing into the world a little child totally dependent on the care of others and leading it gradually to maturity is true defiance of the power of death and darkness. It is saying loudly: For us life is stronger than death, love is stronger than fear, and hope is stronger than despair.
>
> Henri Nouwen, in *Seeds of Hope: A Henri Nouwen Reader**

> Children are a gift from God.
>
> Psalm 127:3 *(The Living Bible)*

The psalmist presents us with an elegant truth that we are inclined to dismiss as a lovely thought. Psalmists should not be patronized. The idea of children as a gift from God is far more than a lovely thought; it is an essential perspective on children that delivers four significant insights regarding the practice of adoption.

THE IMPLICATIONS OF A GIFTS PERSPECTIVE

To begin with, we reasonably presume that gifts are positive. Certainly, circumstances in life strain that assumption—times

---

* *Henri Nouwen. "Resistance." In* Seeds of Hope: A Henri Nouwen Reader. *Robert Durback (Ed.). New York: Bantam, 1989.*

when the news of an expected baby feels more like a burden than a breakthrough—but in our hearts, we know that each child deserves to be welcomed as a blessing. Each time I cradle a baby in my arms, I realize that I am holding the full range of human possibility: past, present, and future. Seven squirming pounds of bittersweet potential. Eyes that search and test the soul. A future senator? A musician? A prophet? Perhaps a gifted social worker?

Author Henri Nouwen, a Jesuit priest with an especially compassionate heart, captures some of the magic of children with this observation: "The children challenge me to live in the present. They want me to be with them in the here and now... I have suddenly discovered the great healing power of children."* Children move us beyond our tedious self-centeredness. Their total dependence excites in us the desire to give ourselves completely to another; they stir in us our own possibilities, our own prospect of a fresh start. Each child is indeed a gift with unique spirit and beauty.

The second thing we learn from this perspective is that children are not deserved and cannot be earned. In our desire to create children, we are ultimately powerless. We cannot produce them on demand. For proud, capable people, this is an infuriating truth. We strive to master our circumstances, but the fact is, children are only available to us as gifts, and all we can do is receive them humbly. Like it or not, the only verb that appropriately brings children into our lives is *receive*. That observation leads naturally to the third insight; namely, the appropriateness of gratitude.

When we receive a gift of inestimable merit, the sensible response is profound gratitude. Consequently, one might assume that gratitude is a major—perhaps even dominant—dynamic in the realm of adoption. But, is it? At its best, adoption brims with gratitude. Most adoptive parents are profoundly grateful and quick to express their thankfulness; but, interestingly, many are not. Curiously, some even express resentment.

When adoption lacks gratitude, something is seriously wrong. The absence of gratitude usually signals a lack of appropriate surrender. The problem is the result of presumption; nothing destroys gratitude more efficiently than a presumptive spirit.

---

* *Henri Nouwen. "Celebrating Children." In* Seeds of Hope: A Henri Nouwen Reader. *Robert Durback (Ed.). New York: Bantam, 1989.*

Casting aside the idea of children as a gift from God, some adoptive parents hold that fate owes them children. They genuinely believe that they deserve children, that they are entitled to children because they have lived according to our culture's prevailing scripts for appropriate behavior. Instead of reveling in the wonder of the gift, they dwell on their inflated sense of worthiness. Given that mind-set, gratitude is unlikely. Adoption that is deficient in gratitude lacks the warmth of appreciation and the lightness of joy associated with adoptions rooted in gratitude.

Finally, the gift perspective reminds us that children belong to God, not us. Parents are privileged to hold them for a while, but they cannot be hoarded and contained. From the day we first welcome children into our lives, we know our goal is to prepare them for the day they will leave. They are entrusted to our care, and it is our responsibility to nurture them toward independence. As parents—biological and adoptive—we are stewards, not possessors. The thought of owning a child is chilling and dehumanizing. With total confidence, we can state that it is better if children are not possessed.

MOVING TOWARD HONOR

The principle of "the best interests of the child" has reigned for decades as adoption's overarching value. According to this principle, everything done in adoption is meant to further the well-being of the adoptee. The Michigan Adoption Code, for example, states that its purpose is

> to provide procedures and services which will safeguard and promote the best interests of each adoptee in need of adoption and which will protect the rights of all parties concerned. If conflicts arise between the rights of the adoptee and the rights of another, the rights of the adoptee shall be paramount.

That raises a very interesting question. If the rights of adoptees are paramount, how is it that even adult adoptees are denied fundamental information about themselves?

Sadly, a noble concept has become an empty phrase. Through the years, the operational definition has become "the rights of the adoptee *as determined by the adoptive parents* shall be paramount." Too often, this is "adopt-ese" for "the best interests of adoptive parents." Seldom have I heard anyone use this language to suggest that birthparents have something vital and beneficial to offer adoptees. Most typically, the phrase amounts to the projection of the thoughts and preferences of adults onto children, and in this form it is particularly insidious. It has the effect of making the child responsible for outcomes even though she has no say. Furthermore, it sets into motion the idea that adults can easily speak for the child. If that mind-set holds over time, it robs the adoptee of her voice. For many adoptees, there is no more discouraging dynamic than that of other people speaking smugly on their behalf.

I believe *honoring the child* is a better expression. It has merit because it puts the responsibility on the adults. The honoring—or failure to honor, as the case may be—is done by the adults. If the adults are successful in their effort to love fully but not possessively, children will be honored and the adults involved will be honorable.

Obviously, this phrase is also subject to interpretation and distortion. It is easily confused with indulgence or overinvestment. Since adopted children are hard to come by, adoptive parents are prone toward overprotection. This fusion between parent and child is the flip side of neglect and is just as debilitating. If we sincerely respect a child, we will provide him with the security of limits and will expand his decision-making opportunities as he grows in responsibility. Honoring a child means listening to him with honesty and understanding; it does not mean that he will rule the household.

The adoption process can honor children in at least five important ways. These applications include a child-centered design, respect for the birth heritage, sensitive handling of information, a developmental perspective, and cooperation among adults. This is far from an exhaustive list. As we grow in our understanding of adopted children and in our willingness to prioritize their needs and interests, more ideas are sure to surface.

A Child-Centered Design

The entire purpose of a child-centered style of adoption is to serve children. As infant mental health specialist Michael Trout puts it, adoption should be "baby-driven."* It is important to state this principle very clearly, for infant adoption is increasingly organized as a service to infertile families with some child-serving language tacked on as an afterthought. When services are organized around the goal of meeting the needs of prospective adoptive parents, there is nothing ambiguous about the preferred outcome. The obvious goal of these services is adoption, and there is significant risk that adoption will be unduly promoted, and highly vulnerable birthfamilies exploited. A system that prioritizes the interests of prospective adoptive families is inclined to underplay the importance of genetics and overplay the significance of environment. It is prone to disregard the feelings of birthfamilies and underestimate the interest that children have in their roots. In such a system, service to children is incidental to the process.

The finest programs, on the other hand, serve children by design; they are intentionally organized to create optimal circumstances for children. That is not to say that a child-centered process neglects the adults involved, for their emotional security is obviously very important. Children are affected by the security or insecurity of the adults caring for them. The security of adults, however, is not the primary goal; their security is a means to meeting the goal of serving children.

The old system of adoption routinely put children into foster care for weeks and months until the legal dust settled. The effect of that practice was to shift the anxiety of the circumstance from the adults to the infant. If we seek to serve children, it is better to avoid the extra step of foster care with an unfamiliar family whenever possible. At-risk placements put prospective adoptive families in emotional jeopardy, but it is worth the risk because adults are better equipped to handle anxiety than the children.

A system designed to meet the needs of children will make an effort to screen prospective adoptive parents. It is very difficult, even controversial work, and many service providers have given up on it. Painful as it may be, most of us recognize that not all persons interested in adopting children are satisfactory prospects for the role. Similarly, we know from experience that some people are not appropriate candidates for open adoption. This is an unpleasant fact that needs to be acknowledged and discussed openly. With assistance, most people can develop

---

* *From a speech entitled, "Adoption Reversals," at the Spirit of Open Adoption conference, Traverse City, Michigan, May 1995.*

appropriate skills and attitudes. Some families, however, choose to actively resist the fundamental ideas of open adoption and consequently are not suited for the role.

Birthfamilies and adopted children deserve to benefit from the knowledge gained from experience. If we are to enjoy peace of mind as professionals, we must be confident in our prospective families. In *Adoption Without Fear,* I noted, "Our program is only as good as the adoptive parents who carry out its ideals." The best designed program in the world will not work if its concepts are carried out by people who lack conviction and sincerity.

Based on our experience, Catholic Human Services has a clear vision of the qualities we look for as we consider prospective parents. We categorize these factors as *indispensable, crucial,* and *complementary.*

Indispensable qualities for participation in our program include

- genuine respect for birthfamilies;
- integrity;
- flexibility and ability to improvise;
- unpossessive attitudes toward children;
- high tolerance for emotional pain; and
- inner strength, or faith.

Each of these variables is necessary for participation in values-based open adoption. If open adoption is attempted by someone lacking any of these characteristics, problems are likely.

Other factors we consider *crucial* include

- relationship skills;
- an unquenchable desire to learn;
- humility, or being at peace with one's imperfections;
- leadership ability;
- compassion;
- foresight;
- intuitive understanding of systems thinking; and
- affirming and inclusive personalities.

Additional characteristics that we find *complementary* include

- humor,
- gratitude,
- gregariousness, and
- "chooseablity."

Chooseability is the ability of prospective adoptive parents to present themselves as interesting and likeable candidates for a rewarding and enduring open adoption relationship.

These three lists speak to matters of the heart and have little to do with traditional eligibility requirements. Screening should not be a matter of indulging middle-class standards; it should be founded on what we know about adoptions of quality. The goal of screening is to discover and admit participants who can bring life to the eight central values of quality open adoption. Ideally, all of our families share these values. Beyond that indispensable commonality, we hope that the families will reflect the wholesome diversity of our community. Although it may appear that we are looking for perfect families, we are not. We are looking for families who have learned from their failings and have been improved by them.

Screening is a difficult and painfully inexact process, but it dramatically improves the prospects for satisfying outcomes. Screening is worth the effort, for in striving to find optimal candidates for open adoption, a program truly honors children. If we give up on screening, if we take the position that experience has taught us nothing about what works and does not work in adoption, we are giving up on intelligence and we are offering children less than our best.

The prescreening by professionals sets the stage for selection by the birthfamily. The care that they put into the selection of the adoptive family must correlate to the consequences of their decisions. The method of selection should dignify the life of the child. Perhaps every introspective person wonders how he or she became part of a particular family, but certainly inquisitive adoptees wonder about this. For the sake of the adoptee's personal dignity, there must be a sensible answer. Given the unparalleled magnitude and duration of the consequences attached to this decision, it is vital that the decision is made with great intelligence, foresight, and care. The idea of a haphazard assignment to a particular family is a devastating blow to an adoptee's sense of personal significance.

Matching has always been a fascinating aspect of adoption. Many questions come to mind. Does any child fit with any family? Does every birthfamily line up successfully with every adoptive family? Should the process of coming together be left to chance, or should there be a system?

Besides dignifying the life story of the adoptee, a careful selection benefits everyone involved. It substantially improves the likelihood that birthparents and adoptive parents will relate to each other comfortably and naturally. Even more importantly, compatibility between the families significantly improves the chances the child will feel that she fits in and belongs. It helps her both integrate and differentiate her experiences. Fitting in sounds like such a simple matter, but it profoundly affects our comfort level. We all can relate on a much smaller scale to the painful awkwardness of showing up for a party inappropriately dressed. Not fitting in, even for a miserable hour or two, is almost more than we can bear. If feeling out of place is a poor way to spend a Friday night, it is certainly a poor way to spend a lifetime. Being cut from the same cloth improves the prospect that things will be workable. On the other hand, if the selection is made carelessly or from too narrow a field of prospects, chances grow that the youngster will feel that she does not fit in. Tragically, she may feel as though she is in exile among strangers. She may be tempted to simply put in her time until she can reconnect to her "own kind."

Another opportunity arises for the system to serve children at the point of separation and transition. If we act as though babies are oblivious to the world around them and are endlessly adaptable, we dishonor and seriously underestimate them. Sandra Musser, a strong voice for adoption reform, helps us to understand the meaning of an abrupt shift in custody with a simple analogy. She suggests, "Imagine all your family and friends—everyone who is dear to you—is on a plane headed for an exciting vacation. The plane crashes and you are the only survivor. You have lost *everything familiar.*"*

---

* *Sandra Musser. "The Ethical Issues Associated with Adoption and Openness." Presented at the conference, Open Adoption Comes of Age, Traverse City, Michigan, April 14, 1988.*

We must learn how not to be abrupt; we need to learn the art of gentle transitioning. In the best of circumstances—which are hard to arrange—the gentleness begins prenatally. Ideally, the relationship issues between the birthfamily and the prospective adoptive family are worked out so thoroughly that an amazing spirit of relaxation prevails. In such circumstances, there is confidence that, regardless of the ultimate decision, the baby will be welcomed and celebrated by everyone involved.

We must treat the infant as though he is fully aware of what is going on around him, because he is. We must give him a chance to gradually adjust to his new circumstances. We must provide time for unrushed good-byes and unhurried hellos. We must be very careful that, in the name of bonding and attachment, we do not traumatize the baby.

A well-designed system of adoption sets up participants for success by careful planning. It attends to the details of the open adoption relationship and clarifies everyone's expectations of each other. Some surprises always arise, but much of the journey is predictable. As witness to the understandings that are worked out, the program adds an extra dimension of accountability to the process.

The final characteristic of a system designed to honor children is that it follows through on the adoptions it launches. By creating a lively open adoption community, it fosters an environment in which the entire extended open adoption clan can thrive. An important aspect of that effort is that it informs and educates the public to better understand and support open adoption families. Many families in open adoptions around the country feel isolated. We often field calls from people outside our system who are enjoying their open adoptions but who find their confidence waning because of the relentless skepticism they encounter. An excellent program continuously learns more about adoption and strives to keep its graduates up to date. More accurately, the learning process is mutual, as professionals and participants share new insights gained through experience. Follow-up also means a willingness to mediate any misunderstandings that may emerge through the years.

HONORING THE BIRTH HERITAGE

For decades, adoption made artificial orphans out of adoptees. *Clean* was the operative word. The adoptive parents were squeaky clean; the birthparents made a clean break; and the adoptee was a clean slate, a tabula rasa. It was all part of an enduring game of pretend. The adoptive family pretended that the baby was born to them, as if they were a biological family. In the "as if" plan, there was no room for a birthfamily. It was best for them to vanish. The game suggested that birthparents pretend that they had never had a baby. In extreme form, the participants in the game never got around to telling the adoptee that she was adopted.

One of the most damaging aspects of this charade was the uncomfortable imposition of the adoptive family's aptitudes and interests on the child. With no regard for their idiosyncratic abilities, adoptees were told, "We've been playing piano for five generations in this family, and you will be the sixth." In the pretend world of adoption, there was little regard for the child's natural abilities. The clean-slate approach dishonors children; it sends them very negative messages about themselves. If we do not respect the child's birth heritage—the stuff she is made of—how can we really love her? What is the youngster if she is not the stuff of which she is made? How can we understand this person if we ignore her origins?

Barbara Trimetiere, a seasoned adoption professional, tells a haunting story set in the hectic days as the Vietnam War pressed to its conclusion.* In a frantic fight against time, children were loaded on planes and jetted to the safety of America. Barb was a leading child welfare worker in Philadelphia at the time. With very little forewarning, she was notified that a plane loaded with children was en route to Philadelphia, and she was asked to assemble a child welfare team to receive them. After calling everyone she could think of to help, she headed for the airport. There she saw an unforgettable scene unfolding. Many children had arrived with writing all over their bodies. Recognizing that in all likelihood they would never see their children again, their ancestry-conscious parents had used their last precious,

---

*   *In* Open Adoption: The Experts Speak Out. *Video produced by Carol Land and Sharon Kaplan-Roszia. Tustin, CA: Parenting Resources, 1989.*

frantic moments of family intactness to write their family histories on their children as final gifts. One can imagine the writing smudged with tears. The social work response? Soap. In the judgment of those present, the children need to be cleaned up. Barb's response, of course, was to find a camera; but treasures of information were lost forever by the time she was able to take action.

This compelling story captures one of adoption's most crucial decisions. How shall we approach the children? Will it be with soap, or will it be with a camera?

Wiping the slate clean is a tragedy for everyone. To lose the birth heritage is to lose something unique and personal. Most of us, if we discovered our house on fire, would grab an armful of family pictures over other treasures. Older people in the process of shedding possessions make the same choice. Faced with the prospect of great loss, our most basic instinct is to somehow preserve what we can of the past. The "clean" approach to adoption forever scrubs away the fragrance and color of horse traders, village chiefs, mad scientists, and saints. It is nothing less than a profound insult to the birthfamily and an indescribable loss for the child.

Sharon Kaplan-Roszia tells with great warmth the story of a particularly lovable 16-year-old who captured his life circumstance with a poignant analogy. "I'm like a cake. The bottom layer is my birthfamily and the top layer is my adoptive family. It's up to me to ice them together, but the bottom layer is so crumbly that the top keeps slipping off."* What sort of cake would there be if there was no bottom layer to work with?

All this is very difficult for those of us who are not adopted to understand. For the most part, we take our family relationships for granted. I became more sensitive to the power of this intergenerational connectedness while strolling for the first time through the little Dutch village where my father was born. Having grown up surrounded with family, and being fully informed regarding our history, I had always felt well-grounded and complete. Suddenly, though, upon encountering powerful symbols of past generations, I felt significantly more complete. I was unprepared for and astounded by the power of that experience.

---

* *Sharon Kaplan-Roszia. "The Ethics of Adoption." Presented at the National Catholic Charities Pregnancy and Adoption Conference, San Francisco, April 1994.*

It was a magnificent moment, a moment that defies description—it has to be experienced to be understood. As gripping as that discovery was, I am sure that, for adoptees, the ancestral connection is significantly more powerful. To honestly complete my story, however, I must add one note. As I stood in that dear village, I had a distinct, bittersweet impression that life had moved on. I believe adoptees experience a more powerful version of that sensation as well.

What a contrast there is between systems of adoption that honor the birth heritage and those that seek to erase it! There is more to love about a child who comes from somewhere. Familiarity with the birth heritage equips adoptive families to respond to and nurture the uniqueness of the child. Adoptive parents who love and honor the birthfamily are sure to love and honor the child. They are eager to preserve the link to the birthfamily because those are his roots. It occurs to them that, without these roots, their child would not exist. They are greedy for information about the his heritage because it helps them understand this person they love so deeply. They realize that background information may help him understand himself better. For that matter, it may help them to respond more effectively as parents.

With tears in her eyes, one adoptive mother told me about a cache of pictures her family had received from the mother of their son's birthfather. Since they had not been able to gain the involvement of the birthfather and did not know him, they were thrilled to have this new information about him. They made a beautiful collage out the pictures so their son could measure his growth as a person against that of his birthfather. They could not have been more pleased if they had won the lottery.

Sensitive Handling of Information

An honoring form of adoption celebrates the adoptee's sense of curiosity. Hopefully, the genuine openness of open adoption will show up in the everyday interaction of the adoptive family. The great message of open adoption is this: "Whatever the issue, we can talk." Unless we believe that adoption is at heart shameful, adoption is nothing to hide. It is astounding to think that home studies from 30 years ago hinged on the question,

"Do you intend to tell your child that she is adopted?" Even the more enlightened version, "When do you expect to tell your child that she is adopted?" is amazing. What does it tell us about our attitudes if we consider this information so horrifying that we have to practice the words 50 times before we say them? How can we in good conscience advertise adoption as a wholesome option on one hand and hide it from children as an unfortunate, woeful fact on the other?

Children deserve the truth. Adoptees deserve the truth. People have an absolute right to information about themselves. It is unconscionable that this institution continue to play shell games with people's identities while fogging the scene with hollow talk of the best interests of children. The great enduring shame of adoption is its reluctance and unwillingness to provide adoptees with fundamental information about themselves.

Children benefit from genuine information. Good information contributes to their sense of trust and security. It helps them move toward greater mastery of their lives. Lacking good information, they fill the gaps with fantasy. Fantasy, of course, is seldom mundane. It lurches dramatically toward the exotic, both positive and negative. How sad to think that the institution of adoption has for decades required adoptees to build their identities on the bedrock of fantasy and speculation.

The great challenge in adoption is to speak the truth with kindness. It is an art form. Sometimes, because the facts are harsh, it is difficult to share information with children in a way that is both honest and kind. Adoptive parents surely cannot paint a savage picture of the birthparent world, nor can they make it too pretty. If the birthparent circumstance is described as a nightmare, it can detrimentally affect the child's self-concept. On the other hand, if all was well in the birthparent situation, why was adoption necessary?

It takes a loving heart to discover ways to share accurate information with the child in a spirit of truth and kindness. It takes wisdom to find the most appropriate perspective. We need to be very sensitive to the messages we send children about themselves. How does an adopted child interpret the idea that the birthfamily gave him to the adoptive family as a "gift"? What does it mean to a child to be a product of a "problem pregnancy"? What goes through his mind when he hears about the "plight of unwanted children"? What does a child make of our offhand comments about the finances of adoption? At one of our conferences, adult adoptees publicly compared their worth with sad humor: "I was a $3,000 baby. How about you?"

Open adoption parents have a great advantage when it comes to sharing information about the birth heritage; namely, the birthfamily. No one, obviously, knows the inside story better than they do. They can provide details that no one else can, and there is no finer authority to answer the important question, "Why?" Crucially, the ongoing involvement of the birthfamily with the adoptive family is concrete testimony to the youngster that they truly do care.

A DEVELOPMENTAL PERSPECTIVE

Adoptees are not perpetual infants. An honoring form of adoption respects the obvious fact that their needs and interests will change over time. It recognizes that as an adopted child matures, she will have a shifting understanding of birthfamilies and adoption. The themes of loss, security, and being different will vary in meaning to adoptees as they move through developmental phases.* Adoption that honors children affords them, in age-appropriate fashion, a growing voice in deciding their life courses. In every dimension of life, young people are expected to assume greater responsibility for themselves as they mature. This principle also applies as they come to terms with their adoption.

As we listen to the children, we must be especially careful in our interpretations of their silence. In the past, some adoptive parents pointed to the silence of their children and concluded, "Adoption is not a problem for our children because they never talk about it." It was a logically precarious conclusion. Similarly, some modern interpreters of the adoption experience point to the same silence and presume the adoptee is in denial. They seem to imply that if she is not perpetually talking about adoption, she is in distress without recognizing it. It is often a tough call to

---

*   *Helpful information about the intersection of developmental and adoption issues can be found in* Being Adopted: The Lifelong Search for Self, *by David Brodzinsky, Marshall Schecter, and Robin Marantz Henig;* The Adoption Life Cycle, *by Elinor Rosenberg; and* The Open Adoption Experience, *by Lois Melina and Sharon Roszia-Kaplan.*

make. Parents need to develop an intuitive sense of the issues. They need to sincerely invite discussion of the feelings, but do so without pressure. Gently, they must find ways to let their children—who can read their parent's pleasure related to adoption and are often reluctant to douse their enthusiasm—know it is safe to talk about these often complicated feelings.

Critics of open adoption are especially wary of the teen years and the accompanying drive toward independence. They point to the "grass is greener" phenomena and predict dire outcomes. Family dynamics are magnified during adolescence, and it is entirely possible that open adoption families will have their hands full—like most other families. In many ways, this speculation insults all of the participants in the open adoption drama. It reveals a resilient distrust of birthfamilies, who, the cynics insist, are simply biding time waiting for the opportunity to sabotage the plan they themselves chose, designed, and benefit from. It denigrates the capacity of adoptive parents to establish and sustain significant, satisfying relationships with their children. It suggests that adolescent adoptees are fickle and heartless, devoid of feelings of loyalty and affection.

It is possible that open adoption's greatest moments may occur during the adolescent years. This is especially likely if families have mastered the art of open discussion. Often, the people who resist the idea of open adoption most vigorously are adoptive parents from the closed system. Open adoption seems to threaten them. Sometimes, though, these parents have approached me after public presentations mourning the unavailability of open adoption in their day. They confess, "We were totally lost during our kids' teen years. We didn't have a clue what was going on. We would have given anything to be able to compare notes with the birthfamily back then. We would have been better positioned to help our kids work through their most forlorn and lonely moments." Wise adoptive parents and birthparents will establish the foundation for effective navigation of the adolescent years during the less perplexing years of early childhood.

The ultimate task for the adoptee as he matures is to establish his unique identity. This is a great challenge for every maturing person, but it has been especially difficult for the adoptee who lacks information about his birth heritage. On the strength of personal familiarity with all the important contributors to his life, the open adoption adoptee can recognize the ways in which he resembles each of his adoptive and birthparents, how he is dissimilar from them, and what his own unique characteristics are.

COOPERATION AMONG ADULTS

The best analogy for open adoption is marriage. Just as one of the best gifts to children is an effective marriage, one of the best gifts to children in open adoption is effective relationships between the adults involved. In the days of closed adoption, when birthparents and adoptive parents were presumed adversaries, adoptees were caught in an emotional cross fire. They could safely enjoy only one set of parents at a time. Curiosity about the birthfamily was frequently interpreted as ingratitude. Open adoption relieves that tension. When birthfamilies and adoptive families respect and enjoy each other, adoptees are free to enjoy all the important people in their lives. The loyalty bind vanishes.

The adults involved in open adoption do the child a great favor when they build satisfying relationships with each other. Naturally they are all keenly interested in the youngster, but they need to enjoy each other as well. If they are unable to build this connection, they may depend too much on the child to sustain the relationship. She may feel a burden to entertain the adults and keep everyone happy. When the adult relationships are comfortable, the adoption develops a natural quality, and the youngster can relax.

It is not a simple matter to honor a child. Sometimes a child's needs are obvious, but often they are subtle. No parent is fully equal to the challenge of reading the signs. It takes a sixth sense to understand a child; and sometimes, of all things, it takes a committee. The more eyes, ears, and hearts that one tuned into a youngster, the better the chances are that she will be understood. Ultimately, though, there is a trial-and-error dimension to the process of figuring out her needs. In the same open adoption family, for example, one child may attend a gathering of the extended birthfamily and enjoy it immensely, while the other child may find that sort of event overwhelming. The only sure way to know is to experiment and monitor outcomes closely.

Parenting in any form—birth or adoptive—calls for sacrifice. It is the first clause in the job description. Participation in open adoption requires getting along with the other persons involved in the plan. Getting along with other people requires flexibility and a pronounced willingness to compromise. A sacrificial attitude requires doing some things for the child even when it is uncomfortable for the adults. I remember a closed adoption mother in the studio audience of a television show commenting on this necessity: "I can see that there are advantages to open adoption for the birthfamily and the child. In all honesty, I'm just not sure I could make the sacrifices myself." If we are serious about honoring children, we will surely be familiar with the pain of sacrifice.

The commitment to cooperation means the adults must work things out when there are disagreements. Like all relationships, open adoptions need to handle disappointment and frustration. In case of sustained disagreement, it makes sense to go back to the agency to work things out. Interaction must not degenerate into win-lose showdowns, since adoptees always lose in such circumstances. A good program will help participants achieve clarity of roles and authority. Most conflict can be avoided if roles are well-defined and respected. Participants who are committed to honoring the child will support and affirm each other's status in the arrangement. Birthparents will support the authority of the adoptive parents, and adoptive parents will defend the honor of the birthparents.

Consistency honors children. In the early years of our open adoption practice, we gave little or no direction to birthparents regarding their obligations. They were free to come and go as they pleased within the comfort range of the adoptive family. For some, involvement with the adoptive family was entirely dependent on the necessities and whims of their lives. If, for example, the birthmother's life was full and interesting, she might be less involved with the adoptive family. If her life was uneventful, she might be more involved. A more evolved form of open adoption is driven by the needs of the child. Children are honored by the predictable involvement of birthparents.

Teamwork between adoptive parents and birthparents is especially important when adoption pain surfaces. In the days of closed adoption, there was no choice but to work through the pain individually. Encouragingly, our experience so far suggests that the usual open adoption instinct in the face of pain is inclusive. Families realize that cooperation dramatically improves the likelihood of finding collective relief. When the team finds the desired relief, the open adoption relationship is reaffirmed and revitalized.

So we have a start. We have at least some beginning ideas regarding what it means to honor the adopted child. We are certain to learn more in the years ahead. It is worth our effort. If we succeed in truly honoring adoptees, we will all be enriched.

Chapter 4

Candor: A Luminous Possibility

> Most people opt for a life of very limited honesty and openness and relative closedness, hiding themselves....It is easier that way. Yet the rewards of the difficult life of honesty and dedication to the truth are more than commensurate with the demands....Open people are continually growing...they can establish and maintain intimate relationships far more effectively than closed people...[they] have served as sources of illumination and clarification. Finally, they are totally free to be....By their openness, people dedicated to the truth live in the open, and through the exercise of their courage to live in the open, they become free from fear.
>
> Scott Peck, *The Road Less Traveled*

> When we mix a little love with our honesty, we tell the right truth to the right person at the right time in the right way. We also tell the right truth for the right reason.
>
> Lewis Smedes, *A Pretty Good Person*

A few years ago, while filling out a grant application for a video project, I encountered the question, "What is innovative about your program?" A simple question requiring a simple answer. "Our major innovation," I wrote, "is a wholehearted commitment to candor. We make every effort to make sure that our clients are fully informed. This commitment puts us on the living edge of adoption." I was ready to move on to the next question, but I could not quite get past what I had just written. Candor as an innovation? What does this say about the others in the field who are not so innovative? We know an institution is in trouble when forthrightness is considered novel.

There is no greater albatross in the world of adoption than secrecy. It hangs conspicuously around the institution's neck, utterly fouling its prospects for vitality. Once secrecy takes hold, it is a difficult liability to shed. I believe adoption is destined to struggle with its image, not to mention its basic health, as long as secrecy perseveres as a significant factor.

I do not argue for the total elimination of secrecy from adoption. We all know of unusual circumstances that appear to pose genuine threat and hazard to everyone involved. In a very high-risk situation, secrecy may be useful, but it needs to be viewed as a tool of last resort. It should be used sparingly—we know too much about secrecy to take it lightly—and only when there is professional consensus regarding its application. The assumption in any healthy institution must be candor, and this assumption should only be overruled for very persuasive reasons. Worker convenience or the casual preference of adoptive parents are not sufficient reasons to install secrecy as an enduring and limiting dynamic in an adoption. And in those rare instances when full information cannot be shared, we can at least be candid about our reasons for not being candid.

THE EFFECTS OF SECRECY

In the past, secrecy was not used as a tool of last resort; it was standard practice. It was routinely applied to even the most benign circumstances. Let us briefly consider what we have learned from this experiment in social engineering.

Secrecy is divisive. By creating "haves" and "have nots," secrecy sets birthparents and adoptive parents apart as adversarial groups with nothing in common and no opportunity to get to know each other. "We" become sacrosanct, and "they" become a little less than fully human. Where there is division, prospects for mutual understanding and support are seriously diminished.

The division created by secrecy is hard on everyone involved, but it is especially difficult for children. It creates for them a painful problem of divided loyalties. In rigorously divided circumstances, they can love only one family at a time. If they have positive feelings for one family, they feel disloyal to the other. Secrecy leaves many adoptees feeling like divided people and that some part of them is not fully acceptable.

Secrecy fuels the dynamic of power. The party holding the secret has obvious power over the uninformed; but, interestingly, the dynamic works both ways. The uninformed party, with his potential to penetrate the secret, also looms very powerfully in the life of the secret holder. An arrangement founded on power easily degenerates into a power struggle. When relationships are worked out in terms of power rather than mutual respect, promising ideas are frequently lost. The only thing that matters is power. Might takes precedence over good sense.

Secrecy generates preoccupation. Since human nature seems to find the forbidden especially alluring, secrecy easily lends itself to debilitating preoccupation. There is nothing quite like the appeal of the forbidden fruit. Many adoptees and birthparents have been unable to press forward with other important life tasks because they are psychologically stuck struggling with the unknowns and unfinished business of adoption.

Secrecy is a gateway to unhealthy living. To seek refuge in the protection of secrecy is to live a fear-based lifestyle. Secrecy is a short-term strategy for dealing with situational anxiety that turns into a lifetime of apprehension and dread. It creates a condition of chronic vulnerability. The defense of secrecy requires constant vigilance and is accomplished only at great psychic expense. Once launched, secrecy is a consuming dynamic that takes on a life of its own. It breeds additional layers of secrecy and builds momentum that is nearly impossible to reverse. Often, it takes a dramatic turn of events to break the spiral of proliferating secrets. Because fear alters our ability to gather and interpret information, decisions are often based on fantasy-enhanced speculation rather than fact. For the adoptee, secrecy can accentuate the distressing feeling of being different from others. She worries about the nature of information that must be contained and hidden away.

Secrecy runs counter to professional value systems. It undermines the value that all human service professions place on self-awareness and healthy disclosure. Denial is considered a primitive and undesirable coping mechanism and is actively discouraged. It is bizarre to consider what may go on under the roof of a family-service agency. An adoption worker in one room may be launching secret-based adoptions while the therapist down the hall labors creatively with stifled clients to unearth repression and denial from their pasts.

Secrecy and confidentiality are often confused for each other. Confidentiality is meant to protect the exchange of information in a professional relationship. It is a limited constraint on information sharing that can be set aside when the client's interests are best served by doing so. When the protection of information is applied universally, whether or not people ask for it, and when it cannot be waived by the "beneficiary," it is not confidentiality; it is secrecy.

Secrecy is obsolete. It has outlived its purpose. In vivid contrast to an earlier era that condemned "illegitimacy," there is presently little stigma attached to pregnancy outside of marriage. The contemporary moral response is a shrug of the shoulders. In this context of moral nonchalance, birthparents and adoptees have little need for the protection of secrecy. If birthparents face any current negativity from their communities, it is rooted in pragmatic and economic indignation, not moral censure. In the debate over the public's willingness to pay for pregnancy outside of marriage, secrecy is not a relevant factor.

Secrecy is counterproductive to its original purpose. While society grew more tolerant of illegitimacy—a word seldom heard these days—it grew much less tolerant of secrecy. In a remarkable twist of irony, secrecy—with its shadowy connotations of unwholesomeness—now generates the very aura of illegitimacy and shame it was intended to overcome.

Secrecy repels. We instinctively react to secrecy with suspicion. We know from everyday experience that healthy activity seldom requires stealth. Unacceptable behavior, on the other hand, routinely craves the cover of secrecy. People prefer to be leveled with, even when the news is difficult, and are quickly disgusted when provided with inadequate information.

Secrecy is unnecessary. If birthparents were fire-breathing monsters, secrecy might be important. Since they are usually average, likable, imperfect human beings, there is, with very rare exception, no need to protect against them.

Secrecy undermines our commitment to truth. In a secretive environment, it is impossible to know whether one is working with facts or fiction, and we quickly become disoriented. When fact and fiction are indistinguishable, there are no facts. After a birthmother from the secretive era signed a release of parental rights, she was told by the judge, "If you are ever asked, whether you had a child, even under oath, you should say, 'No.'" When society's keepers of truth bend it so comfortably, truth becomes elusive, and no one, adopted or not, can know anything with certainty. It is possible to know that one is adopted, but it is not possible to be certain that one is not adopted.

Secrecy is an illusion; it does not really exist. At Catholic Human Services' 1982 open adoption conference, Mary Jo Rillera, then director of a large search organization in Southern California, reported that, in her experience, 90% of the adoptees and birthparents who earnestly search find their counterparts. That observation indicates that there really is no such thing as closed adoption. We kid ourselves if we think information can be contained. How wise is it for adoptive parents to base their emotional security on an illusion?

Secrecy isolates and inhibits feedback. In an environment of isolation, there is little flow of information. That is a very significant deficit, for the health of every institution depends on information and feedback. For many years, secrecy prevented traditional service providers—agencies—from gathering the information they needed to improve their programs. Without impetus for change, agencies stagnated and in many regions lost their positions as primary providers of adoption services.

Secrecy reduces accountability. Hiding behind the impenetrable veil of confidentiality, professionals are seldom challenged to explain their decisions. With reduced accountability, the usual system of checks and balances is impeded, and prospects for error and abuse are greatly elevated.

Secrecy interferes with the adoptee's fundamental right to information about him- or herself. In an extraordinary departure from usual assumptions about individual rights, the institution's affection for secrecy—obsolete, unnecessary, and illusory—blocks a basic human right righteously afforded all other Americans. Coming from an institution that steadfastly claims above all to serve the interests of adoptees, this aberration is especially cruel.

Secrecy impedes the flow of crucial genetic and medical information between the birthfamily and adoptive family. Painful medical tests that could be avoided if current medical information were available are sometimes necessary as a consequence of secrecy. In the most dire circumstances, the lack of information—unavailable because of secrecy—can be fatal.

The toll extracted by secrecy in adoption over the years is incalculable. Thousands of adoptees and birthparents invest their most creative life energy, not to mention countless hours and dollars, to overcome its legacy. Perhaps the cruelest twist of all is that it sometimes necessitates "counter secrecy." Otherwise straightforward people are compelled to enter the world of covert inquiry and deceit to gather basic information about themselves, information that the rest of society takes for granted.

Variations on the Noncandor Theme

Secrecy is not the only impediment to candor in adoption. There are several ways in which facts are distorted. Some forms of adoption, for example, are deliberately deceitful. Promises are made when there is no intention to follow through on them. Birthparents are assured that they will have ongoing involvement with adoptive families, but once the legal torch has passed they find themselves totally shut out. Inverting the victimization, some pregnant women have "played at adoption" to get their medical expenses paid by prospective adoptive parents. Whenever there is a manipulative quality to adoption, deception is part of the problem.

Another variation is double-talk. One birthmother came to us after exploring the possibilities with other programs. She told of a peculiar conversation that she had experienced with a social worker. "If I work with your program," she asked, "will I be able to choose the adoptive family?"

"Yes, you will," replied the worker. "You can choose the adoptive family if it turns out that everything works out in a fashion that allows you to choose the adoptive family."

"Oh. Now, if I work with your program, will I be able to meet the adoptive parents?"

"Yes, you will. You will be able to meet the selected family if a number of factors come together in a form which is of the sort which generates sufficient comfort for everyone involved that they all conclude that it would be okay to meet."

"Oh."

Some programs, it appears, practice something other than full candor.

Another form of noncandor is the withholding of difficult information. This censorship is often a well-intentioned effort to avoid the deleterious effects of self-fulfilling prophecies. Through the years, adoption workers have been tempted to spare adoptive families the gory details. This concern has given birth to countless euphemisms. A birthmother with a D-minus average, for example, became a "struggling student." An unemployed, high-school dropout birthfather would be described as "looking for his niche."

The shortcomings of this strategy are obvious. When families are denied important background facts, they are not positioned to make fully informed choices. Some adoptive families unknowingly open their homes and hearts to children who are not appropriate for them. Not knowing pertinent historical details, they are deprived of the opportunity to prepare themselves for the predictable challenges associated with particular children. A system that withholds information from clients for their own good is patronizing and disrespectful. It underestimates their ability to handle the realities of life. In an adoption culture where there is some prospect that significant information might be withheld, distrust is certain to emerge.

A final variation on the noncandor theme is the overemphasis on the positives of adoption at the expense of truth. The classic example of this is the chosen-baby story, despised by countless adoptees. A pleasant story in which adoptive parents select a particular baby from a long row of unclaimed infants, it served to temporarily bolster adopted children's self-esteem. Later, though, when adoptees discovered that they had built their self-images on total fiction, they felt betrayed. The chosen-baby story has clearly lost favor, but the "everything is wonderful" approach to adoption perseveres. In an effort to bolster adoption's appeal, many people sugarcoat adoption and overlook the pain that resides in its core.

A LUMINOUS ALTERNATIVE

In the early years of open adoption, I often spoke, no doubt more pompously than was necessary, of honesty and truth. Now I use the word *candor.* This is a better word for three reasons. First, it is less arrogant or smug to speak of candor than of truth. Those who claim to have captured the truth can expect to encounter many skeptically raised eyebrows. Second, unlike the word *honesty,* candor does not imply that those who are in secret-based adoptions are dishonest. Participants in closed adoption were taught to be honestly noncandid. The third reason is that *candor* is a splendid word that is rich with helpful nuances.

The Latin root of candor, *candidus,* means "bright," whereas the French word *candere* means to "shine" or "glow." These roots point to the luminous quality of candor. With its candescent nature, candor stands in perfect contrast to secrecy, with its affection for hiding. The two styles are incompatible; they suffer each other's presence. The encounter of candor and secrecy brings to mind the image of unsavory night creatures scurrying for cover when they are suddenly exposed to the light.

Candor is larger than honesty. It is honesty in unreserved form. That means it is proactive; it proclaims itself and goes out of its way to avoid any appearance of holding back. Candor is transparent and forthright openness. It is without guile or duplicity. It is in no manner ulterior, it is not phony, and it abhors counterfeits. In this regard, candor is closely related to humility, a virtue that Episcopal priest Gale Webbe describes as "complete unpretentiousness." He elaborates with the observation that the "humble person adopts no postures. He sees, acknowledges, and accepts himself as being exactly what he is, not more and no less. He is utterly genuine, and interested only in things that are genuine."

Two particularly pleasing definitions of candor are offered in *Webster's Third International Dictionary.* One meaning is "kindliness," and the other is "unstained purity and innocence." Each is listed as archaic, suggesting that in our modern age we have reduced need for words that convey the ideas of kindliness and innocence. For some of us, candor still conveys a hint of kindliness and innocence. There is a charming naivete about candor. Certainly there is vulnerability to it, but those who practice candor have the personal strength to endure whatever rejection they may encounter. Kindness is an invaluable dimension of candor because it tempers the hurtful potential of truth.

Although we usually regard candor as a style of communication, it might better be understood as a view of life. Candor is a predisposition to respect oneself and others. It assumes that trust is an indispensable dimension to successful relationships. A person of candor presumes that the more you get to know him, the more you will appreciate and enjoy him. He wonders how anything of interpersonal substance can be accomplished if people remain strangers to each other. A candid person benefits from the fact that candor is contagious. A warm expression of candor invites a candid response. As a result, for people of candor, getting to know people comes easily.

One of the most healing aspects of candor is its capacity to get beyond the isolating burden of perfection. A truly candid and humble person is, as Webbe pointed out, delightfully unpretentious. Hang around candid people even briefly and you know all about them. Very significantly, you know about their blunders and the lessons they learned from their mistakes. Their ability to live at peace with their imperfections is inspiring. Imperfect people are easier to relate to than those who project an image of perfection. Most people fear they would be rejected if they were fully known. As a result, they insulate themselves and, predictably, end up experiencing the very emotional distance they feared. Candid people, on the other hand, declare themselves and their failings openly and, as a result, end up greatly loved. Writer Henri Nouwen speaks to this phenomenon very clearly. He notes that we are tempted

> ...to use our many obvious failures and disappointments in our lives to convince ourselves that we are really not worth being loved, [when, in fact] the many failures may open that place in us where we have nothing to brag about but everything to be loved for. It is becoming a child again, a child who is loved simply for being, simply for smiling, simply for reaching out.*

Now and then, to grow in our understanding of adoption, our professional staff reviews its top 10 birthparents and adoptive parents and asks, "What is it about them that makes them exceptional?" One conspicuous factor is that they are all easy to get to know. To be in their presence is to comfortably and

---

* *Henri Nouwen. "Failure." In* Seeds of Hope: A Henri Nouwen Reader. *Robert Durback. (Ed.). New York, Bantam, 1989.*

naturally learn their stories. They laugh at their shortcomings without self-consciousness and take credit for their triumphs without boasting. They have an "old shoe" quality about them, and they wear well.

Some people are naturally gifted with a spirit of candor. It is their nature, and they do not know how to be anything other than candid. They are refreshing and inspiring. Most of us, however, need to cultivate the art of candor. It is not easy, because our culture trains us to be clever. It takes conscious effort and true courage to practice candor. Those who successfully move from guardedness to candor are usually rewarded, because it is the nature of old-fashioned candor—innocent, kind, and pure—to generate highly satisfying relationships. A knowable person, after all, is generally much easier to trust than someone who is mysterious.

Candor happens best within reasonable limits. There are times when self-disclosure is not desirable, and there are times when information gained about others should not be shared. The old guidelines for defending against gossip apply. Before information is shared, it needs to pass a few sensible tests. Is it true? Is it necessary? Is it kind?

Candor enhances the communication process. Because it paves the way for comfortable sharing, candor produces high-quality information that is direct, thorough, accurate, and updatable. Everyone involved benefits from information of this quality. Good information ends the unhealthy mystery and fantasy that have characterized adoption through the years. Most crucially, it equips adopted children to understand themselves more fully.

The face of adoption changes completely when it is characterized by candor. As the opposite of secrecy, candor inevitably produces different outcomes. When the participants of adoption—birthparents, adoptive parents, adoptees and professionals—commit themselves to candor, the results can be extraordinary. Where secrecy formerly bred shame, candor now generates trust; and where there is trust, there is potential for intimacy. If we want adopted children to develop a sense of reasonable trust in the world around them, we owe them nothing less than candor.

Chapter 5

Honoring the Pain

We are never more alive to life than when it hurts....
We are never more aware of our need for each other,
never more in reach of each other if we can only bring
ourselves to reach out and let ourselves be touched.
The universal experience of pain is what makes us all
brothers and sisters, the parents and children, of each
other, the story of one of us is the story of all of us.

Frederick Buechner, *A Clown in the Belfry*

If our joy is honest joy, it must somehow be congru-
ous with human tragedy. This is the test of joy's integrity: Is it compatible with pain?....Only the heart
that hurts has a right to joy. Only the person who
cries for the needless death of children has the right
to bless God for the gift of life.

Lewis Smedes, *How Can It Be All Right When Everything Is All Wrong?*

The pain associated with adoption is miserable stuff. It's the
birthfather in the hospital corridor curled up in a fetal ball of
self-blame. It's the doctor saying, "You're pregnant." It's the
doctor saying, "You'll never be pregnant." It's the 80-year-old
birthmother rocking and mumbling, "They shouldn't have done
that to me, they shouldn't have done that to me, they shouldn't
have...." It's the 8-year-old sobbing, "I wish I had started in
your tummy." It's the dazed birthmother standing alone on

the sidewalk as the adoptive family drives away with her two-day old daughter. It's the hopeful couple driving away with their two-day old daughter, leaving their child's birthmother standing alone on the sidewalk. It's the 21-year-old being told he has no right to his original name. It's finding out for the first time from falling-down-drunk Uncle Charlie at the family reunion that you're adopted. The permutations of adoption pain are endless.

We must be careful not to sanitize, sentimentalize, or even glamorize the pain of adoption. It really is miserable stuff, and it is intensely personal. It is internal. The pain of adoption is not something that happens to a person—it is the person. Because the pain is so primal, it is virtually impossible to describe.

In the days preceding open adoption, I would do my best to convey to excited prospective adoptive parents some sense of the prior scene, the withering moment of the birthmother's separation from the baby. With a lump in my throat, awkwardly searching for sufficient words, I would somehow get the story out. The couple would listen politely and, with serious faces but lightness of voice, comment, "That must have been really difficult for her." This response never set well with me. I wanted to scream at them, "Difficult? Is that the best you can do? It was awful! It was horrible! You don't understand!"

It infuriated me to hear the unspeakable agony of birthparents distilled into the feeble word "difficult." Of course, trivializing the pain was neither the couple's fault nor mine. The problem is in the nature of pain; its essence cannot be expressed through words. Words give us some sense of the category of another's pain, some remote sense of what it must be like; but to really understand that person's experience of pain, we must be with them and with it. In that era, which kept people apart, they had not been with each other.

Because pain is so difficult to describe, everyone involved in adoption feels, at least to some degree, misunderstood. This problem is exacerbated by the fact that intense pain makes us very self-centered. Nothing else really matters when we are consumed with pain, and it is tempting to think that no one else has endured pain quite as devastating as one's own. After all, no one truly understands the anguish of parting with a child. Surely, no outsider fully understands the to-the-bone exasperation and helplessness of biological mutiny—hopes relentlessly dashed on a monthly basis. And it is folly to suppose that someone who has not been there can really grasp the interior emptiness that exists when one leaves the clan. And somehow, not being understood makes the pain all the worse.

The many anguished voices of adoption address variations on the theme of disconnection and incompleteness. Disconnection, of course, is larger than adoption, but adoption intensifies the feeling of disconnectedness. Some participants feel the incompleteness more intensely than others, but every participant in adoption must eventually come to terms with this dynamic. It is spiritual pain. Often it takes the form of an aching sense of what could have been. How would a child born to us have acted? How would things have turned out if I could have found a way to raise my baby? What if I had stayed with my birthparents? Adoption wishes it could be perfectly natural, but it is not. It is dogged by the fact that something important—the intergenerational cohesion of biology—is missing. Lovingly crafted adoption can transform extremely difficult circumstances into something beautiful, but it cannot alter the fact that each person's journey begins with loss.

The issue of pain has polarized the adoptive community. Some people believe adoption generates so much pain that it should be abolished. Others believe the pain of adoption is insignificant and does not merit serious consideration. Neither extreme makes sense.

Those who seek to eliminate adoption reason that anything containing so much pain ought to be abolished. There are two errors in their position. First, they overlook the fact that adoption has not cornered the market on pain. The alternatives to adoption are also painful, sometimes more so. Unfortunately, many situations offer nothing but painful solutions, and the sorry challenge is to determine the least deleterious path. Second, they overlook the constructive potential of pain. Although we view pain as the enemy, and no one volunteers for it, we also recognize that pain contributes significantly to the breadth and depth of our existence. It is a necessary element of life, and it is an error to conclude that anything painful should be eliminated.

The other camp, those who deny the pain of adoption, denies the obvious. They are waltzing around the elephant in the living room. Docile for awhile, eventually it will sit on their laps. Christian commentator Thomas Merton knew it was unwise to deny pain. He wrote,

> The more you try to avoid suffering, the more you suffer, because smaller and more insignificant things begin to torture you in proportion to your fear of being hurt. The one who does the most to avoid suffering is, in the end, the one who suffers the most.

Adoption without pain is like religion without sacrifice—shallow-rooted, pretentious, and ultimately devoid of credibility.

People downplay the pain of adoption for various reasons. A few seem genuinely oblivious to it. For some reason, they do not hear those who cry out with voices of experience. Others realize that, on some level, there is substantial pain in adoption, but their tolerance for it is low. The only way they know to handle the pain is to ignore it. We are, after all, part of a culture that avoids pain. Still others overlook the pain because they want to promote the institution. They downplay the pain because they want adoption to be attractive and enticing. Promoters get to the good news of adoption too quickly. They sugarcoat adoption and portray it as innocuous. Focusing exclusively on the "gain" of adoption, they distort the truth and create unrealistic expectations.

As much as we would like to avoid pain, we will not succeed. True denial is a powerful tool of the mind, but it is a mechanism that ultimately fails. We all know this, but we try to ignore the pain anyway. Denial is self-deception. The pain related to adoption is not imagined, and it does not disappear. Eventually, it surfaces—often in altered forms—and demands attention. Denial handicaps the ability of the adoptee to fully process and come to grips with her life story. If we pretend the pain is not there, we cannot work with it to relieve it or heal it. If we deny the pain, we end up handling our incompleteness incompletely.

The impact of pain on children hinges on several factors. The obvious truth—so obvious that it is often overlooked—is that adoptees are not all the same. It is a simple truth, hardly headline news, but it makes an enormous difference in our understanding of the circumstances. Although some adoptees are by nature incredibly sensitive, others are carefree or oblivious to the affronts of fate. For the serious-minded adoptee, adoption may be a dominant theme. The easygoing person, on the other hand, may treat it with a shrug of the shoulders. Furthermore, each loss has many unique aspects. Beyond the personality factors, variables include such matters as the timing of the loss, the reasons for the loss, the opportunity to process the experience, and the availability of support. Each factor affects each adoptee differently.

COMMON REACTIONS TO PAIN

Denial is one of the most common methods of reacting to pain, but it is hardly the only way we respond to it. Let's consider some of the other possibilities, all common in the realm of adoption.

- **Speedy relief at any cost.** Pain often generates desperation, which begs for relief. To resolve the situation, we settle for the speediest remedy, the first available solution. Any potential remedy is better than the continuing pain.

- **Anesthetics.** If the pain will not go away, perhaps it can at least be dulled. Distractions of every variety are welcome.

- **Playing it safe.** It is very risky to care deeply for something or someone. It is far safer to pull into oneself and take no chances.

- **Recklessness.** At times, the pain seems so great that things cannot get much worse. There is really nothing to lose, so why not throw caution to the wind?

- **Exaggeration.** Some people have a gift for dramatizing the pain. As they see it, in the history of humankind no one has seen pain of a magnitude to match theirs.

- **Entitlement.** "I've had more than my share of pain and trouble. I've paid my dues, and now I deserve some positive results. I deserve special treatment."

- **Faultfinding.** Pain often prompts excessively negative thinking. One way to shift the pain is to blame others.

- **Misery loves company.** If I hurt, everyone should hurt. People who have endured great pain sometimes inflict great pain on others. Pain becomes an excuse for irresponsible behavior.

- **Stuck.** Some people become mired in pain. Pain sometimes offers insidious reinforcements. For some, pain becomes an important aspect of their identities, and they never move on.

Our culture takes a dim view of pain. We consider it an unwelcome stranger, the enemy, and we do everything in our power to avoid it. Our fear of pain adds to its negative power. We view pain as a mistake. We see it as one of life's problems instead of as life itself. If pain is a problem, it is, logically, something to be solved; but, somehow, we know better than that. Rather than "solve" our pain, we need to accept it as a part of the normal rhythm of life. If we focus entirely on the negative aspects of pain, we overlook its constructive potential.

Justice Oliver Wendell Holmes once said, "I would not give a fig for simplicity this side of complexity, but I would give my life for simplicity on the other side of complexity."* This is a wonderful thought that captures a major truth about the nature of simplicity. With apologies to Justice Holmes, I like to rework the idea to speak to the issue of pain. I sometimes say, "I wouldn't give a nickel for joy this side of honest pain, but I believe joy on the other side of pain is a priceless gift from God."

After I shared that observation in a public lecture, an adoptive father approached me and admitted, "I'm on this side of the pain. I don't have what it takes to get to the other side." I think he does—the fact that the idea caught his attention is a good sign—but he needs encouragement, and he needs a guide. His comment saddened me, because his inability to go further means something important for his child. If the adults involved can face their adoption pain, prospects are improved that the children will be able to face theirs. If, on the other hand, adults shrink from their pain, chances are that the children will elect to hide theirs. Children look to the adults in their lives for effective ways to handle their feelings.

MANAGING PAIN

If we summon the courage to face the pain, how do we come to terms with it? What are the tools for managing pain?

- **Learning.** Since pain is an inevitable fact of life, we do well to learn to live with it. If we face it, we can learn from it. Pain has meaning; it is instructive. It is important to listen to its message and make adjustments.

---

* *Quoted by Max DePree in* Leadership Is an Art. *New York: Dell, 1989.*

If we learn from pain, we are usually able to prevent even greater subsequent pain. Pain can point the way to healing.

- **Community.** Pain is largely offset when handled in a loving community. Surrounded by small mercies and unglamorous proofs of caring, pain does not seem quite so oppressive.

- **Control.** Even a small measure of control goes a long way to reduce the fears and anxieties that accentuate pain.

- **Meaning.** Senseless pain is the most difficult to bear. If we can identify the significance of our pain, we will bear it more gracefully. We can tolerate much more if we know our suffering serves a purpose.

- **Hope.** To persevere and move forward, we need hope. As long as we have reasonable hope, we can endure. Hope holds open the prospect of reassurance and healing.

- **Faith.** If we have a sense of meaning and hope, we have a measure of faith. We can surrender that which we cannot control and begin to relax. We learn to stop fighting it and begin to incorporate the pain as an important part of our story.

Above, I said that pain adds to the breadth and depth of life. There is danger that we reach that observation too lightly and minimize the devastation of pain. It really is true, though, that pain has positive aspects. The good news in pain does not erase its anguish, but it rounds out and completes our understanding of it. In *Legacy of the Heart,* therapist Wayne Muller writes beautifully of a beneficial way to respond to pain:

> Accepting the pain we are given requires us to soften our hearts and allow the pain to break us open, to acknowledge and to grieve the terrible sadness that comes with abandonment, loss, illness, and disappointment. In this moment we can feel most human, in kinship with all who have felt the deep despair of a broken heart. This is not angry resignation, born of defeat; this is a deep, loving acceptance that what we are given has become our companion and our teacher....

Let's consider some rewards that await those who accept their pain with softened hearts.

Pain Generates Authenticity

Pain shatters our illusion that all is well and that all is fair. Frederick Buechner, a man of faith who has faced the pain in his life, comments in *A Clown in the Belfry,*

> At no time more than at a painful time do we live out of the depths of who we are instead of out of the shallows....We stand a chance of finding in those depths who we most deeply and humanly are and who each other are....

Pain also ends our illusion of self-sufficiency. In the grip of pain, we recognize that we are not self-contained and that we do not have all the answers. Paradoxically, in imperfection and weakness, we discover strength. When we run out of personal solutions, we discover grace. And when we become aware of our own need for grace, we are quicker to be compassionate toward others. Again, with the keen eye and the heart of a pastor, Buechner puts it beautifully:

> What is perhaps most precious about pain is that if it doesn't destroy us, it can confer on us a humanity that needs no words to tell of it and that can help others become human even as they help us.

Linked to Love

I wrote of the frustration of trying to explain the birthfamily loss to adoptive parents. There is no way for them to understand what they have missed. Adoptive parents who have been there with birthfamilies have a very distinctive understanding. Families that have cried together—tears of pain and joy—have different relationships from those who have not.

Pain is clearly linked to love. It is excruciating for prospective adoptive parents to witness the awful moment when the birthparents and baby separate. There is no way to ward off feelings of guilt and intrusion. Nevertheless, it is important for them to be there. The pain of the birthfamily speaks powerfully of the depth of their caring. Most of the dramatic events connected to the adoption will blur over time, but the anguished moment of separation is remembered forever. Adoptive parents who have shared this pain will not happily tolerate insinuations from outsiders that the birthfamily was cavalier in its decision making. There is no mistaking the fact that the pain signals great love.

During everyday family life, the adopted child will very likely at some point share the observation that the birthfamily let him go lightly. The sentiment will be some version of, "She didn't give a rip." The family that heard about the pain of the birthfamily will use the occasion to offer polite reassurance. In noteworthy contrast, the family that shared the wretched moment of separation will flinch. They will be stunned and will have a hard time comprehending the comment. This flinch is an extraordinary gift to the youngster. Without a word, it powerfully communicates that his speculation is completely off base, and that message is marvelous news to the him. A flinch never lies. It tells him in unmistakable fashion that he was deeply loved by his birthfamily, and that feels good to him. It does not make the pain go away, but it soothes the sting. He knows that pain surely signals love.

Linked to Community

I will never forget the anxiety generated the first time we brought together a group of birthparents and prospective adoptive parents. Following the prevailing thought of the era, I presumed they were natural adversaries. Like water and oil, they could not mix. In plain English, I was prepared to referee a fight and then face the fallout for trying something unconventional and professionally unsound. It felt risky; but, convinced that each group would benefit from greater understanding of the other, we thought it was worth the risk.

It took less than a minute for these "natural adversaries" to discover the common ground of pain. As they exchanged stories of loss and loneliness, the body language in the room changed dramatically. They let down their guard, leaned into each other, and entered each other's pain. We had anticipated an electric atmosphere, and, as it turned out, that is what we experienced.

We learned something extremely important that day—we turned one of the major premises of closed adoption inside out. Birthparents and adoptive parents are not natural adversaries. Given an opportunity to explore the pain of their circumstances jointly, birthparents and adoptive parents are naturally supportive. Pain is their common denominator, and anyone who shortchanges the pain of adoption misses one of the vital building blocks of open adoption.

There is little in life that can rival the ability of pain to bring people together. Pain can drive proud people to reach out for assistance, and it can inspire constricted people to touch others with unusual offers of kindness. Although each person's pain is unique, it is also an experience we have in common with others. We are forever grateful for comrades who penetrate the loneliness, hang in there with us, and share our pain. In *Out of Solitude*, Henri Nouwen puts it this way:

> When we honestly ask ourselves which persons in our lives mean the most to us, we often find that it is those who, instead of giving much advice, solutions, or cures, have chosen rather to share our pain and touch our wounds with a gentle and tender hand. The friend who can be silent with us in a moment of despair or confusion, who can stay with us in an hour of grief and bereavement, who can tolerate not-knowing, not-curing, not-healing and face with us the reality of our powerlessness, that is the friend who cares.

We are probably never more self-aware and authentic than when we are in the middle of great pain. We are probably never more compassionate of others than when we are healing and coming to terms with our pain.

Linked to Joy, Linked to Beauty

Pain is linked to joy by mystery. In many ways, this is a surprising, even offensive, observation. It seems that pain and joy would be remote from each other, but we know they are connected. The connection is difficult to explain. Partially it is a matter of contrast, for context makes the difference especially vivid. It heightens each sensation. As Fuller Theological Seminary Professor Lewis Smedes observes in *How Can It Be All Right When Everything Is All Wrong?*, "Maybe there is more joy in Watts than in Palm Springs.... The joy of a person with an inoperable brain tumor can be infinitely deeper than the thrill of a birdie on the eighteenth hole."

Pain invariable breeds hope. We accept the fact that pain is a natural dimension of birth and rebirth, and we recognize that pain often signals the end of the old and the beginning of something new. Transformation is full of pain—it is painful to shed the past, confront the imperfect present, and witness the emergence of the unknowable and untamed future—but we know it is necessary. To its credit, pain makes us unusually receptive to change.

Holocaust survivor Elie Wiesel puts it best: "No one is as capable of gratitude as one who has emerged from the kingdom of night." Fulfillment is always sweet, but on the heels of deprivation, it becomes indescribably sweet. It is more than the arrival of that which was longed for—it is the vindication of hope itself.

Pain is also related to beauty. Perhaps the link is connected to our language deficiencies. I made the point earlier that words are seldom adequate to convey the meaning of pain, but somehow we overcome this deficiency and come together in our understanding anyway. Therapist Rollo May makes essentially the same observation about beauty:

> The strange thing about beauty is that it wipes away all boundaries and inspires us to realize our common humanity....In beauty, we have a language in common to all of us....It is by beauty we feel the pulse of all mankind.

Pain Motivates

When pain fills our consciousness, we are not content with the status quo. Pain makes us intensely and relentlessly aware of the need for relief. It stirs a formidable partnership between our creativity and our determination.

Each participant's pain is significant and deserves to be recognized. For me, though, the worst of it is the pain of the children. That is the pain I most wish to deny. As a professional, although consciously I know better, I am inclined to interpret the emotional pain of my clients as failure. It is hard for me to come to terms with the fact that, ultimately, I can do nothing to prevent adopted children from experiencing pain in some form. I can help preserve the link to the birthfamily, but this does not eliminate the adoptee's sense of loss. I can help generate arrangements that feature extraordinary compatibility between the families, but the adoptee will still feel a measure of differentness. I can help in the creation of an enduring relationship between the birthfamily and adoptive family, but to some extent the adoptee will still feel cut off from her roots. I can moderate the pain, but I cannot make it go away. As much as I want to wish the pain away, and as tempted as I am to ignore it, I believe the effectiveness of any adoption professional is directly related to his or her capacity to "hang in there" with the pain.

Nothing motivates me to search for improvements in the adoptive process like the pain of children. The pain is of two types. Some pain is intrinsic to the experience and cannot be avoided. In our work with this form of pain, the goal is effective relief. We must be relentless in our pursuit of better ways to soothe that pain. There is much to celebrate when adoptions of exquisite quality come together, but the unavoidable pain of children keeps me from becoming too enthused about the creative potential of adoption in any form. The other type of pain is the result of fear and poor preparation. That pain must be eliminated.

The great hope for open adoption is that it will bring the pain closer to the surface where it can be identified, addressed, and shared. To some, it may appear, because it is more obvious, that there is more pain in open adoption. That perspective misses the mark, because pain is part of every adoption, open or closed. Sadly, the critical view overlooks the great advantage to having access to the pain. My experience with anguished adoptees who grew up feeling that they did not fit in suggests that their adoptive parents were emotionally detached and disinclined to attend to their feelings of alienation. That detachment has tragic consequences. Far better that we find the courage to acknowledge and enter the pain, for in doing so we stand a chance to find relief and, in the process, connect to each other in profound ways. We may also find authenticity and joy, and the children will be the ultimate beneficiaries.

Chapter 6

The Blessing of Choice

> To live a full life, I want to be faced with dilemmas, learn
> to come to where the ways part, to risk choices, to
> shoulder responsibility. That makes me come alive,
> use my resources to the full, and be myself.
>
> Carlos Valles, *The Art of Choosing*

> Spiritual power...is the capacity to make decisions
> with maximum awareness.
>
> Scott Peck, *The Road Less Traveled*

When adoption becomes a business, the first casualty is
birthparent choice. Since the most pivotal junctures in adoption are moments of birthparent decision, it is not surprising
that adoption's most ferocious politics swirl around the process of choice. Naturally, everyone claims to honor the right of
birthparents to freely choose, but the claims are often carried
out in peculiar fashion. These days, it seems everyone vies for
the exclusive attention of potential birthparents.

Choice is not an esoteric issue—everything in adoption depends on it. It is foundational. The quality of an adoption is
related directly to the quality of the decision making that goes
into it. If the initial choices are well-considered and solid, all
that follows in the adoption will likely fall into place appropriately. Conversely, if the initial decision-making process is
flawed, everything that follows will likely be defective. The

importance of choice cannot be overstated. It is so vital that I am sometimes a bit cantankerous in its defense.

Recently, I received a call from a professional from a well-reputed agency on the West Coast. After a round of pleasantries, he told me that a family in his program had "discovered" a pregnant young woman in our service area, and he was inquiring if we would be willing to work with this young lady to prepare her for adoption. He concluded his request for assistance with a stunning question: "You aren't going to confuse her with choices, are you?" I indicated that we would be happy to respond to her, and that we would do so in our usual fashion. We would work to expand her options. Our goal would not be adoption; our goal would be that she reach a well-informed decision consistent with her value system—a process that might or might not lead to adoption. If she concluded that adoption truly was the optimal outcome, the next task would be to make sure that she was aware of the full range of possibilities available within that alternative.

One might suppose the professional would have been delighted to learn that the young lady in question would receive service of this nature, but the voice on the other end of the line was not pleased. With carefully measured tones of righteousness, he warned, "It certainly wouldn't be professional to lure a client from one system to another." I found this comment as stunning as the earlier one. Of all things, the caller was claiming the high ground of professional ethics. With equal, if not greater, sanctimony, I stated that it was hardly our intention to "lure" anyone into anything—by the way, how did you happen to run into this pregnant person 2,000 miles away—but we surely respected the right of clients to make decisions based on thorough information. We heard no more from this caller, as he either found "more professional" services elsewhere or simply did without.

Michael Spry, an open adoption parent with a keen eye for shaky ethics, calls this a "predatory" style of adoption. His observation evokes the chilling image of a powerful aerial hunter circling, swooping, and ultimately sinking its clutching talons into unsuspecting quarry. Too often the image fits. Fueled by the unmitigated self-interest of sometimes desperate would-be families, this aggressive style of "outreach" radically disrupts the decision-making process for birthparents. The privilege of choice is being replaced with a system of discovery and capture.

The predatory system of adoption undermines the choosing process in several ways. First, it is extremely presumptive. An expectant mother who says she is thinking about adoption is suddenly treated as though she has made a definitive decision. The complexity of the decision is minimized, and she is treated as though she were fully committed to adoption. In an instant, the machinery of adoption gears up and builds momentum.

Second, her field of choices is narrowed prematurely. The outreach and discovery process would be much less worrisome if it meant that an additional family was added to the pool of prospects. Unfortunately, it does not work that way. Once the extensive and very costly recruitment effort produces results and locates a potential birthparent, the last thing the finder wants to do is acquaint her with additional resources. In a twist that stretches credulity, the predatory system claims that the choice is made from the entire universe of possibilities. "She didn't choose us from a handful of families, she chose us from the realm of potential adoptive parents everywhere." That claim is far from accurate. Instead of choosing from a diversified pool of well-prepared prospects, the birthfamily is urged to "select" from a field of one. To make the process appear a little more acceptable, the mischief of sophistry is employed. Successful recruiters purr, "We helped our birthparent locate us."

Third, decisions with extraordinary and enduring consequences are made from scant, superficial information. When I ask birthmothers who have participated in such systems how they settled on a particular family, they comment, "I really liked the sound of their voices on the phone" or "I thought it was neat that they named their Labrador Retriever 'Joe.'" The depth of consideration is not even remotely correlated to the enormity of the consequences. The likelihood that the involved parties will enjoy significant compatibility is slender.

Fourth, the predatory system intentionally seeks to create a sense of obligation. To "close the sale," it works hard to generate a speedy sense of obligation within the potential birthparent. Instead of respecting the ambivalence that is intrinsic to the birthparent experience and gently working it through, recruiters press for speedy commitment. If they successfully stir a measure of sympathy for the prospective adoptive parents, recruiters proudly claim that they have helped the pregnant woman get beyond her painful ambivalence.

Finally, there is often a very uncomfortable socioeconomic dimension to these circumstances. When families with discrepant financial resources encounter each other, initiative makes a difference. It is one thing for a birthfamily to initiate action in the hope of achieving upward mobility for their child, but it is another thing for the socioeconomically advantaged to approach the less-advantaged. In the best of circumstances, economic disparity between birthparents and adoptive parents creates an awkward dynamic. In less optimal circumstances, it has an exploitative flavor about it.

The predatory system results from desperation and excessive self-interest. A certain amount of self-interest, of course, is necessary for survival, but it becomes worrisome when it is teamed with desperation. It significantly affects the atmosphere of adoption. When circumstances are cast in terms of predator and prey, survival is at stake. If it feels like survival is threatened, defenses are reflexively activated. Once that happens, cooperation and trust is difficult to achieve.

ALL SYSTEMS ARE BIASED

The predatory system of discovery and capture is an especially aggressive threat to the integrity of the birthparent choosing process, but it is not the only threat. In fact, we must recognize that every service-providing system is biased. There is no way to avoid bias. Every program has its own reality—traditions, motives, politics, personalities—and this unique reality is certain to affect its manner of operation. Since every effective system eventually finds a way to accomplish its purposes, it is crucial that every system examine its biases. Although it is simpler and more comfortable to leave them unexamined and uncorrected, decency requires they be winnowed with courage and honesty.

To begin with, almost every adoption program depends on fees generated by adoptive placements. A certain number of placements are necessary for program survival, and this dependence on fees creates, at the very least, a background bias toward adoption. Some administrators put this dependence in the foreground and go out of their way to remind workers of the need for placements. Other programs are profit-making by design and have conspicuous incentives to secure placements. There is little doubt regarding the outcomes they prefer.

It is interesting to see new service providers spring up while many longstanding programs find it difficult to remain viable. These new programs are almost always motivated by a desire to serve infertile families. That is understandable, because those families have great needs and surely deserve compassionate service. Nevertheless, it is crucial for us to recognize that the potential for inappropriate intrusion and imposition on families grappling with untimely pregnancies multiplies when service providers are primarily motivated to meet the needs of infertile families.

Infertility and untimely pregnancy are entirely distinct issues. Those who wrestle with pregnancy at an awkward time in life have absolutely no obligation to bring relief to those who suffer the frustrations of infertility. Granted, there has been an historic connection between these populations, but it should be a link of choice, not of assumption. No one presumes that a person with healthy kidneys owes one to a stranger who stands in need of a kidney. The idea strikes us as bizarre. Somehow, though, when it comes to babies, the idea seems acceptable. These situations appear to be distinguished by the conclusion that one set of possible donors, birthparents, have failed morally and have less right to retain what is theirs. Although few are so bold as to declare who deserves a kidney and who does not, many are quite willing to forward opinions about who deserves a baby and who does not.

The best programs—those least likely to exploit the vulnerability of birthfamilies—offer adoption as an extension of their pregnancy services. The values-based open adoption program offered by Catholic Human Services, for example, exists because of the agency's concern for families working through the challenges of untimely pregnancies. By design, that is our initial bias. We provide an unpressured environment for those families to think their way to outstanding outcomes. Since some of those families are interested in the adoption alternative, we need outstanding adoptive families. Our desire to fully empower birthfamilies motivates us to work hard at screening, educating, and preparing outstanding prospective adoptive families. We consider our adoptive families a resource to our birthfamilies, not vice versa. Our approach to adoption might be summarized in these words: *We serve children by preparing adoptive parents to relate positively to birthfamilies.*

This clarity of purpose has served us well through the years. Over time, though, we have become aware of an unexpected form of potential bias—the bias of unequal excellence. Although we genuinely encourage, support, and celebrate pregnancy decisions that lead to reasonable plans for parenting, the thing we are really good at is open adoption. Excellence is exciting, perhaps even seductive. All of us—professionals and clients alike—delight in the opportunity to be part of something remarkable. Like it or not, there is some hazard that we express the most excitement about the adoption alternative. We are aware of this bias and work hard to counter it. Perhaps it is fair to say that part of our excellence is our awareness of our excellence and the potential for bias that it creates.

A quality choosing process is far from automatic and should not be taken lightly. It is a delicate privilege, eroded by many factors. As we have seen, it is challenged by clever recruiters and systems tinged with bias. Several other factors complicate and confound the decision-making process. To more fully understand the nature of choice, we need to consider the decision makers and the context in which they make their decisions.

The Choosers

Birthparents come from every imaginable background and operate with wide ranges of motives. Recognizing that there are many exceptions to these generalizations, for the moment I will identify three factors that characterize birthparents. Typically, they are young, well-intentioned, and anxious. These factors have important implications for the decision-making process.

In our experience, most birthparents are in their late teens or early 20s. Although they are often mature beyond their years, most of them lack experience in making major decisions. As a function of their age—one of the gifts of youth is an irrepressible zest for the immediate moment—they are likely to think in short-range terms. It is unusual for them to think about the distant future. They are inclined to solve the problem for the moment and worry later about the long-term consequences. Sometimes I wonder if it is humanly possible for a 17-year-old to peer 18 years into the future.

Birthparents want to do the right thing, and they want things to work out well. In age-appropriate fashion, they are struggling to gain greater independence, but they still want the approval of the people around them. This makes them especially susceptible to feelings of obligation. Even strong, independent-minded birthparents are reluctant to disappoint potential adoptive families. Once they realize that the enthusiastic couple's hopes are riding on their decisions, it is difficult for them to change plans.

In the birthparent reality, anxiety is a given. If their circumstances were in excellent order, they would not be considering adoption. Their circumstances are deeply anxious, and predicting how they will handle their anxiety is difficult. Some are quick to ask for assistance, whereas others cover up their distress and keep their worries to themselves. Sadly, many are reluctant to turn to others. As a result, they move through this experience with self-imposed loneliness, a loneliness of great depth. They may fall into a cycle of blaming self and others. Many suspend their usual competence and slip into denial. However they handle their anxiety, it is safe to say that they crave speedy relief and will pay almost any price to achieve it.

The bewildering experience of pregnancy adds to their anxiety. In a phrase, everything changes. The expectant mother can expect changes in her body, relationships, emotions, interests, and priorities. It seems nothing stays the same. Her circumstances are very different from what she previously knew. She will interact with a variety of systems—medical, social, and educational—in ways that are new to her. She will discover that her community views her differently than it did previously. Some may treat her with great deference, while others communicate contempt. Still others may view her as a resource. To say the least, pregnancy takes some getting used to.

It is often difficult for a youthful expectant woman to find the emotional support she needs. The important people in her life are frequently unsure how to be helpful. Many are too directive, whereas many others are too vague. Sometimes, there is so much well-intended diplomacy involved that it is difficult for her to gain a truly accurate picture of what the important people in her life think. Unless someone takes the initiative and speaks to the issues clearly, there will be too much mind reading and too little sensible discussion.

There is much about making this decision that is displeasing to her. Among other things, it can be characterized as self-assaultive. She only considers adoption because she is not sure she can adequately meet the needs of her child. It is painful to focus on one's inadequacies. Furthermore, the decision is frustrating because it is often not possible to fully understand the alternatives. Can someone who has never parented make a fully informed decision about parenting? The decision is distressing for one more reason; namely, it is a matter of choosing between painful alternatives. We are accustomed to choosing between positive alternatives: Will it be chocolate or vanilla? Red or blue? The beach or the mountains? When the choices are all painful, we want to check the box that says, "None of the above."

VARIATIONS ON THE FORFEITURE THEME

The alternative of not choosing has substantial appeal. Some people elect not to choose, preferring to drift into decisions—or better yet, have others choose for them. If choice can be evaded, one can avoid responsibility for outcomes and preserve the prospect of eventually taking on the role of victim. Many are resigned to the view that things work out eventually. They are passive and respondent and do not perceive of themselves as decision makers. Unable to believe in themselves and their ability to make a difference, they simply play the cards they are dealt.

It is not surprising that the enormity of the decision immobilizes many birthparents. Standing at a true crossroad in life, it is normal to hesitate. It is frightening to realize an error in judgment can extract a lifelong price. The choice facing a birthparent is doubly daunting because there is a second, totally dependent life at stake. What is more humbling than holding a child's future in one's hands? The high stakes generate understandable paralysis.

Occasionally, birthparents are totally paralyzed by ambivalence. They feel completely stuck, caught in a debilitating loop of inhibition. They have no appetite for parenting, but neither are they at all drawn toward releasing their rights. The only thing clear to them is that they cannot find peace of mind with either alternative. They are frozen with indecision.

Some birthparents deliberately paint themselves into corners. They welcome a sense of obligation because they want this dynamic to counter the predictable emotional pull toward parenting. This self-trapping trick is a particularly dangerous tactic because it often works and, in the process, disallows and overrides last-minute wisdom to the contrary.

Other birthparents carry hidden agendas and play games with the decision making. They use alternate outcomes as leverage on certain people, which means the decision is not centered on what is best for the child. Rather, it is made with eye toward the impact it may have on others. The youngster's future is hostage to the dramatic politics of unstable relationships. Again, this is a very dangerous and disrespectful game.

The process of choosing is not a simple matter, and it is not wise to accept preliminary decisions at face value. Early decisions needs to be double- and triple-checked and cleansed of distracting factors.

A Fruitful Culture for Choice

The hallmark of an excellent adoption program is that it provides a fruitful culture for choice. Quite possibly the finest gift that professionals can give participants is a context and culture in which good decisions can be made. It is a "healthy decision-making culture," not an "adoption culture." It seeks, honors, and celebrates effective decision making. A fruitful culture for choice provides the safety, freedom, and candor that are conducive to the discovery of creative solutions. It is an unpressured, unhurried environment that appreciates the delicate art and gift of discernment.

- **Options are expanded.** An all-out effort is made to unearth all possible alternatives. Creative energy is expended to customize the options or rework them in unique combinations. There is a conscious effort not to narrow the field of possibilities too quickly.

- **Options are explored.** Information is gathered about each alternative, and each option is given thorough consideration. Sloppy thinking is challenged.

- **Options are preserved.** Decision making is a process, not an event. Alternatives temporarily set aside are revisited from time to time, and the opportunity to change course is defended until a "point of no return" is finally reached.

- **Decisions are not pressured.** The decision maker is defended from outside pressures, manipulation, coercion, and obligation.
- **The process is paced with patience.** Decisions are made in an unhurried fashion. The decision maker has ample time to thoroughly contemplate the implications of the decision before making a commitment. There is a healthy pace to the process—neither dawdling nor hasty.
- **Consideration is multidimentional.** Brain, heart, and soul are brought to bear on the situation. The decision should consider intellect, emotion, and intuition.
- **The decision is value-based.** The decision maker is encouraged to operate with an awareness of her values. Ideally, the decision will proceed naturally from a greater "clarity of purpose" in life.

Of all these important factors, not the least is the freedom to change plans. To defend this freedom, the practitioner must plant the seed of permission to change course early in the discussion and return to it routinely. This is an indispensable safeguard to offset the potential for the creeping sense of obligation that so often accompanies adoption planning. It is wise and necessary to make plans, but we must be careful to recognize that planning creates momentum and sets expectations into motion that, over time, begin to resemble obligations.

Ethical professionals will work hard to help birthfamilies factor the prospective adoptive family out of the decision. Birthfamilies need to be reminded often that, apart from honesty, they owe the prospective adoptive family nothing. They need to be reminded that the prospective family is chooseable and will have other opportunities if the birthfamily changes their mind. They need to be reminded that the prospective adoptive family enters the experience fully informed and well-prepared. If the friendship is real, they will understand. Once a potential adoption is set into motion, one family or the other is slated for loss. We never know who it will be. The loss of the prospective family would be no more tragic than the birthfamily's loss. If the birthparents can rally in the last minute and devise an effective plan for retaining custody of the baby, we view it as a positive outcome.

A fruitful culture should lead to an optimal choosing process. Birthparents typically make adoption decisions at least three times. A preliminary decision usually comes at some point during pregnancy. The birthmother makes a more informed but still preliminary decision in the hospital. A final decision comes later, hopefully after the birthmother has recovered from the rigors of actually giving birth. The final decision should be made with the involvement and protection of someone who is legally disinterested in the outcome.

In the introduction to this book, I suggested that the core issues of the adoption decision have changed through the years. These days, it is seldom a matter of moral and economic necessity. The ultimate question is better understood as a process of finding the path that offers the child the greatest prospect for emotional stability. We must recognize that, often, all the mighty thinking that goes into a decision is irrelevant, because there remains the question of whether a decision maker has the strength to carry out a difficult decision. We all know from personal experience that knowing the right course of action does not necessarily translate into application.

So what constitutes a good choice? A good choice is balanced. It allows for the wisdom of mind and heart. It respects the voice of intuition. A good decision usually enjoys the support of crucial people. There are times, however, when it is necessary to stand alone. In his inspirational bestseller, *The Road Less Traveled*, psychiatrist Scott Peck puts it this way, "The highest forms of love are inevitably totally free choices and not acts of conformity." A good decision has positive intentions. It does not intend anyone harm and is not rooted in fear. Ultimately, a good decision will be consistent with the decision maker's major purpose in life.

A good decision includes at least four factors:

- **It is sensible.** The decision is well thought out and based on good information.

- **It is wise.** The decision is based on foresight. It takes the long view of things.

- **It is loving.** The decision is loving and gentle. It considers the wisdom of the heart.

• **It is right.** The decision is consistent with the chooser's most vital values.

If a decision passes these tests, it is solid. The most crucial factor is consistency with one's values. If a decision is deemed right, it will be a matter of conscience and it will be a decision that can be lived with. As Episcopal priest Gale Webbe so interestingly puts it, "A decision based on honest motives works out so surely for good that it is entirely true to say that even if it is the wrong decision, it will be the right one." His wisdom suggests that we approach decisions in terms of motives, which are knowable, rather than outcomes, which can only be contemplated in terms of probabilities.

BENEFITS OF CHOOSING

The cornerstone of quality open adoption is the commitment to a valid choosing process. It requires tremendous effort, and sometimes it is cumbersome. Is it worth it? I am convinced it is. Let us consider the benefits realized through a genuine process of choice.

Comfort

In the days of closed adoption, birthparents were almost powerless. Adoption was posed to them on a "take it or leave it" basis, and they had virtually no ability to influence its course. It was necessary for them to totally depend on the system. Dependence typically generates fear, hostility, helplessness, and despair. Many birthparents ended up feeling guilty, feeling they had abandoned their children. With greater control over the process, birthfamilies have much greater reassurance. As the other becomes better known, the canyon of trust that must be hurdled shrinks to reasonable dimensions. The opportunity to steer the process reduces the fear. Choice can contribute to long-term comfort. If birthparents are to live comfortably with adoption, they must be extremely clear about their rationale for choosing adoption. This clarity of mind does not mean that adoption is painless, but it does mean that the decision can be endured. Careful choice is an important defense against resentment and regret.

Creativity

Human nature cherishes choice—it is the stuff of life. Carlos Valles, a Spanish-born Jesuit priest who has spent many years in India, says it well in the quotation that opens this chapter: "To live a full life, I want to be faced with dilemmas, to come to where the ways part, to risk choices, to shoulder responsibility. That makes me come alive, use my resources to the full, and be myself."

Ownership

Again, Valles states it especially well: "When I make a choice, I instinctively want to show that my choice was the right one, and therefore I do all I can to make it work." Perhaps the inverse is also true: If a significant decision is imposed on us with no regard for our thoughts or feelings, we may be tempted to sabotage or undermine the decision. When we accept responsibility for our choices, we live with integrity. When we exercise the privilege of choice, we grow in maturity because decision making is always an act of faith.

Blessing and Entitlement

To be chosen from a field of strong prospects is an astonishing experience. It is flattering, but more importantly, it is empowering. The only way that adoption can be truly satisfying is with the blessing of the birthfamily. The birthparent blessing generates a powerful, indispensable sense of entitlement for adoptive parents. The torch of parental authority is passed, and the new parents are permanently installed in the role. Interestingly, the blessing of being chosen is so vital that it is not unusual in our experience for adoptive parents who have been approached by a potential birthparent to ask that she be given information on other available families. They do not want to feel that the birthparent settled on them for lack of alternatives; they want to be fully endorsed.

Compatibility

Through the years, we have seen birthparents consistently select adoptive parents who were "cut from the same cloth" as themselves. It is difficult to overstate the importance this factor. A high level of compatibility between the families makes their relationship comfortable and natural. This goodness of fit significantly improves the prospect that the adoptee will fit comfortably into the adoptive family. If relationships are to have life and vitality, there needs to be a spark of attraction and interest between the families involved.

Cooperation

The many benefits of genuine choice—comfort, creativity, ownership, entitlement, and compatibility—lead naturally to a high level of trust. Cooperation is the offspring of trust. Cooperation produces results that are consistently to everyone's advantage. It is a joy to participate in a cooperative relationship.

Does the quality of choice affect adoption outcomes? Let's juxtapose the possibilities. One path, typically born in desperation, features coercion, obligation, pressure, enticement, and manipulation—factors that lead to second-guessing, regret, resentment, and victimization. The other path, nurtured in a fruitful culture for choice, features exploration, protection, patience, integrity, and freedom—factors that leads to comfort, ownership, creativity, entitlement, compatibility, and cooperation. Framed this way, it is clear that handling of choice is of utmost importance.

Choice and Adoptive Parents

One might gather from this chapter that choice is mostly an issue for birthparents. It seems that they do the choosing and that the adoptive parents are along for the ride. Actually, the decision-making course of the two groups is quite parallel. Volition is a vital issue for adoptive parents as well. If they are pressured to carry out a particular form of adoption for which they have no enthusiasm, they will view their adoptive obligations negatively and look for opportunities to escape them. On the other hand, if adoptive parents freely chose the style of adoption they wish to carry out, they will carry it out comfortably and with enthusiasm. The themes that apply to birthparents usually apply to adoptive parents as well, but there is no way around the fact that adoption decision making starts with birthparents.

A program that treats birthparents with full respect is obviously good news for birthparents. It is also great news for adoptive parents, and wise adoptive parents are quick to recognize that fact. They realize that the comfort and beauty of open adoption are directly correlated to the extent of the birthparent's blessing. Conversely, the open adoption relationship will struggle in direct proportion to the birthparent's discomfort with the arrangement.

There is a wonderful paradox of indirectness involved in treating the participants of adoption with dignity. The greatest gift a program can give to birthparents is access to well-nurtured adoptive parents, and the greatest gift it can give to adoptive parents is well-treated birthparents. Ultimately, well-prepared birthparents and adoptive parents become an enduring gift to the child who brings them together.

Chapter 7

Adoption with Honor: Commitments and Covenants

> Covenantal relationships reflect unity and grace and poise. They are an expression of the sacred nature of relationships.
>
> Max DePree, *Leadership Is an Art*

> To dare to make and keep commitments—this is to live.
>
> Lewis Smedes, *Caring & Commitment*

One of our adoptive parents, Don Spinniken, captured the heart of the open adoption relationship with this comment: "What exists between our birthfamilies and us is a thousand times stronger than a contract. It is a matter of honor. If I somehow violated this relationship, it would change who I am." It is a powerful statement. He is defining open adoption as an expression of his identity, putting it in terms of honor and personal integrity. In his way of thinking, open adoption puts his personhood on the line. It is important for him that his open adoption relationships succeed. If they thrive, he thrives; and if they fail, he suffers. Don Spinniken realizes that he is the sum of the relationships in which he is involved.

Honor is attractive, but honor is far easier to discuss than to implement. Trust enables intimacy, but it is always shadowed by the possibility of betrayal. The prospect of betrayal concerned us from the very beginning of our work in open adoption, and our concern has not abated over the years. In the early days of our program, we thought the primary beneficiary of open arrangements was the birthfamily. Because of that slant, we were mostly concerned about the possibility of adoptive parents arbitrarily setting aside their agreements, and we told birthfamilies they were free to come and go as they pleased. Now, with greater experience, we understand that the most crucial beneficiary of continuing contact is the adoptee. As a result, in current practice we are also concerned about the equally damaging prospect of birthparent betrayal. With the emotional health of children at stake, the faithfulness and dependability of all participants is indispensable.

Betrayal looms as a worrisome possibility because many factors work against continuity and stability. Most open adoption arrangements are born in a context of great immediacy. Time is often short, and all available energy is consumed simply getting through the moment. Everything is focused on the pressing matters at hand, and there is little opportunity or inclination to think about the future. As a result, the long view often suffers. Adding to the tension of immediacy is the pressure that inevitably accompanies a life-altering sequence of decision making. Still more anxiety is generated by the dramatic shift in power from the birthfamily to the adoptive family, a transition that profoundly alters the emotional balance. The situation is further complicated by the extraordinary emotions tied to the experience. There are good-byes and hellos to be said, and great joys and losses to work through. Even the most loving participants find it difficult to sustain the emotional connection to their counterparts when the psychological tasks they face are so divergent. Clearly it is expediency, not long-range planning, that prevails in the early and formative stages of most open adoptions.

Every responsible system of open adoption is concerned with the possibility that participants might somehow betray each other. It is a reasonable line of worry. If adoptive relationships are not sustained, open adoption quickly loses its credibility. This issue is so crucial that, as suggested in Chapter 1, systems of open adoption can be distinguished in terms of their response to this concern. Irresponsible forms of open adoption put no emphasis on the issue, but every respectable system considers it critically important and seeks to defend against the prospect of betrayal.

The safeguards take a variety of forms. The contractual approach, for instance, seeks to remove uncertainties in the relationship between the birthfamily and the adoptive family by organizing the adoption in terms of a well-defined, binding contract. The guardianship style of adoption seeks to reduce the prospect of betrayal of birthfamilies by preserving some legal status for them. In that form of adoption, birthparents have the legal standing needed to seek recourse in the event their expectations are not met. The cooperative approach taps into the good will of mutually beneficial relationships and keeps the benefits of continuing interaction in the forefront of everyone's minds. The values-based system of adoption approaches the issue from a threefold perspective of relational power, commitments, and covenants.

RELATIONAL POWER

The quality of every open adoption obviously depends on how the participants relate to each other. If they relate based on understanding and respect, the results can be exquisite. Conversely, if they relate on the basis of unrestrained self-interest, the interaction can degenerate into singular or mutual exploitation. Theologian Bernard Loomer describes two kinds of power—*unilateral* and *relational*—which are of great relevance to this discussion. He defines unilateral power as

> ...the capacity to influence, guide, adjust, manipulate, shape, control, or transform the human or natural environment in order to advance one's own purposes....The focus is on the individual and his personal goals, not on the relationship conceived as mutually internal and creative.[*]

Extending the concept further, he observes, "The aim is to move toward the maximum of self-sufficiency....Dependency on others, as well as passivity, are symptoms of weakness or insufficiency." He is describing a very familiar form of power, which is deeply ingrained in everyday interaction.

---

[*] *Bernard Loomer. (1976). "Two Conceptions of Power." Criterion 15 (1).*

Far less common is something Loomer calls "relational power," defined as "the ability to produce and undergo an effect." He explains that relational power is a matter of "mutually influencing and being influenced, of mutually giving and receiving, of mutually making claims and permitting and enabling others to make their claims." Writer Michael Duffey expands on the concept and observes that relational power has great potential to broaden our lives and generate personal growth. He notes that it

> ...has as its source the awareness of our incompleteness and our need for the influence of others. This power invites others to bring their truth to us, trusting that the influence of others will help bring us closer to the fullness of life.

It is only available to those who have the inner strength to take the risks of trusting others. Relational power is a dynamic and endlessly creative form of interaction. In Loomer's words,

> What is truly for the good of any one or all of the relational partners is not a preconceived good. The true good is not a function of controlling or dominating influence. The true good is an emergent from deeply mutual relationships. *

The great advantages of relational power is its spirit of openness and its capacity to build relationships of stunning flexibility and depth.

Since unilateral and relational power does not exist in pure form, it is an error to think in either-or terms; nevertheless, it is largely accurate to note that our preference in styles of power has a watershed effect on all that follows. The two forms of power inevitably produce different outcomes. As Duffey points out, "In all of our relationships...we are involved in patterns which tend either in the direction of mutuality or toward patterns of domination and submission that crush the human spirit." Every participant will settle on one form of power or the other. If open adoption is attempted based on self-sufficiency and unilateral power, it will be carried forward as a matter of graceless practicality. As an expression of unilateral power, even in its gentlest and most positive form, it will be a patchwork of

---

* *Bernard Loomer. (1976). "Two Conceptions of Power." Criterion 15 (1).*

people using each other's resources for personal benefit. On the other hand, when participants choose to set aside unilateral power and interact with relational power, they move beyond the constrictions of fear into the richness of mutuality. Founded on relational power, open adoption comes alive and approaches its full potential to affirm and transform.

WHAT IS COMMITMENT?

How do we empty ourselves of unilateral power and shift to relational power? How do we shift from "influencing, guiding, adjusting, manipulating, shaping, and controlling" to mutuality? In her book, *The Human Condition*, internationally respected philosopher and social critic Hannah Arendt provides a key. She writes, "The remedy for unpredictability, for the chaotic uncertainty of the future, is contained in the faculty to make and keep promises." We implement relational power by offering ourselves to others through commitments.

Commitment comprises three essential factors: a deep concern for another person, an investment of oneself in the other, and an intention to apply this abiding concern and investment to contend with the unknowable future.

Commitment begins with a profound concern for another person. It is a significant declaration that the other is both interesting and important. When adoptive parents and birthparents commit to each other, they are establishing an enduring interest in each other. Each is asserting that the other is important; and because of that significance, they are resolved to interact respectfully. They are genuinely concerned how things turn out for each other. We might say that commitment is a willingness to bet on the capabilities of the persons involved. According to psychiatrist Scott Peck's definition of love, they "aspire to spiritual growth for the other."

"Investing" in the other sounds innocuous, but a closer look alters that view. As alternate words like "pledge," binding," "obligation," and "sacrifice" suggest, the investment is decidedly meaningful. Commitment is a matter of heart, mind, and soul. As Loomer puts it,

> Commitment may occur because of the persuasiveness of the ideal. But commitment that is simply

intellectual is partial. If the ideal is to be striven for, the commitment must be organic. The whole self needs to be persuaded. We may be lured or "led" toward a desirable goal. But whether we will 'follow' depends on whether we are impelled to do so from within.*

Margaret Farley, a professor of Christian ethics at Yale University Divinity School, provides a fascinating picture of the process of investing in another.

> To give my word is to "place" a part of myself, or something that belongs to me, into another person's "keeping." It is to give the other person a claim over me, a claim to perform the action that I have committed myself to perform.... When I "give my word"...it is given...as a pledge. It still belongs to me, but now it is held by the one to whom I have yielded it. It claims my faithfulness, my constancy, not just because I have spoken it to myself, but because it now calls to me from the other person who has received it.

Once it is given, it is out of our hands and not easily recalled. This is a powerful description because, with its reference to putting "a part of myself in another's keeping," it describes commitment in a way that literally describes the sacrifice of birthparents. What birthparents do literally, adoptive parents do figuratively.

This convergence of interest and investment provides a mechanism to meet the future. Come what may, those who are committed are prepared to hang in there with their counterparts. It is, as Farley puts it, "promising that I will do all that is possible to keep alive my love and to act faithfully in accordance with it." As it addresses the future, commitment features the amazing quality of being unconditional, a vital and often overlooked dimension of commitment. This "unconditionality" is the brash charm of commitment. Seen in this light, commitment is bold, hopeful, and optimistic. Spiri-

---

* *Bernard Loomer. "The Free and Relational Self." In* Belief and Ethics. *W. Widick Schroeder. (Ed.). Chicago: Center for the Scientific Study of Religion, 1978.*

tual commentator Lewis Smedes comments on this vitality in
Caring & Commitment:

> Commitments live on hope. Not on duty. Not on
> what we are obligated to do, but on hope for what we
> can do. And what others can do for us. Hope is the
> alternative to the seductions of the uncommitted life.

In their book, *Conscious Loving,* Drs. Gay and Kathlyn
Hendricks, partners in marriage and in writing, point out that
"a co-committed relationship rests on several intentions that
are agreed on by both persons." They go on to list six specific
commitments that merge to form the larger commitment:

- I commit myself to full closeness and to clearing up
  anything within me that stands in the way.

- I commit myself to my own complete development as
  an individual.

- I commit myself to revealing myself in the relationship, not to concealing myself.

- I commit myself to the full empowerment of the people
  around me.

- I commit myself to acting from the awareness that I
  am 100% the source of my reality.

- I commit myself to having a good time in my close
  relationships.

Although the Hendrickses include a reminder to be playful
in their list of commitments, for the most part the commitments require honesty, creativity, and courage. Planting and
nurturing commitments is hard work—so much work, in fact,
that we sometimes ask ourselves, "Is it worth the effort?"

THE ADVANTAGES OF COMMITMENT

When concern, investment, and unconditionality are brought
together in commitment, it creates what Margaret Farley po-
etically calls "the way of fidelity." The way of fidelity involves
many beneficial qualities:

Security. In *Caring & Commitment,* Smedes points out that
commitments "create small islands of security for us in our

oceans of insecurity. They make enclaves of steadiness in jungles of change. They give us the only human basis for trusting one another." Commitments go a long way toward making the world more secure, dependable, and manageable. Without reliability, things quickly degenerate into chaos.

Freedom. Security leads to freedom. Though our humor depicts it as imprisoning, robust commitment is actually liberating. In the context of commitment, there is no need to apply scarce resources to the protection of other resources. We are free to press ahead with other projects. Commitments open new possibilities. Contrary to the wisdom of the street, there is more freedom within commitments than there is outside them.

Protection. Commitment is protection. When it is working well, the way of fidelity defends us from outside intrusion and distraction. Perhaps more importantly, commitment helps defend against personal weaknesses. It helps us sustain the most promising course of action in confusing times of high stress. According to Farley, "Yielding to someone else a claim over our future actions provides a barrier against our fickle changes of heart, our losses of vision, our weaknesses and our duplicity." She goes on to say,

> Duty can hold us in relation when all else fails. When our hearts are dry and our vision is clouded, when our memory is confused and our hope is eclipsed in the day, then duty—our sense of obligation in relation to the word we have given—holds us to the deeds of love and to attentiveness to new springs of old love within us.

Commitment can buy the time needed to repair a faltering relationship.

Identity. Commitments help us establish ourselves as persons. Once more, Hannah Arendt helps us understand:

> Without being bound to the fulfillment of our promises, we would never be able to keep our identities; we would be condemned to wander helplessly and without direction in the darkness of each person's lonely heart, caught in its contradictions and equivocalities.

Approaching this concept from a negative vantage point, we recognize that we stand to lose our self-respect if we fail to honor our commitments.

Relationship building. Commitments help us build and sustain our relationships to others. Again, in *Caring & Commitment*, Smedes points out that this is the primary value of commitments: "What makes commitment keeping worth working at is this: it serves the long term good of people in relationships, people who want to live in a caring human community."

Community building. Commitments allow for the possibility of community. Because of the reliability they establish, broader groups of people are able to interact with trust.

THE DOWNSIDE OF COMMITMENT

Contemporary American culture is wary of commitment. We have a ball-and-chain humor about it, and some people refer to it as "the C word." Commitment offends our feeling that we should suffer no limits. We like to keep our options open, and commitment seems to box us in. Most of our fear of commitment results from a mixture of selfishness and cowardice, but it must be conceded that some concerns are founded on reality. Commitment has its hazards—most notably, a tendency toward stultifying passivity and a withering inclination toward joyless duty.

Commitment is meant to be dynamic and lively, but it sometimes takes a 180-degree turn toward passivity and laziness. Departing from the ideals of relational power, some people treat commitment as a mechanism to capture others. If they can pin their counterparts down with commitments and constrict their options, they are satisfied. Commitment of this type is designed to imprison. Because they believe the commitment is irrevocable and inescapable, they see no reason to extend themselves and nurture their relationships. Given this unhealthy line of reasoning, commitment is more likely to kill a relationship than serve it. An unnourished relationship is predictably mortifying.

Many of us find it hard to believe that commitments are liberating because we have seen so much evidence to the contrary. Commitment often strikes us as joyless duty. Farley warns that when commitment loses its vitality and degenerates into duty, "we veer dangerously in the direction of resentment, rancor, hypocrisy, and despair." Relationships based on capture and duty and that drone on joylessly are often destructive to everyone involved. If a relationship is flavored with "resentment, rancor, hypocrisy, and despair," it obviously requires drastic attention. Although it is always painful to review and rework our understandings, there are times when healthy people need to rearrange and sometimes even exit their commitments.

We worry that making a commitment is akin to promising to be perfect the rest of our lives. This thinking discourages the forging of commitments, because we know we cannot honestly make promises of perfection. This perspective distorts the nature of commitment and portrays it as unattainable. Commitments are not about perfection; they are about wholehearted intention. We are capable of greater fidelity than we recognize, and in those instances where we fail each other, forgiveness can bring restoration. Healthy commitment is continually creative. New triumphs and failures are continuously factored into relationships as they lean into the future they will shape.

ENTERING AND MAINTAINING COMMITMENTS

Once we assess their benefits and hazards, commitments appear mostly attractive, but they should be approached intelligently. Most problems associated with commitments are problems of premature commitment. Again, we encounter the importance of fully informed choice and high compatibility. As far as possible, we must know what we are getting into before we get into it. It is vital that we not be hasty. We are at much greater risk of entering foolish commitments if we are in a desperate mode. We ought not enter commitments unless we are optimistic about our ability to cope with the future. We can only know so much about the person to whom we are committing. We should take the time to gather that information; then it is up to us to mutually invent a future that is to our shared advantage. Where the knowing ends, a willingness and enthusiasm for learning must begin.

When our commitments are working well, we are usually unaware of them. They quickly become assumptions—givens. This feature allows us to direct our energies outward. In *Our Greatest Gift,* Jesuit priest Henri Nouwen observes, "I have always been impressed with the thought that people are only ready to commit themselves to each other when they no longer focus on each other but rather focus on the larger world beyond themselves." Becoming conscious of our commitments suggests that our relationships are stressed and that we should attend to the commitments in a preventive manner. Sometimes, our commitments need to be clarified and modernized. Other times, they need to be rejuvenated and renewed. The repair of commitments can be awkward and time-consuming, but it is far less painful than their dissolution.

All constructive relationships need some wiggle room. Commitments need some elasticity if they are going to cope with whatever challenges the future holds. Allowances for expansion and shrinkage need to be built into the original understanding. We do well to anticipate with good nature that people and circumstances will change. From the beginning, for example, we know that the open adoption commitment will be affected by the emerging voice of the child. If we want our relationships to be alive and vibrant, we need to apply lavish portions of common sense and flexibility. An important aspect of this common sense is tolerance for imperfection. Sensible commitment is built on sincere personal investment, not perfection.

COVENANTS

Covenants are commitments tinged with the sacred. In *Leadership Is an Art*, business writer Max DePree speaks eloquently of covenants in the workplace:

> Covenantal relationships...induce freedom, not paralysis. A covenantal relationship rests on shared commitment to ideas, to issues, to values, to goals....Words such as love, warmth, and personal chemistry are certainly pertinent. Covenantal relationships are open to influence. They fill deep needs, and they enable work to have meaning and be fulfilling. Covenantal relationships reflect unity and grace and poise. They are an expression of the sacred nature of relationships.

DePree is writing about the workplace, but he could easily be describing the ideals of values-based open adoption.

Obviously, a covenantal relationship is not a run-of-the-mill, lackadaisical connection between people. It is a sacred commitment. This linkage of commitment and the sacred is an enormously potent combination. Commitment has great potential in its own right, but the addition of a sacred dimension assigns an important additional layer to the commitment. It is the inexplicable something extra that makes violation unthinkable. Covenants are the supple and muscular bonds that give open adoptions the ability to endure and serve their participants over the long haul.

One of adoption's trickiest words is *real,* as in *real parents.* What makes a family real? What is the glue that holds a family together? The answer is found in the realm of commitments. The reality of a family is found in the power of its commitments, in the sacred mystery of its covenantal integrity.

Reclaiming the Power of Commitment

We have seen the substantial benefits and beauty of commitment; yet somehow, it fails to fire our imaginations. It is the virtue no one seems to love. In the great drama of life, commitment plays the role of killjoy because it has the audacity to do the thing we like the least: It limits us. In an age of irrepressible individualism, commitment needs a public relations agent.

We need to recover the notion that commitments are attractive. I believe we can return the luster to commitment by emphasizing two important motivations—our desire to see the people we love thrive and flourish, and our powerful need for self-respect.

Covenantal relationships are very different from the pragmatic or utilitarian relationships to which we are accustomed: They are spiritually pleasing. A covenantal relationship features unusual equality and accountability. It is not a one-up, one-down arrangement based on status, because, in covenantal relationships, everyone is simply a child of God. Birthparents are not beggars, they are full partners. And so are the children. Covenantal relationships establish environments characterized by security, respect, and openness—an optimal atmosphere for growth. When we apply ourselves to the nurture of the covenantal relationships of which we are a part, we bless the lives of the people we most care about, and the nurturing has the feel of a "want to" rather than a "have to."

The currency of commitment is respect—for self and others. It is interesting that we use the word *honor* when we refer to commitments. In this fashion, our language puts us on a promising trail. Commitments are honor in action. We are honorable or dishonorable according to our handling of our commitments. Honoring commitments is a matter of personal integrity. Author Stephen Covey makes an interesting observation about honesty and integrity in *The Seven Habits of Highly Effective People:* "Honesty is telling the truth—in other words, conforming our words to reality. Integrity is conforming reality to our words." To live with ourselves, to perhaps even enjoy a measure of inner contentment, we need self-respect. That is to say, peace of mind depends on our effectiveness in honoring our commitments.

Are commitments important? Are they meaningful? Let's give Smedes, from *Caring & Commitment,* the last word on the subject:

> Commitment is our unique human power to stand up against the whims of fate and circumstance. It ranks alongside of, maybe even above, the other noble faculties that civilized human beings applaud themselves for having—intelligence, great feeling, and imagination....The truth is none of us is ever more Godlike than when we simply make and simply keep commitments to each other.

are less guarded than most and, as a result, ingest more of what life offers—bitter and sweet. They are familiar with the hazards of trust but believe that the gains outweigh the setbacks.

Healthy openness has its limits, however. Receptivity to new information does not mean that every new idea is endorsed; it does not mean that anything goes. Openness means that new ideas will receive fair-minded consideration, but many will surely be found wanting. This is an important clarification, for, as Jones warns in *Passion for Pilgrimage*, "Openness to everything means commitment to nothing."

IMPEDIMENTS TO OPENNESS

One way to understand the spirit of openness is to contrast it with antithetical factors. There are many:

Comfort. Perhaps the most common impediment to openness is something we are all familiar with—comfort. Change requires effort, and we prefer not to expend energy making the necessary accommodations. We prefer familiarity. Comfort takes a variety of guises. Sometimes, it is special affection for the status quo and a reluctance to rock the boat. Other times, it is old-fashioned laziness and a willingness to settle for the easiest course of action while spurning excellence.

Oversimplification. This perspective holds that adoption can be understood and mastered quickly and effortlessly. People who take a simplistic view of adoption reduce it to a few elementary factors and are oblivious to its remarkable breadth and depth.

Certainty. Respected business writer Peter Senge astutely observes, "Nothing undermines openness more surely than certainty. Once we feel as if we have 'the answer,' all motivation to question our thinking disappears." Certainty is based on two amazing premises: that things remain static long enough to be grasped, and that one can be so capable as to know and comprehend an issue of substance. In this regard, certainty is both shortsighted and arrogant. Certainty has another worrisome quality: Not only is it uninterested in learning, in ambitious form it is inclined to impose itself on others.

Elitism. Certainty can lead to elitist thinking. Elitists lack humility. Overestimating their grasp of the issues and discounting the value of "outsiders," they have access to very limited input.

Cynicism. For some, the very idea of cooperation, sacrifice, or honor is peculiar. In their view, there is nothing worth being open to. Henri Nouwen makes this observation in *The Return of the Prodigal Son:*

> For me it is amazing to experience daily the radical difference between cynicism and joy. Cynics seek darkness wherever they go. They point always to approaching dangers, impure motives, and hidden schemes. They call trust naive, care romantic, and forgiveness sentimental. They sneer at enthusiasm, ridicule spiritual fervor, and despise charismatic behavior. They consider themselves realists who see reality for what it truly is and who are not deceived by "escapist emotions." But in belittling God's joy, their darkness only calls forth more darkness.

No one achieves perfect openness. We all lose heart from time to time and fall prey to one or more of the impeding factors. Proponents of open adoption can be as closed-minded as anyone else. If open adoption becomes too comfortable, too describable, or too obviously right, it is in danger of becoming, of all things, a closed form of open adoption.

Factors Contributing to Openness

Openness comes more easily to some than others. Most of us need to work at it. We work at it by overcoming the impediments and concentrating on the factors that contribute to a spirit of openness:

Security. Openness is a consequence of courage and faith. Security is different from certainty. If a person has a clear grasp of his standards and feels secure about them, the contemplation of new ideas poses little threat to him. In this fashion, security generates tolerance. When adults feel secure in their ideals and relationships, they can comfortably address and relieve the insecurities of the children.

Curiosity. Open people are blessed with natural curiosity. They find delight in the mystery of human interaction and joy in the process of learning. They transform aggravations into adventures. Because of their irrepressible urge to learn, curious people seldom become complacent. Curious parents know that their children will not remain static, and they are eager to watch their personalities emerge and mature.

Optimism. Those who are open do not worry about new information; they believe it will enhance and enrich what is already known. They are receptive to change, perhaps even enthusiastic about it, and welcome the prospect of sensible innovation. Optimistic parents are not sure what questions their children will raise, but they look forward to them and are confident that reasonable answers can be found.

Humility. The spirit of openness is humble. In *Between God and Man*, Rabbi Abraham Heschel observes, "There are two kinds of ignorance. The one is 'dull, unfeeling, barren,' the result of indolence; the other is keen, penetrating, resplendent; the one leads to conceit and complacency, the other leads to humility." No one ever "arrives," for the journey moves on. Even in those rare and wonderful moments when we grasp a sliver of truth at least briefly, it soon slips through our fingers. Humble parents know they will make mistakes and realize they will need their children's forgiveness.

Respect. Open people respect the inherent dignity of others and are naturally interested in their ideas. Respectful parents look forward to what their children will teach them.

THE FRUITS OF OPENNESS

Where a spirit of openness exists, there will be fruitfulness. The rewards for the effort and courage of openness are significant and satisfying. They include awareness, learning, approachability, transformation, and adaptability.

Adoptive parent Dan Wolf observes, "The average open adoption participant has more awareness of ethics than the next 10 people." The open adoption relationship—with its exotic mixture of interdependence, fear, attraction, socioeconomic disequilibrium, hope, and sacrifice—presents a kaleidoscope of situations that feather out one's values. People who enjoy learning about themselves appreciate open adoption as an experience that will test their wits and their souls. Designed to defeat denial, open adoption requires that we face ourselves in all our smallness and in all our magnificence.

Awareness is important in adoption. It sharpens our sensitivity to the breadth of our capabilities and those of others. It enhances our understanding of the relationships in which we participate. Theologian Bernard Loomer comments, "Our readiness to take account of the feelings and values of another is a way of including the other within our world of meaning and concern."* Awareness keeps us mindful of personal responsibility and conscious of the fact that change always begins with oneself. It is a crucial dimension of the sixth sense that parents need to discern whether the issues their children raise are related to adoption.

In the quotes leading into this chapter, Anne Morrow Lindberg, wife of aviator Charles Lindberg, and Henri Nouwen eloquently make the point that life is never stagnant. They know this from personal experience—Lindberg from the traumatic kidnapping of her first child, and Nouwen from his restless search for community. In *Community and Growth*, Jean Vanier, a gifted builder of community, and founder of the world-famous l'Arche community for the mentally disabled and their helpers, echoes their view: "A human heart is either progressing or regressing. If it is not becoming more open, it is closing and withering spiritually." Openness is growth, and the key to growth is the willingness to continually learn. As long as there is a desire to learn, there is the prospect of progress. If this desire flags for even a moment, forward movement stops.

The heart of openness, then, is the desire to learn and grow. There is so much to learn about open adoption. Our present understanding is primitive. I believe the brightest and most experienced practitioners know less than a small fraction of what there is to know about it. Open adoption is surely too fresh and deep to yield to simpleminded capture and compartmentalizing. The extent of our ignorance is overwhelming, but it is also exciting. Open adoption exists as a fantastic landscape of profound human interaction waiting to be charted, a circumstance and opportunity that tantalize those who revel in the process of discovery.

One of the great hopes of open adoption is that the spirit of openness will generalize to other relationships, most particularly within the family. Open people are very approachable. They have

---

* *Bernard Loomer. (1976). "Two Conceptions of Power." Criterion 15 (1).*

an aura of candor that communicates that issues can be discussed with them safely. If the open adoption parents are genuinely filled with the spirit of openness, they will be approachable. This vital quality will provide these families with the opportunity to help their children in processing the issues of adoption.

TRANSFORMATION

Different styles of adoption affect people in different ways. A mechanical style of adoption, for example, leaves participants uninspired and indifferent. An ill-conceived, careless form of adoption can devastate participants. It can be the worst experience of a lifetime, laced with uproar, regret, and resentment. Heartbreaking circumstances can bring out the worst in people. Effectively implemented values-based open adoption, on the other hand, is capable of transforming its participants and bringing out their best.

In his doctoral thesis, Timothy Uhlmann, the leader of the formative early years of Catholic Human Services' open adoption program, writes of transformation in vivid, picturesque terms:

> For adults participating in open adoption the experience is one of encountering complexity, drama, transition, and transformation that is accessed only by committed participants. It is as though they have become the material that alchemists of old placed in their retorts to heat and otherwise suffer in hopes of finding the secret of how to make gold. The experience progresses through a series of well-defined musical movements which have identifiable beginnings and ends. Each movement contains distinctive themes, rhythms, and tones. Some of these distinctive movements are turbulent, like an ocean squall, stormy and disquieting. Others are serene and meditative. Like a boat at sea caught in a violent storm, participants experience anxiety and fear. Tears flow. Tranquillity is not possible. The tragic components will not allow it. Just as menacing storms make master sailors out of the uninitiated, adult participants in open adoption undergo a transformation, after which there is no going back. They will never be the same.

Having encountered the tragic, unnerved and swept over by intense distressing emotions, they find the dark night is replaced by dawn.

Participants appreciate that they have been moved, changed over time. There is a continuum. With clear before and after demarcation, there has been an initiation. The ordeal has moved participants both along and up. They marvel at the "old me–new me" split in self perception. After this storm subsides and everybody checks with everybody else, discovering that all have suffered but are well, other storms of life that loomed large in the past seem relatively small. The initiation complete, participants have a sense of belonging to a special group. Their meaningful suffering has bestowed upon them a new status. They have new eyes, especially when viewing others. Participants come away with awareness of the role of pain in bringing light into darkness, and its power to transform the tragic into something beautiful. For some, after many years of pain avoidance based on an assumption of not being strong enough, the realization that there is no coming to consciousness without pain is considered a spiritual experience. All participants ultimately considered the experience a gift. [*]

Anyone who has been involved with genuine open adoption will resonate with Uhlmann's colorful description. It is impossible to be genuinely involved in values-based open adoption and remain unaffected; to step into the open adoption drama is to be transformed. The values we have considered so far— centering on the child, candor, appreciating pain, choice, commitment—are potent; and they make a difference to the people who put them to work. Transformation begins with authentic concern for children. If we are sincere in our desire to serve children, we are not easily deterred. The catalyst for transformation is pain. Pain puts us in touch with authentic feelings and moves us beyond superficiality. Those who focus on children and learn from the pain are well-positioned for

---

[*] *Timothy J. Uhlmann. "The Adult Experience of Adoption with an Open Protocol: A Phenomenological Investigation." Unpublished doctoral thesis, The Union Institute.*

respectful interaction with others, and candor becomes an ideal mechanism for the expression of this respect.

The potential of open adoption is remarkable. Anyone who has seen the healing and harmony that it can stimulate is reluctant to settle for less. In Chapter 1, I defined open adoption in four factors: birthparents choose the adoptive parents, the families meet, identifying information is exchanged, and an ongoing relationship is established. Transformation is the fifth ingredient of open adoption. If there is no transformation, there is no spiritual connection, and there is no vitality to the open adoption relationship. If participants are not somehow stirred and improved by the experience, they have not truly invested themselves and are going through the motions mechanically. True open adoption is never mechanical; it is alive. It has heart, soul, and the breath of life.

Transformation can take many forms. Some people are completely taken by surprise. They were fretful skeptics at the outset but were eventually absorbed, overwhelmed, and converted by the allure and sweep of the experience. Others are completely receptive to the open adoption process from the beginning. They typically find that open adoption affirms them and extends their beliefs in new directions. Still others find the transformation intensely painful and humbling. The adoption journey confronts them with unnerving feelings of imperfection, dependence, and exploitation. They probe their souls with somber questions of worthiness. Transformation is best understood as a consequence of all of these processes—seduction, affirmation, and humility.

However it happens, transformation is the glory of open adoption. In broadest terms, it is a shift from self-centeredness to a sincere concern for others. It is movement from a pattern of caution and self-protection to a fully alive, "go for broke" style carried out within the limits and liberations of one's value system. It is a shift from unilateral power to relational power. Transformation is a double pleasure that begins with liberation from factors that constrict our effectiveness and ends with multidimensional growth. Open adoption is not an event. Rather, it is a continuing process of learning and renewal.

Quality open adoption liberates participants from unwarranted fear and defensiveness, and it relieves them from the draining claims of shame. It releases them from the burdensome illusion of independence and the isolation that accompanies this illusion. Values-based open adoption frees participants from the desperate temptations of pretense, manipulation, and exploitation. It calls us out of stagnation and mortifying comfort.

Participation in a loving adoption rekindles the exhilaration of idealism, of aspiring to the noble and honorable. It stirs the strong interior delight associated with integrity and living according to one's ideals. Involvement in quality open adoption leads to the joyful rediscovery of cooperation—it is still possible. It produces a startling encounter with sacrifice and the deep satisfaction of participation in a covenantal relationship, meaningful and sacred. Suddenly, unexpectedly, we find ourselves feeling like the people we were meant to be.

Participants enter the experience of values-based open adoption with a well-defined task to accomplish and come out of it as better people. Their conscience is intact and approving. The fear that almost paralyzed them in the early phases is replaced with a determination to serve. Self-centeredness is exchanged for generosity. Participants in transforming open adoption awaken a new understanding of themselves and the important people in their lives. Many of them gain personal confidence, new respect for their families, renewed faith, new friends, expanded kinship, a cause, and a reconnection to the sweetness of life. By openly facing their imperfections and the painful realities of life, they drink from the chalice of joy in a new way. They cannot help but respond to these gifts with gratitude, an appealing state of being that can sustain the process of transformation.

The final fruit of openness is adaptation. Those who operate with a spirit of openness recognize that everything in life changes quickly and requires new solutions from us. To meet the future with confidence and joy, we need to be flexible and adaptable. That is the subject of the next chapter.

Chapter 9

The Creative Challenge: Adaptability

> Power offers an easy substitute for the hard task of love.
>
> Henri Nouwen, *In the Name of Jesus*

> Love is fair when it builds up both the lover and the beloved, when it increases both and diminishes neither, when it brings them close and lets them be separate, when it nourishes both and leaves neither wanting.
>
> Lewis Smedes, *A Pretty Good Person*

There is much about open adoption that is difficult. There are many moments along the way when participants do not have their usual control. Reflecting on an early visit of a birthgrandfather, an adoptive father mused, "I'm so glad he didn't smoke in my house. He could have—he knew it, and so did I—but he chose not to. He's a good guy." Sometimes we are most thankful for small mercies. Until trust is fully installed, there is a wariness, an undercurrent of awareness that the birth and adoptive families could make each other's lives miserable. They are acutely conscious of the other's power. Furthermore, absent the cover of secrecy that used to be part of adoption, there is not much anyone can get away with. There is no hiding from results with open adoption; shortfalls are soon discovered, and our cozy pretensions of perfection cannot be sustained. Open adoption compels us to face the reality of our relationships. Open adoption begins with courage and choice, but its enduring creativity and vitality are found in the adaptations that participants make as their lives move forward.

The old approach to adoption has the odd effect of freezing people at a point in time. Birthparents are forever irresponsible teenagers; adoptees always powerless children; and, perhaps on the up side, adoptive parents forever an energetic 35. The reality is obviously very different. People change. Relationships change. Communities change. Social norms change. To remain vital, adoptions must have the capacity to respond to swiftly changing realities. If open adoption is going to meet the needs of children as they grow toward independence, it must be able to improvise and adapt to new and unforeseeable circumstances. The hallmark of open adoption is the ability to improvise within values. An attitude of genuine openness, as discussed in Chapter 8, anticipates change and prepares for it. Adaptation is the ongoing application of openness.

An effective adoption program does its best to get things off to a coherent, respect-filled start and to provide the tools that enable participants to meet the predictable challenges of the future. At some point, however, responsibility must be passed to those who will live out the experience. Moving beyond the program's field of nurture like eager but wary adolescents leaving home, adoptive parents and birthparents strike out on their own. The success of the adoption depends on their continuing creativity. The goal of the process is that each open adoption clan will become a unique, self-governing team.

Others have written about adoption from a developmental perspective, so that is not necessary here.* We will approach open adoption from a perspective of tasks that triad members must accomplish individually and in relationship with others if the open adoption relationship is to flourish. Participants are faced with enormous and sometimes conflicting emotional tasks. Impossible as these tasks appear at the outset, open adoption families routinely respond to them with impressive strength of character.

---

* *David Brodzinsky, Marshall Schecter, and Robin Marantz Henig describe the intersection of developmental issues for children and adoption in* Being Adopted: The Lifelong Search for Self. *In* The Adoption Life Cycle, *Elinor Rosenberg describes life-cycle issues for the larger triad. Lois Melina and Sharon Roszia-Kaplan consider the issues of open adoption in a developmental context in* The Open Adoption Experience.

Tasks for Birthparents

Every open adoption begins with birthparent planning. Their initial decisions set the course for all that follows. A birthparent hoping to establish a healthy open adoption faces many daunting tasks. If these tasks are well-handled, prospects for a satisfying and enduring arrangement are enhanced. To call the birthparent experience emotionally strenuous is to understate the circumstance. It can devastate a person, or it can produce unparalleled personal growth. Often, it does both.

Preparation

Ideally, the open adoption process begins prenatally. Even in instances in which the birthmother copes with her distress by denying her pregnancy, the work of preparation happens at least to some degree unconsciously. The birthmother may begin to steel herself for the difficult course of separation, but this does not require distancing herself from the baby. If she has negative feelings about the birthfather and the circumstances leading to conception, they must be distinguished from feelings about the baby. It is best if she thinks well of the baby and enjoys and affirms him in utero.

Many adoption promoters worry about this advice, fearing that it may undermine her resolve toward adoption, but it is obviously in the child's best interests to be fully appreciated from the earliest possible moment. Ideally, the prenatal period is used to carefully fashion the details of the adoption plan—leaving room, of course, for a change of heart. The prenatal time provides opportunity to learn about the role of birthparent and to build the relationship with the prospective adoptive family. If the families can establish their relationship prenatally, they will be able to work together more comfortably in the highly anxious transition phase after the baby is born. Birthparents can use the time of preparation to anticipate the loss, but we must recognize that their imagination consistently falls far short of the reality they will later experience. Imagined pain is easier to endure than actual pain.

Gentle Transition

The "clean break" approach to separation still has its devotees, but it seems clear that children benefit from a gradual, gentle transition. We easily embrace the wisdom of bridge building in arranging adoptions for older children but ignore its importance with infants. The birthfamily's first project is to welcome and celebrate new life and revel in their amazing role in the process. As the only person with whom the baby is initially familiar, the birthmother is a unique source of comfort for the baby—comfort that should not be withheld.

The birthmother's work is unimaginably emotional. She must simultaneously celebrate the baby's arrival and start making room for and involving the new parents. Almost impossibly, she is saying "Hello" and "Good-bye" at the same time. Birthparents and their supporters must not allow themselves to be rushed in this lonely and tender process; they must assert their unique sense of pace. Although they may not immediately recognize it, birthparents who are whisked through a hurried separation process will surely feel profound resentment later.

Grieving

Birthparents are confronted with a loss that exceeds anything they imagined. It is a peculiar loss by any standards and is unlike anything they have previously faced. The loss is massive, largely self-inflicted, and in some ways incomplete and ongoing. Furthermore, the loss is often misunderstood, underestimated, and unsupported by their usual cast of supporters.

Handling this highly unusual loss is a formidable piece of emotional work. The first task of grieving is to acknowledge the loss. With the joy of the adoptive parents readily available, it is tempting for birthparents to highlight the gains of open adoption and deny their loss. It is better to resist the temptation. The next task is to define the loss. It is best described as a loss of their role as parent. Putting it that way, however, is too antiseptic; it sounds too light. The loss that birthparents experience through open adoption should never be minimized. It is the loss of the most consequential, perplexing, and rewarding role in all of life: namely, "Mom" or "Dad." It is the loss of many incomparable moments of novelty and pride. For many, it is the loss of self-esteem and self-respect.

Like all grievers, birthparents must handle the loss at their own unique pace. Although there are no shortcuts, they can keep the grieving process moving forward by facing the moments of pain courageously. Even far along the path toward resolution, there will be moments—some predictable and some unforeseeable—of renewed grief. Since new aspects of loss are revealed with each new developmental stage the child enters, the grieving process never ends. Each stage stirs a new sense of loss to be worked through.

Working Through Regret

Somewhere along the way, birthparents will face inevitable moments of regret. It may be a flickering thought or it may be lingering preoccupation. Whatever the form, regret is debilitating and discouraging. The best defense against it is clarity about the reasons for the adoption decision. Birthparents need to document in detail the context in which they made their decision and capture their rationale in writing. They must realize that they make their decisions at particular points in time and that it is often surprisingly difficult to accurately reconstruct those contexts in later years. Some birthparents torture themselves unreasonably by revisiting their adoption decisions in the context of subsequent and dramatically altered circumstances. As Judy Tatelbaum, an authority on grieving, puts it in *You Don't Have to Suffer,* "We need to remember that we always do the best we can at any given moment, even though it may not look that way in hindsight."

Committing to Success

At some point, birthparents need to substantially resolve whatever ambivalence they feel about their decision, accept personal responsibility for the adoption, and commit to doing everything within reason to make it work. They must decide to invest themselves in the relationship fully and embrace the adoptive family with a full measure of respect. Even if other aspects of their lives are unsettled, they do well to assign the highest priority to the adoption and commit their best and most positive energy to its success.

Finding the Basic Role

Although the loss of the parental role is indescribably painful, for many birthparents it is also a great relief to responsibly transfer the responsibilities of parenting to a trusted and fully prepared person. Because the responsibilities of birthparenting are quite limited, compared with those of parenting, open adoption birthparents who might have felt overwhelmed in the parental role may fill the birthparent role quite competently and feel successful in it. Describing the role of the open adoption birthparent precisely is difficult because it is in many ways idiosyncratic. Each birthparent creates the role with varying degrees of personal investment and creativity.

The role has two major reference points: the adoptive parents and the child. Relative to the adoptive parents, the role is that of friend and little sister, with a touch of mother-in-law included for good measure. The artful mother-in-law, after all, knows when to speak up and when to keep her opinion to herself. In relation to the child, the birthparent is a marvelous conglomeration of special adult friend, aunt, big sister, historian, and genealogist. The role is inherently worthy of respect, but it does not usually involve any special authority beyond that generally afforded to someone older. Wise birthparents are not presumptive about the status of their roles. They recognize that most of the available affection and warmth in the relationship will be earned. Depending on the energy and creativity she brings to the role, the tone of her interaction with the youngster can range from drab to electric.

Nurturing the Relationship with Adoptive Parents

A wise birthparent works hard to build a positive relationship with the adoptive parents. She makes an effort to get to know them as individuals and takes interest in what is important to them. She makes herself knowable so it is easy for them to connect to her. If this crucial relationship grows, everyone benefits. It adds to the likelihood that the child will perceive his adoption in positive terms. When the relationship between the birthparents and adoptive parents is positive, the focus is broader than just the child. This cordiality relieves the adoptee of pressure he might otherwise feel to make the arrangement flourish.

Self-Acceptance

To find peace of mind and the freedom to enjoy the open adoption relationship, birthparents must come to terms with the inner voice of shame and doubt. They must also reckon with the magnitude of the trust they granted. This can take a long time. They cannot simply rationalize their adoption decision; they must believe in their rationale. If birthparents are to feel personal growth and restoration, they must know in their bones that they made an intelligent, loving, wise, and moral decision. It is also necessary, if they are to know peace of mind, that they release any resentment associated with the experience that they may be holding. The disappointments that led to and in many ways culminated in adoption are profound and plentiful. Release happens through forgiveness. Odd as it seems, prominent among those whom they must forgive are themselves. If birthparents are unable to forgive, they become accomplices to their own discomfort.

Moving Ahead

An important aspect of the adoption plan is the opportunity for the birthparents to move ahead in life. If this prospect is squandered, a significant portion of the rationale for the adoption is thwarted. Forward movement honors the child, who has then an effective birthparent to whom she can relate and in whom she can take pride. To a large extent, this process of getting on with life is a matter of choice. Tatelbaum observes that "suffering is perpetuating the pain of the past and carrying it into the future." She goes on to point out that "grief and loss are unavoidable, and yet how we grieve and how long we suffer is truly our choice, no matter what our circumstances." If birthparents have full and satisfying lives, they are likely to have balanced relationships with the adoptive families. If, on the other hand, they have empty, unfulfilled lives, they risk wearing out their welcome by focusing too intensely on the child and the adoptive parents.

Responding to the Child

The foremost goal of open adoption is to honor the child. An important way to accomplish this is to preserve the extraordinary relationship between the birthparent and child. Early interaction with the baby can be difficult for birthparents because it stimulates the feelings of loss; nevertheless, it is desirable for them to be involved in the youngster's life early enough to make their presence natural, an unquestioned fact of life, a given. A later entrance is, of course, possible, but it runs the risk of generating unnecessary drama and anxiety.

Birthparents hold great quantities of important information for the adoptee. Children love to hear stories of the pregnancy and their birth, and they savor accounts of how everyone reacted to their arrival. It is only natural for a child to be curious about the circumstances leading to his adoption. As he develops as a person, his judgments about the birthparents may vary dramatically. Birthparents need to be prepared to handle everything from profound gratitude to searing accusation.

Giving Emotional Gifts

Highly effective birthparents fully endorse the adoptive parents they have chosen. They bless them with the message: "You're exactly the parents I hoped my child would have. I'm very pleased, and I want you to know that I will never undermine your authority. I don't want you to baby-sit this child. I want you to parent her." They will also fully acknowledge and affirm the child. It is enormously gratifying to a child to know she is a source of pride to her birthparents rather than a mistake to be hidden.

Developing a Spiel

Since open adoption birthparents do not live in hiding, they are subject to endless questions from curious acquaintances. To handle these questions gracefully, they do well to hone their skills of explanation. With practice, they will concoct a repertoire of responses, including a polite but swift conversation-stopper, a 20-second summary, a five-minute explanation of the basics, and an extensive, "aren't you sorry you asked," no-holds-barred account of the experience. They will find themselves balancing the need for public education against their own reasonable need for privacy.

These tasks are distributed over the normal challenges and opportunities of life, as birthparents go on to establish themselves. They will likely experience a variety of jobs, growing economic independence, new friends and significant others, educational and personal growth, children, and assorted family issues. Each of these factors affects their availability for full involvement in the open adoption.

Tasks for Adoptive Parents

After birthparents design and organize the initial plan of action, adoptive parents usually step into the leadership role. The tone of the ongoing open adoption relationship is directly related to their comfort and enthusiasm. In an unanticipated windfall of warmth, we have seen countless adoptive families take emotionally broken birthparents under wing and nurture them so that their full potential is restored. The contributions of adoptive parents are too often overlooked. The truth is, more than any other factor, the steadiness and compassion of adoptive parents makes open adoption possible.

Preparation

The first task for the adoptive parents is putting their emotional house in order. They must conquer their feelings of fear, desperation, and self-interest and settle on a course of action that honors the other participants in the process. They accomplish this by connecting to basic values, becoming well-informed, and finding appropriate hope. They must be clearheaded about the risks that accompany the open adoption process and be prepared to handle a change of heart by the birthparents. Prudent prospective adoptive parents take the time to educate their circle of supporters to the risks they are taking.

Gentle Transition

It is not a simple thing for adoptive parents to step patiently and respectfully into the parental role. In the transition phase, they face the impossible task of fully welcoming a long-awaited child on one hand, while bracing for a change of heart by the birthparents on the other. It is difficult to know how emotionally involved to become. In the hospital, it feels like they are walking a tight rope between too much involvement with the birthfamily and baby and too little. In charting their early course, they learn to skillfully read the birthparents. Similarly, once they assume the parental role, they learn to read the baby's needs.

Although adoptive parents typically have private doubts about their ability to fall in love with "someone else's baby," these misgivings quickly yield to the enormous appeal of the infant's dependency. The pull is so powerful, in fact, that there is a real hazard that they will feel an unanticipated impulse toward exclusivity and latch on like a miser finding a new treasure. It is an impulse to be resisted, for there is far more joy in celebrating the baby's existence with all who love him, including, of course, his birthfamily. Ironically, if they yield to the temptation of exclusivity, they will end up feeling less secure about the adoption.

Committing to Success

At some point, adoptive parents must make a fully informed decision to do everything within reason to make the arrangement work. They decide to risk the vulnerability of trust, invest themselves fully, and embrace the birthfamily with a full measure of respect.

Finding Security

From the earliest moments in the process, adoptive parents are confronted with questions of worthiness. The system does not presume they are wonderful, requiring instead that they prove themselves. Hopefully, as they work to convince professionals and the birthfamily, they convince themselves as well. Later, in moments of deep privacy, as they cradle the mesmerizing infant in their arms, they wonder whether they truly have a right to be part of her life. To move ahead with comfort, they must establish the feeling that they are entitled to parent the youngster.

Security starts with self-appraisal. Adoptive parents must search their hearts and determine that they have been straightforward and honest in their interactions with the birthparents. Beyond this, they must depend on the birthparents for permission to parent. Although they once wondered whether they would be chosen and feared the process, they now find pleasure and reassurance in having been chosen from a field of impressive candidates and in knowing the choice was entirely unpressured.

Coming to Terms with the Importance of Biology

Adoption observers have noted through the years that adoptive parents downplay the importance of biology. It is possible that this tendency is a form of denial, but more likely it is a natural consequence of their interaction with the child. Staring into a baby's eyes and feeling overwhelmed with a jarring passion unlike any they have felt previously, they transcend and leave behind their previous thoughts about the importance of biology. For them, biology is no longer an emotionally meaningful factor, and they find it difficult to understand the fuss others make about it. The task for adoptive parents, then, is to relearn the importance of the biological connection and regain their understanding and respect for the importance that others attach to it.

Parenting

Although adoptive parents have extra issues to deal with, they also have all the usual challenges of parenting. Secure parents feel appropriate authority and feel free to do what needs to be done. They are not tentative or fearful in their parenting.

Interpreting the Experience

An important task facing adoptive parents is explaining adoption to their children. If adoption is truly the positive experience it is advertised to be, it is not a problem to be hidden or even something to be nervous about. For adoption to take on a tone of normalcy, it is desirable that the adoptee grows up having always known. In a relaxed, normalized form of adoption, there is no dramatic moment of truth. The interpretation of adoption is not a onetime event. Rather, it is a process that evolves in response to questions and issues that emerge as the child grows older.

Nurturing the Relationship with the Birthparents

Because of the maturity that comes with age, adoptive parents are logical candidates to provide stability and leadership in the relationship. A spirit of inclusion and welcome—not just polite talk, but heartfelt longing—sets a warm, inviting tone for the relationship. It also helps when they establish reasonable and understandable boundaries. Since the relationship with the birthfamily is obviously not their only relationship, adoptive parents need to find a reasonable place for this unique relationship in their larger constellation of relationships. By establishing a congenial connection in the early years, when the adoptee makes few demands on the relationship, the adults build a solid foundation for the potentially more complicated years when the adoptee is a full participant in the arrangement.

Handling Emotional Indebtedness

To achieve a full measure of comfort with the adoption, adoptive parents must come to terms with the fact that their joy is a consequence of the birthparent's pain. It is an unnerving realization. Ordinarily, we try to handle unbalanced circumstances by trying to even the emotional ledger through reciprocation; but in adoption there is no way to do this. Healthy adoptive parents accept the gift with profound gratitude. If they do not discover an appropriate sense of gratitude, they may feel profound guilt and end up forever over an emotional barrel of indebtedness. There is an enormous difference between appropriate support generated by healthy gratitude and codependent behavior stirred by unprocessed indebtedness and guilt. Gratitude is a response of joy, whereas indebtedness is linked to oppression and duty.

Giving Emotional Gifts

There are at least three significant emotional gifts that adoptive parents can give to birthparents. The first is uncompromising respect for their honor. Grateful adoptive parents will not tolerate any disparaging remarks about birthparents or insinuations that they are in any way uncaring. Another gift of inestimable value is the attitude of inclusion. This legitimizes the involvement of birthparents and tells them it is okay to be involved in the child's life. The third gift is affirmation. Adoptive parents routinely end up in the birthparents' corner. Like few others, adoptive parents are aware of the strength of character that resides in the birthparent's heart, and they believe deeply in her greatness.

Of course, open adoption is not the only thing going on in the adoptive family's life. It is a challenge for them to manage the open adoption relationship while meeting all of the other demands of life. They must deal with the substantial demands of a new baby, but they must handle all the usual vagaries of life— job changes, moves, illnesses—as well.

Tasks for Adoptees

Open adoption also presents the adopted child with a succession of tasks. His influence in the relationship corresponds to his growing competence and maturity. If the adoption is to truly meet his needs, he must grow in his ability to articulate his concerns.

Understanding the Facts

The world is a strange and wonderful place for a child. Among the many realities for her to comprehend is the fact of adoption. First she learns the word, and later she learns that she was born to a birthmother rather than to her adoptive mother. As she grows older, she will learn the facts of reproduction along with obvious and subtle social and economic realities. Fortunately, with the birthfamily involved, she is spared the mysteriousness that formerly plagued adoption. In the open system, adoption is a fact of her life that no one tries to disguise.

Understanding the Relationships

An important task for the growing youngster is to determine how he is related to the various people in his life. As he becomes more alert to the social reality around him, he learns to make distinctions between family, friends, neighbors, and strangers. A particularly complicated relationship for him to understand is his connection to his birthfamily. The extended birthclan offers an intriguing cast of characters of varying interest to the adoptee. Perhaps the most interesting and complex of these relationships involves his birthsiblings. How will he relate to them? Quite possibly, it is a question he will never completely resolve.

Understanding the Feelings

The facts of the adoptee's life and the relationships that organize it are subject to interpretation and will likely generate a variety of emotions. Her earliest feelings about adoption are likely a positive response to the impression that she is special. Later she may interpret *special* less positively. She may grapple with the issues of rejection and feeling different. As her understanding grows about her birthparents and the circumstances they faced at the time of their decision, her appreciation for their courage will likely grow.

Growing in Autonomy

As the years go by, the adoptee will develop greater awareness of his adoption. Hopefully, he will learn to take the initiative and become appropriately assertive. As he matures, he will move toward full partnership in the open adoption relationship. It is also possible, in a surprising open adoption twist, that some adoptees will prefer not to have an active relationship with their birthfamilies.

Establishing Identity

Every growing person develops a sense of identity as he or she moves toward personal autonomy. For adoptees, this is a more elaborate project than for those who are not adopted. Since establishing personal identity requires understanding the contributions of various parties in one's life, the link to birthparents that open adoption provides is an enormous help. The adoptee must determine how she is similar and dissimilar to her birthparents and her adoptive parents. The rest of the process is figuring out how she is unique and distinct from every other person, including parents and grandparents of every sort.

Assenting to the Plan

Ultimately, every adoptee reaches a conclusion about his adoption. Perhaps he will conclude that his adoption was a mistake, and he will put in his time until he can stand alone. Far more likely and more happily, however, he will accept the arrangement and will own it as his life story. It is difficult for adoptees to assent to their adoptions emotionally when they are dealing with many unknowns. An important advantage of open adoption is that the adoptee has at an early age the information he needs to own his life experience.

Giving Emotional Gifts

The adoptee's very existence as an emotionally integrated, healthy person is a never-ending source of pleasure for both her birthparents and her adoptive parents. The healthy adoptee can say, "I love you" to each set of parents. These are words that adoptive parents fantasized about through years of lonely infertility treatments. They are words that birthparents wept over as they made their plans, because they were sure they would never hear them.

The tasks of open adoption are distributed over the usual issues of life for the adoptee. She must weave them through the various demands and activities related to growing up.

THE ADOPTIVE PARENT–BIRTHPARENT RELATIONSHIP

It is no small thing for adoptive parents and birthparents to become family to each other. Writer Denise Lang captures a portion of the significance with the comment, "Ah, families! No other social group is as loved, despised, imposed upon, bragged about, concealed, revered, dissected, ignored, or elevated. They can triple our pleasure or devastate a holiday or special occasion." When participants commit to an open adoption, they add to their clan, and in doing so they add an amazing new dimension to their lives.

As in every significant relationship, the number of variables involved in the relationship between adoptive parents and birthparents is astronomical. If they are doing well in handling their individual open adoption tasks, chances are their relationship will be in good order. There is more to it, though, than individual tasks. Issues can be taken only so far individually; then they are better understood in the catalytic interplay of relationships. The pace and style of birthparent grieving, for example, will profoundly affect the early years of this relationship. If the birthmother elects to handle her grief privately and withdraws, there may not be much interaction with the adoptive family. On the other hand, if she decides to lean on the adoptive family in her time of grief, as often happens, the pace of the early interaction may be brisk.

The issues that need to be worked out in the open adoption relationship are numerous and appear in every phase of the experience. Some challenges are in the basic nature of the relationship. Other tasks appear in the early phases of the arrangement, whereas still others only emerge as the relationship ripens. If they are not worked through, they can severely limit the potential of the relationship. On the other hand, successfully managing these tasks can add to everyone's sense of accomplishment.

Discrepant Emotional Needs

Adoptive parents and birthparents begin with completely different realities. One thinks, "I need a baby so badly that I cry all the time," whereas the other thinks, "I need relief (independence) so badly that I cry all the time." They are expected to connect, though their needs are completely different. Their psychological realities are so different that it is extremely difficult—even for the especially empathic—for each to fully tune into their counterpart. One's personal needs and insecurities predominate and interfere with the usual ability to empathize.

Incompatible Perspectives on the Nature of Parenting

The adoptive mother in particular has an impossible message to convey to the birthmother. In brief, she is saying, "It's okay for you to let go of the maternal role; but trust me, I never will." If the adoptive mother is in the camp of "forever mothers," can she understand the reality of a mother who is transferring her responsibility? If she can truly understand the possibility of setting aside the maternal role, can she be trusted to hang in there come what may? It is not an easy bind to work through.

Unbalanced Initial Status

It is irrational to arrange an adoption unless it constitutes some sort of progress for the child. Consequently, it is the inescapable assumption of adoption that the adoptive parents are a better resource for parenting than are the birthparents. This assumption divides. It means that every adoption begins with a "one up, one down" imbalance in the relationship between adoptive parents and birthparents. Since relationships usually sustain their initial balance or imbalance over time, this dynamic makes it difficult for birthparents to grow into equality and full partnership with adoptive parents.

Working with Grief

Early in the relationship, the predominant feeling for birthparents is grief, whereas the prevailing sensation for adoptive parents is joy. Because each experiences the adoption so differently, it is difficult to for them to find each other emotionally. Many adoptive parents worry that their joy is offensive to birthparents, that their delight is a form of rubbing it in. They are commonly tempted, for example, to withhold the cutest pictures of the baby because they fear these images will torment the birthparents. It is difficult for adoptive parents to understand that most birthparents find consolation in the joy of the adoptive clan.

The discrepant emotions can spawn a devastating spiral of misunderstanding and fear. If the birthparent's grief is intense and her need for reassurance great, she may seek an increasing level of involvement. The adoptive parents may feel pushed or crowded and start feeling twinges of insecurity. If they respond to these feelings by distancing themselves, it can add to the birthparent's insecurity and prompt her to seek reassurance more aggressively. A cycle of insecurity is launched. Since neither party is fully conscious of the pattern, it may require professional assistance to interrupt the spiral of negative interaction.

One more issue merits comment. Adoptive parents can usually respond to the grief of birthparents with understanding, but regret is a different, far more threatening dynamic. When birthparent grief crosses the line and becomes regret, the predictable reaction of adoptive parents is self-protection, not compassion. Regret is the one dynamic that adoptive parents cannot directly assist birthparents in working through.

Claiming Issues

An important question lingers in the background, surfacing uncomfortably now and then. Whose child is this? The birthfamily and adoptive family can easily be at cross-purposes on this question. Birthparents, trying to reassure themselves in their grief and insecurity that they are still important, may cling tenaciously to their claim on the child. Sometimes, it is a matter of getting their share of the credit for his splendor, but in a more serious vein it can signal an unwillingness to relinquish the parental role.

If birthparents overstate their connection to the youngster, they can interfere with the crucial adoptive parent claiming process. To step fully into the parental role, adoptive parents must unabashedly declare in their hearts and to the world, "This child is mine. I live and die with this child. My very identity as a person is invested in him."

The challenge for adoptive parents is to wholeheartedly claim the child without owning or possessing him. They are stewards, not owners. A healthy course of events is revealed in the pronouns used. To begin with, birthparents rightfully claim, "This is *my* child." Then they give a great gift of permission when they instruct the adoptive parents "to enjoy *your* child." Adoptive parents positively luxuriate in the word for a moment, then respond with a thrilling correction: "I think you should say *our* child." It is then the birthparents' turn to soak up the beauty of a simple word. There can be no shortcuts in this pronoun journey; each parent must authorize the other, and there is no collective "we" until that happens. As one astute adoptive father put it, "It is as though the reality of each family is first disassembled and then reassembled as a new unified entity."

Establishing Basic Compatibility

If the initial choosing was done carefully from a pool of diverse candidates, chances are good that the families will be very compatible. The good will they feel toward each because of the selection process is usually enhanced by the dramatic experience of welcoming a new life, which they shared in the hospital. When those dramatic times pass, they must face again the issue of basic compatibility. It is a twofold matter of finding the interests they have in common and achieving a respectful tolerance for their differences. If this is not accomplished, the relationship has limited potential. It will likely become a formal open adoption and little more.

Learning the Dance

It takes a while for participants in a relationship to find a rhythm and establish a comfortable pattern of interaction. They need to learn each other's ways and discover each other's peculiarities. Each must place value on pleasing the other and learn the art of accommodation. Common courtesy is especially helpful in the early stages of the relationship. Keen readers of cues can learn the dance quickly, but participants with lesser social skills may find this process of trial and error very difficult. These participants benefit from explicit descriptions of the boundaries. As they work to clarify the boundaries of the relationship, they develop their problem-solving abilities.

Defining the Relationship

Open adoption participants must determine who they are to each other. They must figure out, for example, how they introduce each other to outsiders. That is a first step in developing the language they will need to describe the relationship. When the dust settles from the placement process, it is important for them to work through what they owe each other. What is the underlying dynamic? Indebtedness? Obligation? Gratitude? Friendship? Do they feel fully committed to each other? Is the arrangement covenantal?

Having recognized the capabilities of the birthparents, adoptive parents are sometimes tempted to help them get on with their lives. They must be careful about this relationship. It is helpful for them to be supportive and encouraging, but they must be careful not to impose their agenda on them. If the relationship is to mature, adoptive parents must open themselves to the influence of the birthfamily. As they spend more satisfying time with each other and trust grows, they will find a mutually comfortable level of familiarity and intimacy.

Worthiness

The relationship contains a subliminal element of threat. The other's success is desirable, but it is also scary. If the adoptive parents, for example, flourish in the role—a development that birthparents hope for—it is also possible that the birthparent will feel dispensable and that she has nothing to offer. Some small part of her wishes they would foul up and make her useful again. The adoptive parents, on the other hand, genuinely want the birthparent to prosper. They think well of her and recognize that her effectiveness reflects well on the child. When birthparents thrive, however, it appears to erase the original rationale for adoption and makes the adoption seem unnecessary.

Birthparents and adoptive parents alike wonder how they compare and whether they can hold their own with each other. They know it is an important issue because some day the adoptee will compare them. Depending on whether the birthfather is involved, the feeling of threat is often greater for the women. The issue of worthiness can complicate the relationship between adoptive mother and birthmother. Many adoptive fathers who are not confronted by their counterparts, the birthfathers, have difficulty understanding their wives' insecurity. Since their relationship with the birthmother is usually straightforward and uncomplicated, they may view their wives' insecurity as an hypersensitivity.

In secure relationships, the question of worthiness is ultimately addressed in a breakthrough conversation. At some point the adoptive mother may confess, "You're young and full of life. You're contemporary and you're cool. You scare me. I'm afraid that some day Suzy will turn to me and think, 'What a dud.'" The birthmother will react with astonishment, "What? You're married and successful. You're a tender mother. You're everything I hope someday to be. I wish I were half the woman you are." Having shared their secret envy and insecurity, they find their relationship strangely cemented.

Resolving the Power Dynamic

Another obvious thread of threat woven into the relationship is the issue of power. Power is a conspicuous dynamic early in the arrangement. If it is well-handled at that stage, it will likely be handled well later. After the legal transfer has occurred and the statutory provisions for recourse have elapsed, the power dynamic becomes more subtle. If they are not careful, adoptive parents and birthparents can hold each other hostage to issues of power. Adoptive parents have the power to control the birthparent's access have to the child and are positioned to heavily influence the child's attitudes about the birthfamily. Birthparents, on the other hand, can undermine the arrangement subtly or directly. They have the power to mount some form of late legal challenge, which, at the very least, would be expensive and anxiety-producing for the adoptive parents.

Power is the issue of fear revisited. Fear gives the other great power. As Henri Nouwen states with great insight in the quotation leading into this chapter, "Power offers an easy substitute for the hard task of love." If the open adoption is to achieve a level of comfort, each family must completely set aside the potential leverage of power and choose to relate based on cooperation, trust, and honor. When trust is fully installed, or to use Nouwen's language, when the hard task of love is in effect, power ceases to be an issue. Unilateral power is set aside in favor of mutuality.

Relaxing

At some point, it occurs to participants that the relationship is working, that it is natural, enjoyable, and genuinely desirable. It is a soul-tickling, joyful realization. Interestingly, though, that joyful awareness creates a new worry. Participants who find their open adoption relationships deeply satisfying now have something precious to lose. They fret that something might come out of nowhere to interfere and undermine the relationship. As is true in all meaningful relationships, they become vulnerable because they care.

Friendship

As relaxation sinks in deeply, the stage is set for the relationship to be fully enjoyed. Instead of relentlessly laboring at the relationship, adoptive and birthparents find it brighter and more spontaneous. It becomes fun. They recognize there is much more to their relationship than the fact that they love the same child; they celebrate each other and the fact that they are friends. They must, of course, continue to work at the relationship, but it is a joyful and rewarding undertaking.

The Committee

The good will and trust established in the momentous and amazing early phases prepares participants to work together, if necessary, in subsequent times of greater complexity. If, some day, the adoptee is experiencing great distress, perhaps because of adoption dynamics, the adoptive parents may find the perspective and support of the birthparents helpful as they search for answers.

The importance of the families working together with effective communication became clear to me recently in half-comical fashion. The occasion was an open adoption banquet, and I was seated at a table with birthparents and adoptive parents who were partners in an open adoption. In the conversation to my left, the birthmother was sharing her opinion that one of the great things for birthparents about open adoption is that the adoptive parents are on duty to handle the child's tough questions regarding why the adoption was necessary in the first place. Two seconds later, I joined the discussion on my right just in time to hear the adoptive mother explain that the great thing about open adoption is that birthparents are on hand to handle the really difficult questions. I suggested they might want to compare notes on the issue. The point is, tough questions must be handled by both families, not one or the other.

THE RELATIONSHIP BETWEEN BIRTHPARENTS

Birthmothers come from every sector of life and are motivated by a variety of factors. For most, there is a pronounced economic dimension to their decision. They reach the sad conclusion that they are unable to provide a satisfactory environment for their children. For some, the baby is a child too many. They have managed to get by with an earlier child or children but fear that another child will push the family over the edge. Others are significantly oriented to the future. They see youthful single parenting as a dead end for the baby and themselves. Many birthmothers are motivated toward adoption by a awareness of their own unreadiness. They juxtapose their emotional, educational, social, and financial readiness with the needs of a baby and sorrowfully conclude the baby would be better off in the arms of a family that is more prepared for the rigors of parenting. Another important factor that often motivates birthmothers to consider adoption is the importance of fathers. Most birthmothers place great value on the enrichment that a father brings to the life of a child, a belief likely inspired by the role her own father did or did not play in her life. Since a leading reason for birthmothers to choose adoption is their belief that children need fathers, the baby's father—involved or uninvolved—is always a central and emotional figure in the drama.

Enter adoption's villain—the birthfather. Birthfathers are adoption's symbols of disappointment. Given the exceptional appreciation that most birthmothers have for fathers, his unavailability to fill the role in her baby's life disappoints the birthmother deeply. If he responds to the pregnancy with disdain and distance, she is understandably indignant and disillusioned. If he responds to the pregnancy positively and with great interest, but is not of a mind to step into a parental role, she may find his tenderness and, to her way of thinking, his unfulfilled potential all the more frustrating.

He is an easy target. "Anyone can be a father," critics are fond of pointing out, "but it takes a man to be a dad." Others are quick to add, "He's just an impregnator," making clear their opinion that conception has little if any emotional meaning for many men. Although birthfathers are largely regarded as shadowy figures, most people have some image of them. There truly are some villains—dangerous and lacking conscience—numbered among their ranks, and we respond to such men with understandable disgust and fear. On the other end of the stereotype is the "harmless" rake—a dapper, happy-go-lucky fellow who enjoys his Friday evening fun with no regard for future consequence. For decades, we have responded to this fellow with an insincere reprimand and a wink. The reality is seldom found in either stereotype. Most birthfathers fall into the category of "average Joe," and that is the group we consider in this discussion. Even in narrowing the field to average Joes, we must bear in mind that the diversity of personalities and motives involved makes generalization hazardous. Without some generalizing, however, we cannot discuss the issues.

"Joe" has a mixture of feelings about the pregnancy and about the proposed adoption. He sips from a peculiar stew of pride, anger, guilt, fear, and helplessness. He feels vague male stirrings of reverence, responsibility, and protection, but does not know what to do with them. Given the awkward union of a pregnancy and a futureless relationship, most men are not sure how to act. There is no script for appropriate behavior for him to follow. He is bewildered and ambivalent, a combination that may produce confusing fluctuations in his behavior. One moment, he tries to evade all responsibility, and the next he attempts to muscle his way into the picture and throw his weight around.

If the birthmother was not already ambivalent about the baby's father, there is a good chance that his own ambivalence about the pregnancy and the relationship would activate it in her. In her hurt that he is not unreservedly pleased about the pregnancy, she may tell him to get lost. We must remember that this relationship is usually charged with the mystery and intrigue that are associated with interaction between the sexes. Communication becomes multilayered, and unspoken messages frequently override denotative meaning. The "get lost" message is often a disguised request that he get involved. Even when he is resolute in his resolve to end the relationship, she may nevertheless wait for him to have a change of heart and save the day. Perhaps it is my imagination, but I believe I have seen birthmothers, moments before signing release papers, take one last pitiful look over their shoulders at the court room door to see if the birthfather might somehow show up in the last minute. She may despise him, but the intensity of her feelings testifies to his importance to her. So often lost in the interpersonal politics is the fact that there was something between this couple at one point. How sad that it could not endure, but their fateful intersection, however brief and however exasperating, is biologically commemorated in new life. If the baby's father cannot be engaged, we are all diminished.

We put birthfathers in a classic catch 22. On one hand, when he is unavailable, we disapprovingly wonder where he is. On the other, when he steps forward and shows interest, many observers are annoyed at the complication he represents. Clearly, he is a very discounted person, yet we are surprised that he seems wary and suspicious. Too often, we who organize this institution are oblivious to our part in this problem. Note, for example, how late in the book this discussion occurs. Sure, birthfathers were referred to earlier in a footnote, but that only illustrates the point. To the institution's discredit, birthfathers are usually considered little more than a footnote to the experience.

Birthfathers have few advocates. We are so impatient with them. We have so little compassion for their confusion, their ambivalence, their unevenness, their dramatics. They are adoption's outsiders and orphans. Sometimes, they are distant by choice, but often they are left out by design. In our all too speedy concessions to everyday reality—"birthfathers are never around," we claim; "they are hard to find"—we fail to raise the standards for what could be. We expect nothing from them, and our prophecies are routinely fulfilled. Chapter 8 observed that quality adoption transforms its participants. When birthfathers are uninvolved, by choice or by exclusion, they miss a remarkable opportunity for growth.

If birthfathers cared, many reason, they would be available and involved. Do we think it is really that simple? Do we really want to be so quick to assume paternal disregard? Do we really want to lightly set aside the usual presumptions attached to biology? If he is to be excused so easily from his rights as a parent because he is not involved, shall we as quickly excuse him from his responsibilities for child support? There are issues of basic decency at stake. Shall we deny him an opportunity to come forward and hold his child? Shall we, in our zest for adoption, summarily relegate him to the realm of the unknown? If birthfathers are discountable and disposable, shall we discount and dispose of adoptive fathers as well?

We must stop vilifying birthfathers. If we wish to move beyond institutional shame, if we truly wish to serve children, we need to become institutionally hospitable to them. Instead of thinking about nasty birthfathers, it is better that we think in terms of the occasional nasty person who happens to be a birthfather. If we allow the generic birthfather to be depicted as a jerk, logically we are led to the highly offensive conclusion that adopted children are genetic half jerks.

If we are determined to find villains in the adoption drama, we should look at adoption promoters who systematically exclude birthfathers from the process. As they abridge the most fundamental human rights of birthfathers to suit their own purposes, they are denying children half their birth heritage and recklessly putting them in circumstances of legal jeopardy because of the poor legal foundation established for the adoption.

So if we do the right thing and engage him, are we home free? Hardly. Successful engagement of the birthfather in the decision-making and planning process launches a new round of effort. It is important to help him process his ambivalence about the situation. It is crucial that we are available to the birthcouple as they attend to the murky emotional currents running through their relationship. If they fail to resolve their issues, the politics of their relationship could haunt an open adoption indefinitely. Negative interaction between birthparents can cause adoptive parents and children great discomfort.

It is a hard fact that, in some cases, the birthmother is drawn to adoption because it enables her to sever any connection to the birthfather, a fact that is of great importance to her. She reasons, "He will never be out of my life if I raise this child." We must admit that open adoption potentially confounds her goal of disengagement. In such a dire circumstance, it may be necessary to separate them and treat them as entirely distinct individuals. This unfortunate dynamic becomes, obviously, a challenge for the adoptive parents, and ultimately the child, to handle.

To participate effectively in an open adoption, birthparents must work through certain tasks:

Resolving the Dangling Issues

In secretive adoptions, many birthparents are left with unfinished business about their procreative partners. Things end so abruptly between them that there is little if any sense of resolution. Simple misunderstandings can haunt for a lifetime if not discussed. The unprocessed disappointments and frustrations they feel for each other can negatively affect the numerous other people in their lives—past, present, and future. They need to work through as many disagreements as possible, if not for their own sake, then for the sake of others who care for them—most notably the child.

Forgiving

If there is to be peace of mind and healing, it is important that birthparents forgive each other and let go of hostilities and resentments. If they can forgive, their outlook can shift from hostility to a spirit of acceptance and inclusion.

Coordinating the Approach to the Adoptive Family

It is helpful if the birthparents coordinate their approach to the adoptive family. If they do not visit the adoptive family together, they must be sensitive to the fact that their separate involvement consumes a larger portion of the adoptive family's social and recreational time.

Defending Each Other's Honor

If enduring hurts have not been forgiven, the birthparents must contain their negative opinions of each other for the sake of the child. He will surely draw his own conclusions regarding each of his birthparents based on their behavior over time. As is true in divorce, to denigrate the other parent is to unfairly burden the youngster. In the eyes of many young people, the critic loses more prestige than the criticized.

THE ADOPTIVE PARENT–ADOPTEE RELATIONSHIP

The relationship between adoptive parents and adopted children includes all the usual joys and aggravations of family life.

Adoptive parents change as many diapers and haul kids off to as many soccer practices as biological parents. For all parents, the responsibility of parenting is an involved and convoluted process of preparing the youngster for independence. It is a profound, enduring, and richly satisfying relationship. Adoptive parents in open adoptions have several additional issues to tackle.

Accepting the Relationship

Going into adoption, many parents wonder whether they will be able to fully love "someone else's child." The child and the parents must look each other in the eye and conclude, "Yes, it is right that we are together." They become "real" to each other and fully identify with each other.

Establishing Rightful Authority

Adopted children are hard-earned. As such, they are candidates for spoiling, overprotection, and indulgence. Adoptive parents must feel fully installed in the parental role, or they may feel like baby-sitters or grandparents who lack the authority to act appropriately. Adoptive parents who feel fully entitled to the parental role can withstand the predictable testing that comes with the territory. Inevitably, they can expect to field the challenge: "I don't have to listen to you, you're not my real parents anyway!"

Normalizing the Adoption Theme

Every adoptive family must learn how much emphasis to place on the adoption theme. Since it is an error to either under- or overemphasize the issue, handling it well is an art form. This is a special challenge for families that have been especially private or public about their adoptions.

Establishing a Spirit of Openness

The great hope of open adoption is that, because of its exceptional comfort with the birthfamily and its normalized perspective on adoption, there will be exceptional ability within the family to talk about adoption issues when they come up. Among other things, this ability may give the family the opportunity to share the sadness they feel about the fact that they are not biologically linked. This shared sadness may bring them closer together than ever.

Assisting the Child to Define Her Relationship with the Birthfamily

If the youngster is to feel comfortable in her interaction with her birthfamily, she needs the blessing of her adoptive parents. Allowing for her personality, the maturity of her judgment, and her comfort with her birthfamily, it is important that her adoptive parents encourage and support her emerging ability to manage her relationships.

THE BIRTHPARENT–ADOPTEE RELATIONSHIP

The true heart of open adoption is the unique relationship between the birthparents and the adoptee. If the adoptee grows up having always known his birthparents, the relationships feel normal to him. In some of these relationships, the chemistry between them is palpable. In others, it is negligible. This variety of outcomes is hardly surprising, since some birthparents are far more comfortable with children than others.

When children grow up knowing their birthparents, their relationships with them are significant, but less dramatic and anxious than those who are accustomed to closed adoption might expect. In the closed system, birthparents are mysterious and only approached through fantasy. They are the forbidden fruit of adoption, alluring and dangerous. In open adoption, birthparents are real and knowable persons with all the strengths and quirks that define their humanness.

Both the adoptee and birthparents must handle a few tasks for the relationship to thrive:

Building Trust

As the adoptee gradually comprehends the full meaning of adoption, she may eye her birthparents with a measure of doubt: "Why should I expect you to endure in my life when you stepped aside when I was a baby?" The birthparents' most convincing answer is performance. Trust grows as a result of affirming behavior reliably demonstrated over time. If trust is to grow, honesty is indispensable. Although it can be tempting for birthparents to make exciting promises, perhaps because of unprocessed guilt, it is important to offer only possibilities that they can actually meet.

Building Understanding

The child deserves explanations. He will want to know in great detail the circumstances leading to the adoption decision. He will also want to know how the birthmother felt about the adoption. It is important to help the adoptee understand the birthmother's reality, but this is tricky territory. Too much sadness can seem to undermine the wisdom of the adoption decision, whereas too much happiness can trivialize the significance of their separation. Open adoption birthparents may occasionally confront the adoptee's anger. At an open adoption banquet, an adoptee rubbed his water glass in the margarine and commented to his birthmother, "Aren't you glad you're not my mother anymore?" As the relationship matures, there will likely be some tender moments spent considering what could have been.

Defining the Relationship

Birthparents and adoptees must figure out who they are to each other. It is challenging for birthparents to exhibit genuine interest in the adoptee and yet steer clear of appearing parental. If they slip and offer themselves as parents, they put the adoptee in a very awkward position. If the adoptee feels any confusion about parental authority, she is certain to feel great anxiety. Without knowing all the implications, birthparents must be willing to give the adoptee a growing voice in the relationship and honor her preferences. It can work either way. It may mean stepping into a larger role, or it may require stepping back for an unknown time.

APPROACHING THE PROBLEMS OF OPEN ADOPTION

It is important that the problems associated with open adoption be considered in a spirit of fair-mindedness. This is not easily accomplished. Over the years, the discussion of open adoption's merit has been laced with emotion. Critics are inclined to exaggerate. They suggest that everything that can go wrong will go wrong every time and to the maximum degree. Proponents, on the other hand, are tempted to minimize problems. Because of the tension between the two schools of thought, little reasonable discussion on the subject has taken place.

In the early years, the debate was mostly speculation. Now, based on substantial practice over many years, we can comment on experience. Some observers have been suspicious of open adoption because it is relatively new. For the same reason, many others view it favorably. Members of the adoption reform community have cautiously supported open adoption because it constitutes a significant improvement over the secretive system. As the secret system winds down, the open system will enjoy less good will generated by discontent with the old approach. It will rise or fall according to the triumphs and problems it generates, apart from comparisons to other approaches to adoption.

A reasonable consideration of problems is a difficult prospect for at least three reasons. First, there is an unavoidable subjectivity to any discussion of problems. What is a problem? Observers will declare the existence of a problem at very different points depending on, among other factors, their tolerance for ambiguity. It is often a matter of degree. Sometimes, there is a thin line between success and disaster. Hopefully, the positive mind-set of well-prepared open adoption participants will predispose them to interpret complex circumstances in constructive terms.

Second, detecting the source of problems is often difficult. Problems sometimes are clearly linked to adoption in general or open adoption in particular, but many other times problems may have very different sources. The third factor making the discussion difficult is the many variations on the open adoption theme. Some styles of open adoption are far more inclined toward significant problems than others. Each form of open adoption will generate a unique pattern of benefits and problems. Variations that lack trust may encounter more trouble because misunderstandings and frustrations multiply quickly when restrictions are artificially governing the relationships.

We must put our exploration of problems in a context of normality. Problems are a normal part of life. To say that open adoption has problems is merely to say that it exists, that it is real. It has problems, as does every other system of adoption. Fortunately, few of them are serious. Most of the problems are minor, and most of them can be prevented or remedied. Unlike closed adoption, which is limited in its ability to address problems, open adoption has the wonderful capacity to confront the problems it encounters.

Relationship Problems

What can go wrong in open adoption? The answer, of course, is "everything." This is more than a cute answer; it is the truth. Everything that afflicts relationships is possible in open adoption because it is, in fact, a relationship. This is a chilling answer until we finish the thought. Everything delightful about relationships is also available through open adoption. Put that way, a dilemma is posed: Shall we play it safe and avoid problems by avoiding relationships; or shall we live dangerously, and wholeheartedly enter relationships with all their potential to hurt and heal us?

Sometimes, families interact in ways that, instead of complementing each other, bring out the worst in each other. Let's consider some forms that problems take.

Misunderstandings

It is difficult for each family to learn how things work in the environment of the other family. Misreadings, particularly if they are repeated, can be very annoying. Participants must respect each other's views in especially sensitive areas related to religion, politics, sex, and money—potential land mines in the terrain of every relationship. The realm of parenting, with its maze of competing philosophies and tactics, can be almost as volatile. Lifestyle clashes and fundamental incompatibilities can make it very difficult for participants to understand and trust each other. The way different people view time, for example, clearly illustrates the potential for misunderstanding. Some families are very punctual about their appointments, whereas others may set times for meetings with plus-or-minus factors of eight hours. If families cannot accommodate each other's styles, friction is inevitable.

Half secrets

Sometimes, if the birthparents are still caught in the web of shame, they try to maintain an open adoption relationship without informing the other people in their lives. This "half secret" style is contrary to the spirit of open adoption and is likely to confound the interaction with the adoptive family. These secrets limit the ability of the families to communicate comfortably.

Outside anxiety

Many more people are involved in an open adoption than the primary participants. As they get to know the other's extended family, participants may discover "open adoption relatives" that they do not enjoy. Anxiety from other relationships may spill over into the open adoption. Adoptive parents may find themselves, for example, fielding unsolicited commentary from the birthmother's Aunt Gertrude about subjects ranging from cloth diapers to the birthmother's dating habits. The link between the families can enable a highly anxious family to discharge anxiety into the other family system. And, of course, within each clan, there may be people—friends, families, and significant others—who do not support open adoption and miss no opportunity to foist their negative opinions on the participants.

Social calendars

Some especially gregarious participants may find it difficult to put their social calendars in sync. This is particularly true when more than one adoption is involved and the adoptive family is connected to several birthfamilies.

Latecomers

Naturally, the participants in an open adoption move forward in life and go onto experience a variety of future relationships. Some of these new relationships will enrich the web of open adoption connections, but others may seriously detract from it. A fellow who marries an open adoption birthmother, for example, may resent the entaglements of the adoption and its reminders of his wife's prior life.

The harmony that open adoption participants establish can be challenged by the belated introduction of new players who are often completely bewildered about their place in the arrangement.

They may find it very difficult to understand the context in which the relationship originated and are not personally invested in its success. Some latecomers have lifestyles that do not mesh easily with the beliefs of the others.

Unequal levels of contact

If an adoptive family adopts more than one child, it is unavoidable that the relationships with the birthfamilies will be unequal. Every experienced parent knows that children spend most of their day measuring and comparing their duties and privileges to those of their siblings. Doses of Kool-Aid must be identical, and no one will wash one dish more than another. The fairness theme can be painful in an open adoption family because equivalency in relationships is impossible. The child whose birthfamily is less involved, less generous, or less affirming can suffer miserably from the inevitable comparisons. It is important for birthfamilies to be aware of this dynamic and do their best not to fuel it. It is desirable for birthparents sharing an adoptive family to get to know each other and coordinate their interactions with the family. Sometimes, for example, the more-available birthfamily can stand in for the other. Some adoptive families are tempted to handle the unequal involvement of birthparents by slipping to the lowest common denominator. Better, we think, to aspire to the highest common denominator by inviting the less-involved birthparent to greater involvement.

Sibling relationships

One of the most interesting relationships facing the adoptee in an open adoption involves siblings who remain in the birthfamily. Very likely, they will function as cousins to each other. It is an important and intriguing relationship that will usually be experienced positively, but there is significant potential for them to at least occasionally experience confusing feelings of envy and guilt. These sibling relationships are a great open adoption frontier. This is an area where much of importance remains to be learned.

Manipulation by the child

If birthparents and adoptive parents do not communicate clearly, there is room for children to play them against each other. Sometimes, the manipulation is an effort to gain leverage toward some goal. Other times, it can become an unhappy form of entertainment. If the relationship is plagued with any unprocessed insecurity or guilt, it is especially susceptible to manipulation.

Relationship drift

If open adoption is considered a matter of convenience rather than a matter of necessity for the child, if the initial commitment is vague, or if the maintenance energy is low, the arrangement can suffer from "relationship drift." Unfortunately, this condition is quite common. Once friends drift out of contact, it can be awkward for them to reengage.

Anxiety in Participants

In the normal course of interaction, each person in the extended open adoption family system absorbs and generates anxiety. This anxiety typically moves through the system, waxing, waning, and spilling over into other systems. Sometimes, though, it coalesces and afflicts a particular member of the system. Some personality types—the especially sensitive, imaginative, or insecure—are particularly susceptible to this prospect.

Anxiety and adoptees

As the focal point of the process that merged the family systems, the adoptee is a particularly likely candidate to absorb the anxiety. If he is in pain, obviously everyone in the system is affected and shares the pain. Not every problem encountered by adoptees, of course, is related to adoption. Nature's usual percentage of physical and psychiatric disturbances are distributed across the population of adoptees. A child's emotional problems can significantly exacerbate the painful issues of adoption. Birthparents typically feel some irrational guilt about the condition, whereas adoptive parents struggle with feelings that fate has tricked them one more time. A child with serious impairments can seriously tax and overwhelm a family's resources, practical and emotional. In such circumstances, it may well take the cooperation of both concerned families to meet the challenges that the child poses.

Some very bright children are drawn to the complexity of life and are inclined to take a serious view of things. For them, nothing is easy. A child of this nature is a candidate to define her adoption—closed or open—as a problem worthy of relentless probing. Although these exceptionally inquisitive and articulate children can wear everyone down, they surely have much to teach us about the psychology of adoption.

The most profound and common concern that the early practitioners of open adoption faced was the possibility that the children would find the situation confusing. Although that worry was understandable, it failed to respect the ability of children to make sense of their lives. Well-designed open adoption does not create insecurity in children, but the concern is reasonable in arrangements that come together in haphazard fashion. If adoptive parents do not fill their roles with authority, or if there is competition for the parental role, children may feel insecure. Adoptive parents should feel secure in their roles, and birthparents should not offer themselves as alternate parents. Cooperation between adoptive parents and birthparents reduces the loyalty bind that adoptees may feel, but competition between them makes it worse than ever.

At various points in life, children just want to fit in and avoid any factors that set them apart. There may be times when interaction with the birthfamily makes the adoption theme more visible than they prefer, thereby prompting them to diminish the extent of their contact.

Anxiety and birthparents

Birthparents are also strong candidates to absorb and generate anxiety of various degrees. For some, it is mild, but for others it is all-consuming. Birthparents obviously vary greatly in their capacity to deal with anxiety. When birthparents have difficulty managing their anxiety, it creates difficulties for adoptive parents and the child.

Some birthparents never grow beyond their ambivalence. The adoption decision is so overwhelming that they find it impossible to fully assent to. They may see it as necessary and helpful, but they are also repelled by the magnitude of the loss. Their ambivalence is understandable but costly. It paralyzes the entire system and puts all the relationships on hold. There is hazard that, eventually, the adoptive parents may lose patience and resent the emotional limbo created by the ambivalence.

Some birthparents find it difficult to follow through with their open adoption relationships because their grief is significantly greater than they anticipated. They may find it necessary to retreat to recover their equilibrium. Having stepped back for some time to heal, they may find it difficult to reengage the adoptive family at a later date.

Some narcissistic birthparents are difficult to work with because they do not share the child-centered orientation. They are only concerned with "what's in it for me?" They are not capable of mutually rewarding relationships. The adoptee may experience them as an embarrassment. Other birthparents, because of long-term deprivation, psychiatric conditions, or substance abuse, have little regard for standard interpersonal boundaries. They are unpredictable and frequently ignore conventions of courtesy. When some thought related to the adoption occurs to them, they act on it without further deliberation. Their impulsivity can easily alarm and exasperate the adoptive family.

Open adoption with particularly difficult birthparents requires particularly effective adoptive parents. This fact by itself documents the need for the involvement of experienced professionals. It is best if potentially perplexing birthparents are recognized before the initiation of an adoption process, because it takes special adoptive parents to respond to them. Open adoption with difficult birthparents works best with warmhearted adoptive parents who can see the beauty of the birthparents through all their warts. It takes adoptive parents who are flexible and tolerant yet who can also negotiate and maintain sensible boundaries. We have long thought in terms of adoptive parents for special-needs children. In an open adoption era, we also need to respond to "special needs" birthparents. It is crucial that, as far as possible, adoptive parents know the implications of their commitment to a birthfamily before they make it.

Anxiety and adoptive parents

If adoptive parents find themselves overwhelmed by the dynamics of open adoption and have difficulty in carrying out their responsibilities, the impact on birthparents and children is dramatic. Open adoption elevates everyone's expectations, and frustration is predictable if hopes are not met. A variety of problematic styles of open adoption parenting are associated with anxiety.

Some adoptive parents offer little understanding or compassion to others; they are only concerned with themselves. People like this only respond to others when they find it convenient and useful. Frequently, they are unpredictable and fickle, sometimes charming and other times unfriendly according to which mode best suits their purposes for the moment.

Some adoptive parents act as if there is a limited amount of love that a child can offer, and it is their intention to collect all of it. Some treat all of their relationships this way, whereas others are surprised by the intensity of their protective response to the youngster. Possessive parents distrust the influence of outsiders. To justify their exclusive view of parenting, they are inclined to minimize the importance of the birthfamily.

A few adoptive parents become "stringers along" They are involved in open adoption because it was required of them, not because their heart is in it, and they are not committed to it. They put up with birthparents but do not nurture the relationship in any fashion. They do nothing to disguise their hope that the birthfamily will go away and leave them alone.

Inflexible adoptive parents find it difficult to adjust to changes that occur over time. They rigidly carry out the terms of the initial agreement and fend off change, even if it is to everyone's advantage. They have a "my way or the highway" attitude.

For a variety of reasons, some adoptive parents are unable to overcome their insecurity. They are so frightened that they are not able to achieve a sense of worthiness. Their anxiety may take the form of excessive accommodation. Because of their anxiety, they have a difficult time setting reasonable boundaries and saying, "No." Parents of this stripe are hard to enjoy, because it is difficult to know who they really are and what they really believe.

Serious Concerns

Most of the challenges, although potentially annoying, are manageable. A few possibilities, however, rank as serious. Thankfully, serious problems are rare in conscientious forms of open adoption. There are four major concerns that merit special attention.

Betrayal

Some people choose to unilaterally set aside all of their open adoption commitments. With no regard for the interests of the others involved, they simply do whatever they please. Either the adoptive parents or the birthparents can betray the other. Both circumstance are painful. Betrayal shifts the spirit of the relationship from cooperation to hostility. When adults betray each other, the child suffers. Lost in the conniving is the very real possibility that a day will come when the adoptee learns all of the facts and holds the betrayer accountable.

Defeated purpose

The ultimate purpose of adoption is upward psychological mobility for the child. What do we do when this purpose is obviously defeated? How do we honor children when the adoptive parents become stricken with disease, divorce, bankruptcy, or abuse, while the birthparents flourish in every dimension of their lives? The closed system does not face this dilemma because outcomes are unknown for 20 years. In open adoption, outcomes are known and must be acknowledged. Obviously, there are no easy answers, but in those circumstances in which the initial effectiveness of the families is inverted over time, it will be more important than ever for the two families to work together to serve the youngster.

The open adoption from hell

Open adoptions are painful if any of the participants is perplexing and unpredictable, but it is possible to imagine a configuration in which every member of the arrangement presents pronounced dysfunctions. Imagine the dynamics in an open adoption comprising an exceptionally manipulative adoptee; extraordinarily insecure and possessive adoptive parents; and a needy, chronically regretful birthparent with poor impulse control. To complete the nightmare, add an inexperienced, controlling adoption professional. If all of the participants are self-centered and are either uninterested or unable to attend to the issues of the other persons involved, chaos is predictable. As large numbers of open adoptions are arranged, situations approximating this exaggerated convergence of personal liabilities can be expected.

Criminal activity

As is true in all human experiences, it is possible for an open adoption arrangement to completely breakdown and degenerate into destructive and illegal interaction. All things are possible in the realm of relationships. If we allow our imaginations to wonder, extortion and kidnapping come to mind as exotic and frightening possibilities. To date, to the best of my knowledge, no such incidents have been reported. If criminal actions some day rise out of the open adoption experience, they should be treated like any other illegal activity.

Response to Problems

Clearly, open adoption is not problem-free. Inherent in the process of bringing people together is the prospect for misunderstanding and conflict. Fortunately, the converse is equally true. By bringing people together, open adoption offers the prospect for creative adaptation. Its great advantage over the previous system of adoption is its access to problems. As long as they can be identified and addressed, there is very reasonable hope that solutions and improvements can be discovered.

There are five broad dimensions to the open system's response to problems:

Prevention

The best way to attend to problems is to prevent them. Most problems can be anticipated and avoided. If adoptions are arranged carelessly, it can take years of very difficult negotiations to put it on a satisfying course. It is far wiser to craft them wisely from the beginning. A crucial aspect of prevention is making sure that promising combinations of people are brought together. Compatibility is difficult to orchestrate, but it is worth aspiring to because it brings so much comfort through the years. If an arrangement begins with little sense of compatibility, the relationship will likely struggle and need propping up by outside supports. The other basic element of prevention is preparation, the value of which cannot be overstated. Well-prepared participants are not driven by desperation or fear. Preparation gives them a feeling of control, and control generates a sense of ownership. Fully invested in the experience, they feel responsible for its success.

Clarity of purpose

Well-crafted open adoptions are not haphazard relationships lacking sense of purpose or direction. To the contrary, they are very intentional in their focus on the shared desire to nurture and bring out the best in the child. Although there is room for disagreement abcut what that means in particular situations, the shared purpose brings general unity to the relationship. The mutual desire to nourish the multidimensional health of the child gives birth to the commitment that adoptive parents and birthparents make to each other. Commitment enables participants to stay engaged even when patience runs low. When there is a common purpose and shared resolve, there are persuasive reasons to address and resolve problems.

Respect and trust

Chapter 1 noted that this approach is more attitudinal than behavioral. The key to effective open adoption relationships is the formation of constructive attitudes. If the families involved view each other with respect and trust, the adoption will surely be satisfying. The families will make sure it thrives because they care for each other. Respect provides the motive, and trust provides the opportunity. When respect and trust are well-established, participants are willing to tackle the hard work of tolerance, forgiveness, and cooperation.

Maintenance

Elegant open adoptions look effortless, but they are always the result of great emotional exertion. If each participant is working through his or her tasks, the open adoption will function smoothly. The operative word is *work*. It takes work and courage to address the little irritations that arise in a relationship before they grow into major problems, and it takes work and courage to override the temptations of fear and laziness. Wise open adoption families will take the time to review their arrangements annually to fine tune the relationships.

Problem solving

We are forever looking for symbols or images that help people to understand open adoption. Perhaps the best symbol of open adoption—not very elegant or sexy—is the kitchen table. The kitchen table is a place for caring people to gather and work through issues of importance. Like closed adoption, the open approach will have problems; but unlike the closed system, open adoption has the capacity to address and solve them. When creative, committed people want to work things out and are able to speak directly to the issues, chances are excellent that solutions can be found. Some problems can be solved through simple compromise. Others are worked out through a process of synergy. Dynamic open adoption relationships, with their emphasis on openness and respect for differences, are well-suited for synergistic processes. The creativity of ideas collectively generated by all of the participants will very likely exceed the creativity of any singular problem solver. As the extended open adoption family finds relief for various issues through its synergistic efforts, it grows in competence and confidence. Consequently, the family is increasingly able to operate from the dynamic perspective that problems are opportunities for learning.

There is deep satisfaction found in authentic open adoption relationships. When they are continuously adapted to new realities, they stay vital. Robust open adoption relationships bring participants together in ways that make them more effective and loving than they would be apart. The capacity to creatively adapt to new situations enables open adoption families to experience the reassurance and joy of community.

Chapter 10

The Open Adoption Community

> Vision and intellectual understanding are important to the life of a community. But intellectual consciousness must always spring from wonder and thanksgiving, which must remain at the heart of the community.
>
> The spirit of community is like a gentle fire giving light and warmth, communicating itself through hearts in communion one with another.
>
> Jean Vanier, *Community and Growth*

In the days when I practiced closed adoption, I felt vaguely uneasy about the direction of my work. For a long time I was not sure of the source of the discomfort, but it did occur to me that if a truck ran me down they might put on my grave, "Here lies Jim Gritter. He separated people with the best of them." That was a distressing thought—both the truck and the separation. Now, in the era of open adoption, that uneasiness is gone. If that truck tracked me down today, they could write, "He brought them together with the best of them." Good social work, good people work, is always a matter of bringing people together, and this is the energy of open adoption. While the old system separated with vigor and encouraged distance, the new system convenes and encourages intimacy. Because it is not mechanical, because it is immensely human, quality adoption happens best in the supportive company of others. Adoption is meant to create community.

THE PAIN OF EXCESSIVE INDIVIDUALISM

Community is being rediscovered these days because, in part, the alternative is so dreary. Rugged individualism may be the cornerstone of Americanism, but social commentators have begun to question its capacity to produce satisfying results. When the country was organized socially based on tightly knit clans, religious enclaves, and ethnic neighborhoods, individualism held great appeal because it had the look of personal freedom. In the contemporary context of social mobility, it feels different. Although we continue to laud individualism as a great ideal with our words, our actions suggest that we are increasingly searching for affiliation. Perhaps it is time for us to reconsider our affection for individualism. In the conclusion of their classic study of American society, the authors of *Habits of the Heart* observe, "The culture of separation, if it ever became dominant, would collapse of its own incoherence." Individualism in extreme form is not viable. They also comment on excessive self-interest, a variation of individualism: "Few have found a life devoted to 'personal ambition and consumerism' satisfactory, and most are seeking in one way or another to transcend the limitations of a self-centered life."

If we tell the people around us long and insistently enough to leave us alone because we can do it ourselves, we may get our wish. Once that happens, we begin to wonder whether we are apart by choice or whether it has been done to us. Henri Nouwen does not view the excessive separateness of modern life as an ideal. Quite to the contrary, he sees it as a form of suffering: "In the Western world, the suffering that seems to be the most painful is that of feeling rejected, ignored, despised, and left alone." Unbalanced individualism leads to withering alienation.

We continue to receive calls from readers of *Adoption Without Fear* wanting reassurance. They report that they are excited about the open adoptions of which they are a part, but eventually they grow fainthearted because the important people in their lives persistently question and undermine their beliefs. It is the same with social workers entering the open adoption arena. They immediately feel that they are on the right track but eventually lose confidence as they are continually second-guessed. For all our affection for individualism and doing our own thing, we find it difficult to stand alone. No matter how firm our convictions, we long for affiliation and support. The participants of open adoption are most content when they are surrounded by people who understand.

UNDERSTANDING COMMUNITY

The word *community* is used in various ways. It is applied in situations ranging from communes featuring total interdependency to very loose associations of people sharing some incidental commonality. In *Creating Community Anywhere*, Carolyn Shaffer and Kristin Anundsen, writers with a passion for their message, sharpen the focus with a clear definition. As they describe it,

> Community is a dynamic whole that emerges when a group of people:
> * participate in common practices;
> * depend upon one another;
> * make decisions together;
> * identify themselves as part of something larger than the sum of their individual relationships; and,
> * commit themselves for the long term to their own, one another's, and the group's well-being.

Shaffer and Anundsen also identify five phases that characterize the life cycle of communities. Communities start with *excitement,* a time of enthusiasm when everyone is impressed with the possibilities. It moves to a phase they call *autonomy,* a time of jockeying for power as issues of leadership and purpose are worked through. The middle phase is *stability:* Roles and structures are settled into with some comfort, and more people become involved; the community is sufficiently developed to withstand changes and challenges. The fourth stage is *synergy,* a potentially productive time as the group unfolds, diversifies, and explores new possibilities. The final phase is *transformation:* Ultimately, each community has to determine its future; the usual options are expanding, segmenting, or disbanding.

In the realm of open adoption, there are several layers of community or subcommunities. Each open adoption—a profound coming together of families—is, in its own right, a step toward community. There is a community of open adoption adoptive parents and a growing community of open adoption birthparents. It is exciting to watch the community of open adoption adoptees emerge as the children grow older. As they find each other and compare notes, they will add important information to our understanding of open adoption. Like the other participants, professionals also delight in sharing their experiences and learning from each other. Community comes alive most fully when all of these subcommunities come together in shared appreciation.

Satisfying community happens best with face-to-face interaction, a fact that works to the advantage of those who are geographically close to each other. In an electronic age, however, a national open adoption community is starting to develop. The allure of affiliation is so powerful that innovative members of the national community are inventing ways to find each other and establish dialogue despite the barriers of geographic distance. Because the rewards for connecting are so significant, the effort is moving ahead with vigor.

THE JOY OF BELONGING

In the early years, skeptics thought that adoptive parents would not enjoy open adoption. They miscalculated. They assumed that adoptive parents, apart from their need for children, had totally fulfilling lives. This assumption did not consider their normal needs for affiliation. Many adoptive parents approach open adoption as an opportunity to expand their extended families. In their pursuit of economic opportunity, many left their clans behind, and they miss them. They are hoping to find people nearby with whom they can relate in familial ways. Similarly, many birthparents, temporarily or chronically frustrated with their families, are also looking for new family-like affiliations. The desire to relate to others in a familial fashion is a healthy alternative to a milieu of alienation.

A wise adoption worker recognizes this receptivity to affiliation and works with it. He or she provides opportunities for participants to affiliate and feel shared identities. An effective program promotes cooperation and discourages internal competition. The experience stays on a high plane through a culture of cooperation. Framed in this constructive fashion, families will naturally to turn to each other for support and encouragement.

To build this culture of cooperation, the effective professional identifies and features the commonalties:

Shared values. One great advantage of values-based open adoption is its focus on values. Its values base is clearly articulated, and this provides a significant basis for consensus. The values bring people together. Each value—honoring children, candor, respect for pain, protection of volition, commitment, openness, and adaptability—is an item to rally around. The values stir and inspire. Each one brings us further out of our tempting shells of protection. Chapter 8 noted that the combined values have transformational power. Transformed participants are prime candidates for community because they are full of enthusiasm they can hardly contain and want to share.

Shared experience. Open adoption participants share a unique and incomparable experience. They know what it means to be in the trenches of open adoption; as a result, they feel they are part of an exclusive fraternity. They are insiders, and they feel instant rapport with others who have been there.

Shared pain. Pain is another common denominator. Although each person's pain is unique, it is something we all understand. It generates authenticity, an important ingredient in community. Pain motivates us to be open to others. As master community builder Jean Vanier puts it, "Community is a safe place. At last some people really listen to us; they stand at the door of our wounded heart.... We are broken, but we are loved."

Shared weakness. To fully enjoy the delight of community, we must set aside pretension. Writers Earnest Kurtz and Katherine Ketcham observe,

> Among those who accept their imperfection there seems to be a special sense of likeness or oneness in their very mutual flawedness.... In such a context of shared weakness, qualities in other people that might, in different circumstances, irritate or anger instead

elicits compassion and identification. Shared weakness: the shared honesty of mutual vulnerability openly acknowledged. That's where we connect. At the most fundamental level of our very humanness, it is our weakness that makes us alike; it is our strengths that make us different. Acknowledging shared weakness thus creates a rooted connectedness, a sense of common beginnings.

Recognition of shared imperfection reduces the tendency toward "we-they" thinking. We are in the experience as peers and equals.

Shared excellence. Tom Morris, a philosopher from Notre Dame, makes a pertinent observation in his interesting book, *True Success.* He notes, "There is a fellowship of excellence among people who really care about what they are doing." A shared vision of and commitment to excellence inevitably brings people together.

Membership in the open adoption community cuts across the usual lines of association. I was fascinated by the composition of an especially effective study group of adoptive parents—many of whom contributed chapters to *Adoption Without Fear*—who went through our program. In the social history forms that prospective adoptive parents fill out, we ask them to indicate where they fall on a continuum from conservative to liberal. One person extended the line beyond conservative to the edge of the page and put his mark there. Another member of the same group responded to a question about three wishes with the remark, "I wish Russia was not the first large country to apply the ideas of Marx." Despite their political polarities, each of them rank among the most committed and compassionate adoptive parents to have gone through our program, and they respect each other as members of the open adoption community.

These unlikely comrades illustrate a statement that Common Cause founder and former Secretary of Health, Education, and Welfare John Gardner made at a Stanford commencement address:

> [Your goal is] not to achieve wholeness by suppressing diversity, not to make wholeness impossible by enthroning diversity, but to preserve both. Each element in the diversity must be respected, but each must ask itself sincerely what it can contribute to the whole. I don't think it is venturing beyond the

truth to say that 'wholeness incorporating diversity' defines the transcendent task for our generation.*

When the open adoption community is at its best, it provides this "wholeness incorporating diversity."

We benefit from belonging in two important ways: We gain identity and we transcend isolation. We worry initially that we will lose our individuality in community, but actually we find it. As Vanier puts it, "Community is a place of belonging, a place where people are earthed and find their identity." A sense of belonging is indispensable to all of us, but it is especially important for adoptees. It can provide relief in that painful phase where they feel unhappily different from others. It is comforting to know that one fits somewhere and that there are others who understand. Because the feeling of differentness is one of adoption's most painful sensations, the sense of belonging is an important benefit of community.

MATURING THROUGH COMMUNITY

Not everything about community is pleasing; there are difficult dimensions to involvement. Successful community requires some sacrifice of individual rights for the collective good. Vanier says, "A community is only truly a body when the majority of its members is making the transition from 'the community for myself' to 'myself for the community.'" For a generation nursed on the ideology of individualism, this is not an appealing prospect. Perhaps, though, it is in the service to children that we still have a shred of willingness to sacrifice. There is no better place to begin. Accepting the call to sacrifice is an important aspect of maturing because it moves us beyond the narrow thinking of self-interest.

Participation in community is often painfully revealing as it brings out every aspect of our personalities. We learn to perceive ourselves and our relationships in new ways. Again, as Vanier points out,

> Community is the place where our limitations, our fears and our egoism are revealed to us. We discover

---

* *Quoted by James M. Kouzes and Barry Posner in* Credibility. *San Francisco: Jossey-Bass, 1993.*

our poverty and our weakness, our inability to get on with some people, our mental and emotional blocks.... While we were alone, we could believe we loved everyone.

Fortunately we are not left to stew in our newly discovered limitations. Kurtz and Ketcham put it well:

> To be related to any other human being is to be both healed and hurt, both wounded and made whole. Our choice is not between whether we will be healed or hurt but, rather, to which of those always present realities we shall attend.

If we can acknowledge our limitations, we stand a chance to make corrections. Community really is a place for healing. It is a place where we can transform our weaknesses into strengths.

THE GENEROUS COMMUNITY

Grief expert Judy Tatelbaum gives voice to a well-known truth:

> Nothing I know of makes a greater impact on our self-esteem than this. Contributing to other people is a potent secret for healing, feeling good about ourselves, and for having a life worth living. Whether we give ourselves to individuals or to the world at large, in serving others we discover or recapture the best that we are.

This truth holds for communities as well. An effective community is concerned with more than the needs of its members. Again, Vanier speaks to the issue with great clarity:

> Communities are true communities when they are open to others, when they remain vulnerable and humble; when the members are growing in love, in compassion, and in humility. Communities cease to be such when members close in upon themselves with the attitude that they alone have wisdom and truth.

As the open adoption community grows, its membership becomes more diversified and its potential to serve others grows. Some members are more committed than others. Commitment to the open adoption community is often correlated to the degree of transformation that individuals have experienced. If the experience has profoundly moved them, they are inclined to stay involved and give something back to the institution. Investment in community is typically a mixture of meeting personal needs, expressing gratitude, and finding pleasure in the opportunity to make a difference.

The service that a community provides to others can take many forms. Sometimes it is simply availability. Most open adoption participants are very willing to share their experience with others. They offer themselves and their stories in a very personal way. Others embrace open adoption as a cause. They feel a sense of responsibility to share what they have learned with others. They are intrigued by the potential of this emerging movement and are interested in building the broader open adoption community. Members of the community who are both invested and articulate find themselves broadly addressing public understanding of open adoption. They are prophets sharing the riches of personal experience. Because they testify with their lives, they are the movement's most credible voices.

THE CHALLENGE OF SUSTAINING COMMUNITY

It is easy to forget that the work is not done when an adoption is in place and running smoothly. It is actually just beginning. Initially, community meets the short-term needs of adoptive parents and birthparents, but it is long-term community that most benefits children. Community serves maturing adoptees by offering them the prospect of affiliation. It also offers the blessing of normalcy. Where open adoption is common, it does not draw the attention typically accorded the exotic. Constituents who take the time to nurture the broader open adoption community honor their children in an important way.

It is not easy to sustain community. People enjoy each other's support in anxious times because it meets their needs, but in calmer times the motivation to affiliate is less intense. Once the drama surrounding placement passes, interest in community often diminishes. Everyone is busy with the tasks of everyday life. Adoptive parents are preoccupied with the delights and demands of parenting, whereas birthparents often withdraw, at least initially, to grieve in private. Once community momentum is lost, it is difficult to regain.

People are far too busy to get together just for the sake of getting together, as pleasant as that is. Builders of community need to provide opportunities for the constituency to come together with purpose. The community needs rallying points; it needs to be needed. Those within the community are eager to give something back and will respond if asked. In addition to responding to crisis, the community is pleased to gather to celebrate its accomplishments.

The commercial influences sweeping the adoption world do not contribute to the building of community. They organize adoption as a short-term transaction and often cast adoptive parents and birthparents as adversaries. Tragically, highly publicized adoption disputes divide the community of birthparents and adoptive parents and generate enormous fear. They stir insecurities in even the most solid arrangements. These influences have the potential to seriously undermine the open adoption community; but, more hopefully, they also have the ability to rouse this remarkable entity to greater levels of service.

So far, our efforts at community-building are rudimentary. We have much to learn about building and nurturing the open adoption community, and it is important work. The open adoption cause will stagnate unless we grow in our ability to support and learn from each other. The ultimate experts in open adoption are those who live it; they have the credibility of experience. Progress depends on the dissemination of what they are learning. If open adoption is to enjoy its full potential, it must successfully create community. Although we have a long way to go, we can celebrate the rich affiliations that already exist. Where once there was only isolation, now, because of open adoption, there are "hearts in communion one with another."

Chapter 11

The Art of Adoption: Leadership

> The real enemy is fuzzy thinking on the part of good, intelligent, vital people, and their failure to lead, and to follow servants as leaders.
>
> Servant-leaders are healers in the sense of making whole by helping others to a larger and nobler vision and purpose than they would be likely to attain for themselves.
>
> Robert Greenleaf, *Servant Leadership*

The 21-year-old college student called deep into her pregnancy—two weeks before the baby was to be born to be exact. She had kept the pregnancy to herself so that no one would try to influence her thinking. At the end of her private decision-making process, she resolved to press ahead with adoption plans. She selected an outstanding family, loving and confident, to adopt her child. They met, hit it off like old friends, and in an amazingly relaxed spirit given the brevity of time, made plans for the future. It came together with ease and grace. In their words, "It was beautiful." And the social worker wonders, "Who needs me? What do I bring to the party?"

Very necessary questions, and, in truth, a little frightening. The answers are not as easy or as obvious as they once were. Clearly, many participants can, in fact, work out many details on their own. And just as clearly, professionals have much to learn. Nevertheless, I am convinced the professional plays an indispensable part in the open adoption process.

As a product of the 1960s, it is difficult for me to put it this way, but I believe things unfolded positively in the opening scenario at least in part because of our system. Chances are things would not have been quite as simple without professional assistance. The decisions and plans they worked out were preceded by some important activities. They had the advantage of meaningful preparation and, as a result, operated with a mind-set that sought to balance the interests of everyone involved. Beneficiaries of the experience of others who preceded them, they were familiar with the usual course of events. They proceeded boldly because they had real confidence in the process in which they were participating.

CHANGING ROLES

These are crazy days for adoption workers, times of doubt and insecurity. We feel less powerful but more accountable. We routinely put the reputation of our programs in the hands of our families, and it is difficult to let go of our inclination toward control and over-responsibility. For many open adoption professionals, it feels like there is more work to be done, less time in which to do it, and less appreciation gained for the effort. The truth is, social workers preach change but have as hard a time dealing with it as everyone else.

Adoption is in flux. As the system shifts from closed to open, the roles for workers are changing dramatically. In the old system, the worker is essentially a czar. She has total power—life altering and unchallenged. The fate of the participants is entirely in her control. That overarching role is being replaced with the role of leader, a very different concept as we will discover. In the closed system, the worker is a protector, and the most important aspect of this protection is making sure that birthparents and adoptive parents do not get too close to each other. The new role follows a very different course. Instead of separating participants, the contemporary professional brings them together. She is a convener and mediator, forever searching for improved ways to launch birthfamilies and adoptive families into satisfying relationships. In the old system, it is important for the worker to contain information. Now she spends her days finding ways to dispense information as broadly as possible. The worker's most crucial role in the closed adoption system is as evaluator or judge. Although that role has not been eliminated, in open adoption it has been significantly diminished and replaced by the role of educator and facilitator.

The transition can be characterized as a move from unilateral power to relational power. Instead of being based on authority, the professional's role is now based on service. This completely redefines her method of operation. The worker is no longer center stage. Whereas the process formerly assumed that the worker would solve any dilemmas that developed, the current effort is to equip participants to handle situations as they come up. The worker realizes that the enduring relationship will be between the adoptive family and the birthfamily. Thus, her most lasting contributions are those that enhance that primary relationship.

In the era of open adoption, the worker seldom operates from a position of traditional authority; most of her efforts take the form of influence and persuasion by providing information. The astute professional quickly learns that there are moments of optimal influence and other times when she is along for the ride. Recognizing the difference, she knows when to assert herself and when to let things run their natural course. She does not hold center stage in the drama of adoption; most of her work is offstage. Consequently, her efforts are inconspicuous. There is a subtle inverse relationship between effectiveness and the appearance of being necessary. The worker who is conspicuously directing traffic may appear to be a very helpful player but may actually have handled the preparatory work poorly. Often, the greater the worker's effectiveness in preparing clients to manage their own circumstances, the less conscious consumers may be of her influence.

The contemporary focus is less on the individual psychology and more on systems. Open adoption is less fascinated with pathology than is closed adoption and is more interested in affirming the health of the participants. An important aspect of this positive emphasis is the building of community with and among the participants. The professional is not separate from the adoptive community; she is a full member of it. The old game of the system versus the people, full of separation and distrust, does not make sense in open adoption.

As the system shifts, the worker's purpose shifts also. Participants no longer view the worker as a supplier of families or babies but rather as provider of preparation and opportunity. Her goal is to create a culture in which participants can thrive and function optimally. The open adoption professional functions as a guide, preparing adventurers for and leading them through a formidable and largely unmapped wilderness of possibilities.

SELF-DETERMINATION

The unmentioned theme underlying the discussion so far is self-determination. In the closed system of adoption, self-determination is virtually nonexistent. Adoption is an assembly line, and each adoption is accomplished in identical fashion. There is no opportunity for individuality. In the open system, adoption is very client-driven, and self-determination rules. It usually marches under the flag of empowerment, and it has great contemporary luster. It is something for which many of us have longed and worked hard to achieve. Now that we appear to have it, how well do we like it? What happens when self-determination moves beyond a point of balance and dominates?

Let's consider some ways it can be distorted:

- **Imposition of professional agenda.** The most common worry related to self-determination is that the professional may somehow impose his agenda on his clients. If this happens, the clients are robbed of their will and opportunities to grow. They grow dependent and less able to handle future challenges.

- **Clever planting of ideas.** It is possible to accomplish professional mischief consciously or unconsciously in the name of self-determination. In their early interaction with clients, professionals can plant ideas that participants later parrot as their own. This can be an insidious way to justify almost anything, because once an idea is expressed in the voice of the client, it is largely beyond attack. The underlying question is whether the participants really own the idea.

- **Professional handwashing.** Excessive reliance on self-determination can be a professional cop-out, a professional washing of one's hands. It can be a way for professionals to evade responsibility. With wide-eyed innocence, he may chirp, "Don't look at me, it wasn't my decision. Can I help it if they weren't thinking clearly?"

- **Promotion of unmitigated self-interest.** Careless handling of self-determination with a narrow focus can play into and promote selfish, short-range thinking. A systems perspective suggests that the self-determination of one party can come at the expense of the other members of the triad. The claim of self-determination can lend the appearance of legitimacy to an unbalanced, even exploitative agenda.

It is difficult to balance the issues of self-determination. Momentum seems to take things from one extreme to another. We have accomplished much by bringing participants more fully into the process, but much could be lost if the trend is taken to an extreme and professional judgment is minimized or excluded. Just as reworking the issue of confidentiality has taken years, gaining a healthy perspective on self-determination will likely take time.

Well-understood and practiced, self-determination creates a partnership between the professional and the participant. It is not a matter of the participant's or the professional's will prevailing, but a merging of their experience, ideas, and values. A combined effort produces a beneficial blend of superior foresight and practicality.

We must address three important factors—preparation, timing, and balance—if self-determination is to produce optimal results in the adoption arena. The first of these, preparation, refers to all the work that contributes to an optimal choosing process. Effective decision making is a matter of personal awareness and full information about the broadest range of options. Chapter 6 discussed the process of choice at length, so we will concentrate here on the remaining factors of timing and balance.

Self-determination is better understood as a question of when participants make their decision rather than if they will make their own decisions. Key questions emerge quickly: Are participants ready for self-determination when they first enter the process? Are they cool, calm, and generous-spirited? Some may be, but in my experience most are significantly distracted. As I first get to know birthparents, I anticipate some predictable challenges. They vary, of course, from person to person, but I expect to encounter some combination of denial, short-range thinking, and shame. They crave relief and want it instantly. The heart of my work with birthparents is wrestling these demons to the ground. If any of these dynamics—denial, short-range thinking, or shame—persist, the potential of the adoption will be significantly diminished.

With prospective adoptive families, I expect to encounter a similar sense of desperation. They typically come to us roughed up and wounded from their costly and exasperating pursuit of fertility. They are afraid of the endless factors out there, which seem to defy control, and many have a keen sense that time is slipping away from them. These combined factors make for a perfect script for desperation. Better decisions result when choices are deferred until the desperation is attended to and brought under control.

Balance is a critical aspect of healthy self-determination in adoptive practice. The interests of each party must be balanced with the interests of the others involved. If the interests of one party are advanced without consideration for the others, the system chafes and becomes less effective. To bring added balance to a proposed adoption, the social worker becomes an advocate for the child, who may otherwise have no voice in the plan. In carrying out this role, the worker may actively seek to curb some initial preferences of birthparents and adoptive parents. In taking on the role of an advocate, the professional strives to create balance, not undo it. If a professional advocates narrowly for one of the adult parties involved, the balance of the arrangement is jeopardized. In contemporary practice, this hazard is most frequently attached to adoptions facilitated by enthusiastic advocates for impatient adoptive parents.

Balance must also be established in the relationship between participants and the professional. Whenever a professional is involved, there is some imposition of his opinion on the process. If this were not so, he would have little value. His ideas are usually welcomed. If participants had all the information and perspective they needed, they would not likely seek professional input, unless, of course, they are going through the motions to gain a necessary blessing or stamp of approval.

Dare we inconvenience our clients when we encounter short-range thinking? Dare we not? Part of the responsibility of any professional, whether participants like it or not, is to point out the liabilities and hazards in a proposed course of action. If their wishes go unchallenged and things work out poorly, they may return and wonder why they were not forewarned. Participants sometimes want to play it both ways—"Don't tell me anything I don't want to hear, and be thorough about it"—but that is only possible if professionals let it happen. Clearly, professionals are obligated to be thorough and to present perspectives that run counter to the client's initial preferences.

A thoughtful consideration of self-determination raises a host of issues and makes obvious the fact that self-determination cannot be reduced to simple formulas. How do we factor in the varying levels of effectiveness that participants present? Does the nature of the professional's agenda affect the agenda's "impose-ability"? How do the politics of decision making affect our judgment? How does self-determination relate to power? Once begun, the questions are endless.

Indisputably, professionals must be careful about issues of influence. This is especially true with very passive, gullible, or otherwise vulnerable clients. Some clients ask for and appear to need more direction than others. Some are paralyzed with fear. In such circumstances, workers must often take active or more imposing roles to initiate movement. The point of the intervention is to rouse clients from their paralysis and coax them into taking charge of their lives again.

The nature of the professional's agenda makes an obvious difference. If his agenda is to help participants reach well-informed decisions consistent with their value systems, the agenda is inoffensive. If, on the other hand, the worker has a standard solution for all the situations he encounters, the agenda may be a major imposition. If professionals have predetermined answers, they must make them conspicuous at an early stage. That enables clients, if they wish, to avoid or escape the worker and his solution without losing vitally important time.

Each worker must be aware of his standards and must know which principles are negotiable and which are not. He must know with great clarity what he is trying to accomplish. We need to know what attitudes and behaviors we are trying to accelerate and which we are trying to overcome. Whether we are conscious of it or not, our preferred outcomes will affect the processes we orchestrate. If, for example, we think adoption is the best solution for untimely pregnancy, adoption will be promoted. On the other hand, if the goal is well thought out decision making, an entirely different course of action will follow.

There is an inescapable political aspect to the handling of self-determination. We are inclined to judge the appropriateness of the process according to how well we like the outcome. Although none of us take pleasure in admitting it, we are inclined to ignore or tolerate imposition if we agree with the agenda being imposed. If a process produces ideas and outcomes we support, we call it "effective preparation." If the same process produces outcomes that we oppose, we see it as "brainwashing." Rare is the observer who challenges sloppy thinking leading to favored outcomes with the same vigor used to challenge sloppy thinking leading to less-preferred outcomes.

When self-determination is confronted in rawest terms, the question is, who is in charge here? The social worker does not seek to control clients but must also be certain not to be controlled. The process short on respect can become a struggle for power. The worker must operate from strength. If adoption is entirely client-driven, it runs the risk of degenerating into survival of the fittest, an everyone-for-themselves free-for-all. If professionals are to contribute, we need to assert our standards.

Self-determination means that clients make the final decisions. They do, of course, whether we want them to or not. This does not mean professional neutrality on all issues. If our convictions are meaningful, conscience requires that we make ourselves clear about them. Sharpening the argument, if we believe children deserve a dynamic link to their past, then, as a matter of professional integrity, we must encourage sincere consideration of open adoption. Anything less would be unprofessional. The principle of self-determination holds a lofty position in the hierarchy of professional values; but, unquestionably, it must defer to the higher value of honoring children. Imposing our convictions on clients unreasonably, of course, would be equally unacceptable. We must be willing to discuss and negotiate the possibilities honestly. Ultimately we defer to the client, but that does not mean we endorse all outcomes. Nor does it mean we must assist in carrying out decisions we consider unacceptable. If a client is committed to a plan that the worker cannot support in good conscience, a referral to another service provider is in order.

In an era of competition, social workers do not have the exclusive power we once held. With an abundance of alternate service providers available, we fear that clients will avoid us if we do not indulge their wishes. There is a very positive aspect to this pressure, because it forces us to pay more attention to the needs and desires of our constituency. We must involve participants to a greater degree and learn from them, but these improvements do not require abandoning our principles. We must be careful that we are not so accommodating for the sake of our own preservation that we set aside the knowledge and standards gained from the experience that shapes our practice. Like everyone else, we must take our chances in the marketplace. It is possible that the consuming public will prefer the simplicity of a nonreflective process to the prospect of long-term quality. One likes to think, however, that the public may have room in its heart for accountable services centered on children, founded on enduring values, and concerned with long-term outcomes. Hopefully, they appreciate services that balance the interests of all the parties involved, build community and harmony among participants, and reduce socioeconomic tensions.

This brings us back to the beginning question: What does the social worker bring to the party? His first gift is his value system. Until theory is more thoroughly formulated, adoption must find its direction from values, and that is the strength of social work. Drawing from a rich pool of values known to be helpful in a variety of circumstances, the social worker sets the moral tone and establishes the spirit of open adoption. Values give rise to procedures, which are fine-tuned through experience. Without this vital information, each contemplated adoption is bereft of all that has been learned previously. Experience enables the skilled social worker to stake out the norms of adoption and distinguish the usual from the unusual. He helps in the interpretation and in the application of what is generally known to the unique features of a particular situation—the personalities and the quirks of context. The professional bears in mind the larger picture and strives to keep the emerging family system in balance. He helps defend against personal excess by emphasizing the importance of collective action and community.

Frankly, not all social workers bring something to the party. Many have little interest in the art of adoption, preferring to approach it from a technical perspective. They simply fill their customers' orders. Technicians are often esteemed because they are accommodating and unchallenging. They accept things just as they are and cheerfully carry out the initial set of instructions. They are glad for the dynamics of denial, short-range thinking, and shame because they make the march toward adoption all the easier. Artists, on the other hand, view these powerful blocking forces as formidable challenges. Piercing the denial takes work—substantial and often initially unappreciated—and, if accomplished, it has the unrewarding effect of creating additional rounds of work. The role of technician is tempting, but conscience requires something greater from us.

LEADERSHIP

The new role of social work can be best characterized as leadership. This seems a strange idea to many social workers. We often think of leadership in heavy-handed terms, a matter of bossing people around and imposing demands on them. In that form, it is the opposite of self-determination. That line of thought suggests that we have a lot to learn about leadership. With his concept of servant leadership, respected business executive Robert Greenleaf presents a very different picture of leadership. As he describes it, the ideal leader is a servant first, and the test of leadership is its effect on those who are led: "Do they, *while being served*, become healthier, wiser, freer, more autonomous, more likely themselves to become servants?" Leadership in this form is obviously compatible with authentic self-determination.

Leadership is an enormous and humbling subject. The more we learn about it, the more our shortcomings become painfully obvious. None of us has all the desired qualities; nevertheless, if we seek to grow in our ability to serve, we need to gain a clearer understanding of this demanding role.*

Leaders Challenge the Process

The first major quality of a leader is that she challenges the process. A true leader cannot be happy with the status quo; there is no way, to her way of thinking, that the present reality

---

* *The structure of this section is borrowed from James M. Kouzes and Barry Posner.* The Leadership Challenge. *San Francisco: Jossey-Bass, 1987.*

is good enough. She is intrigued by the unorthodox and has the nature of a constructive rebel. A leader is haunted by the idea that there has to be a better way to get things done. To a leader, the choice between change and the absence of change is a choice between adventure and extinction. In her eyes, nothing is more appealing than a better idea, and nothing is more repulsive than stagnation. The truly challenging leader never "arrives"; she is forever involved in a loop of improvement. Foremost among the ideas she challenges are her own.

A leader is a chronic learner. Whereas many settle for formulas and answers, a leader is far more intrigued with provocative questions. To her way of thinking, every situation teaches something. It breaks new ground, confirms an earlier impression, or does both. Since there are no identical circumstances, something new and interesting is always happening.

A leader has a bias for action and the courage to experiment and take risks. That is not to say she is reckless, for the risks she takes are based on careful assessments of potential gains and hazards. As a person with unusual skills for anticipating problems, a skilled leader provides reasonable safeguards to reduce the likelihood of problems and cushion their destructive impact if they do occur. She is not afraid to fail, because she knows that is a normal part of growth. Setbacks energize her because they are exceptionally instructive. She studies all outcomes, negative and positive, so new discoveries can be implemented.

The challenging leader is certain to encounter resistance. Her message that things need to change steps on people's toes, and not all people will react graciously. Resistance can be instructive, frustrating, and sometimes nasty. One predictable method to discredit ideas is to discredit their representative. To persevere, the leader must have great conviction and inner strength. She is able to withstand tremendous pressure to conform and give up. The challenging leader might be fairly characterized as "constructively stubborn."

Hopefully, the process of challenging the process leads to an awareness of a better way, a vision of new possibilities.

Leaders Build Visions

The second major responsibility of a leader is to build a vision. This involves at least four factors: foresight, inventiveness, idealism, and credibility. To begin with, a visionary leader needs an exceptional sense for the future. He must also have the intelligence and imagination to discover the full range of possibilities that exist in her field. He discerns which possibilities are desirable and which are not. As he sizes up the possibilities and identifies the ideal, he factors in a generous measure of practical, realistic thinking.

An effective leader has an uncanny sense for what is around the corner. As Greenleaf puts it, a leader must have "a sense for the unknowable and be able to foresee the unforeseeable." This ability is more an innate gift than a skill, but to some extent it can be cultivated. A visionary leader is acutely aware of and sensitive to trends in the field and in related fields. He is also very conscious of historic patterns. Visionary leaders face the unknown future respectfully but with confidence and eagerness.

The visionary has greater awareness of the possibilities than less-imaginative persons. He is able to suspend his critical inner voice and entertain new combinations of factors. Using his imagination, he alters particular variables and spins out the consequence of the alteration in her mind. He envisions ideal outcomes, identifies obstacles to their realization, and invents ways to overcome the obstacles. The visionary leader takes a deep interest in problems because they yield information and opportunity. In a similar vein, he pays close attention to the arguments of those who offer opposing opinions.

Since visions typically spring from a process of challenging the established system, they are often initially stated in negative terms. That analysis is helpful; but a true vision, if it is to come fully alive, has to offer more than criticism. Visions need to be expressed in positive terms. Actually, *positive* is an insufficient word, because visions are concerned with ideals. The visionary leader has an irrepressible passion for quality and a determination to approach the ideal. He has a vivid sense of the most ethical course toward the most moral goal.

Although the visionary leader offers a way that is idealistic and rich with potential, it is not a way of perfection. In a spirit of candor, he must frame the process truthfully. If the vision is to be credible, it cannot be all good news. The leader can identify and speak to the cost of the vision. Anticipating that additional negative information will be gathered as plans are carried out, he preserves the opportunity to amend the vision accordingly.

If a better way—a way of vision—can be formulated, it must be communicated engagingly if it is to take hold. That requires inspiration.

Leaders Inspire

A leader is not ashamed to ask people to change for the better. Popular sentiment says, "Accept me just as I am." But an inspirational leader calls his constituency beyond their usual functioning. She assumes there is a dimension in everyone that longs to contribute and be part of something uniquely meaningful, and she speaks boldly and directly to that longing. The inspirational leader invites people to step into an experience of excellence, an experience that extends them and moves them closer to the living edge. She creates an environment that makes risk-taking safer than usual. She has a way of softening people up for a tenderness of spirit to emerge.

How sad that the process of preparing for adoption has been somber, dull, and predictable for so many years. The message of quality adoption is exciting, and the method of expression ought to match it. It need not be unpleasant; the inspirational leader makes the preparation interesting, fun, and useful. She earns the right to get to know the participants by respecting them. Tickling, cajoling, and teasing, she learns to "teach when the teaching is good."

Again, Greenleaf describes the challenge well: "One must have facility in tempting the hearer into that leap of imagination that connects the verbal concept to the hearer's own experience." Imagination is the key; it is absolutely crucial. In the words of Notre Dame philosopher Tom Morris, "Only imagination has the power to engage the emotions, the attitudes, and the will over the long run. Only the imagination can really motivate us and sustain us with the energy we need to achieve difficult and worthwhile goals." Or, as Brother David Steindl-Rast, a priest with extraordinary spiritual insight, puts it in *Gratefulness: The Heart of Prayer,* "Even goodness and truth will not be convincing to the human heart unless they are gifted with a gracefulness and ease that makes them beautiful." Great ideas will languish if they do not appeal to the imagination. We must be patient in this process because, as Christian commentator Thomas Merton observes in *Contemplation in a World of Action,* "The imagination should be allowed a certain amount of time to browse around."

To stand a chance to stir the imagination of her constituency, the professional must be totally committed. There is a noticeable difference between living one's vocation and "eight-to-fiving" it. Professional vitality happens when ability and interest meet, in passionate form, need and challenge. In *Wishful Thinking,*

Frederick Buechner expresses this point with particular beauty: "The place God calls you to is the place where your deep gladness and the world's deep hunger meet."

It is crucial that a leader love her work. In *The Grace of Great Things*, University of Oregon Professor Robert Grudin makes this important observation: "The courage of innovative thought is not a distinct virtue that can be practiced in and of itself. It is a by-product, a strength that is the simple consequence of loving our work and knowing why we love it."

Do we love our work? We all complain, of course, but the adoption workers I respect truly do love their work. It is not a matter of power, prestige, or money—the thought would make them laugh. The opportunity to serve in a meaningful way at a meaningful time is what makes the work satisfying. There is beauty in the work. Grudin helps us to understand this beauty:

> Every professional field ...offers opportunities for the flash of insight....Beyond this are all experiences involving justice. Human justice, which might be described as a kind of symmetry in time, resembles the natural symmetries and reciprocities that strike us as beautiful. To speak or act justly is to create a symmetry between self and experience. Thus, fairness is beautiful, because it suggests a symmetry between what people deserve and what they get. Frankness (in measure) is beautiful, because frankness equates what we say with what we feel. Humor is beautiful, that is, when humor can convey elegantly and creatively things that are impossible to put frankly. Precise expression of any sort has beauty because of the symmetry between reality and the signs that convey it. In short, anyone who performs difficult tasks inventively, justly, and with humane expressiveness works in the presence of beauty.

Grudin's observation captures much of my delight. The joy of the work truly is related to insight, justice, frankness, humor, and precise expression. Adoption is astonishingly undeveloped territory, and there is much to learn. A person could spend 10 careers exploring its nooks and crannies and never cover the same ground. It is rich with complex, three-party dilemmas that stretch one's ideas of justice. It is a field that yearns for candor after decades of secrecy. Adoption has been such serious, somber, shameful business for so long that it is ripe for lightheartedness. It is so polarized and politicized that it craves unhysterical clarity. I watch in wonder as participants affirm, sacrifice, and cooperate with each other, and I am encouraged and energized.

Love for the work generates passion, and nothing inspires like passion. Lofty ideals fire our imaginations, but passion stirs the juices. No one says it better than highly regarded business writers Tom Peters and Nancy Austin in *A Passion for Excellence:*

> Courage and self-respect are the lion's share of passion: It's hanging in long after others have gotten bored or given up; it's refusing to leave well enough alone; it means that anything less than the best you can imagine really bothers you, maybe keeps you awake at night. It usually means sticking your neck out: daring to give your best shot to something you care about and asking others to do the same is self-exposing. It asks you to pick sides, to wear your passion on your sleeve, to take a position and remain true to it even under the scrutiny of an audience, when the wish to please, to be accepted, welcomed, can compromise the clearest inner vision. Passion opens you to criticism, disappointment, disillusionment, and failure....

Through imagination, conviction, and passion, the inspirational leader invites constituents to consider the vision, become involved with it, own it, and improve it. It begins with catching their attention and intriguing them, then moves to enlisting their commitment to the shared vision. The prospects for enrollment are improved if the leader models the way, the third quality of leadership.

Leaders Model the Way

Ideally, the leader exemplifies the qualities desired in the constituency. His efforts are most compelling if he is a model of multidimensional health and conscientiously attends to his physical, mental, social, and spiritual health. Credibility demands that what is expected of participants is expected first of the leader. The leader must be consistent with the message. That observation prompts renewed consideration of the eight values of values-based open adoption—the message—and how the leader handles them:

- **Child-centeredness.** The effective practitioner has a tender and vigilant heart for children. He has a knack for understanding situations from the perspective of the child.

- **Candor.** He is able to share difficult, unpopular truths in a kindly manner. The people who count on him know where he stands.

- **Respect for informed self-determination.** The leader encourages and defends the opportunity for participants to reach well-informed, unpressured decisions that are consistent with their own value systems.

- **Honoring the pain.** He has the courage to face the pain of adoption. As Buechner puts it in *A Clown in the Belfry*, "Maybe the teacher's main business is to teach gently the inevitability of pain." His effectiveness will be directly related to his capacity to hang in there in moments of intense and raw emotion.

- **Honoring commitments.** A credible leader models great integrity. In *Leadership Is an Art*, business writer Max DePree notes that integrity is "a fine sense of one's obligations." He is consistent, trustworthy, and reliable.

- **Openness.** A relentless learner who stays current with information in several fields, the gifted practitioner is comfortable with uncertainty and believes in cooperation. Most crucially, he allows himself to be touched by the process.

- **Adaptability.** An authentic leader is an effective problem solver and is able to assist in finding synergistic solutions. He is tolerant of conflict and directs it toward productive exchange. He seeks and grants forgiveness.

- **Receptiveness to community.** A credible adoption worker enjoys diversity and is aware of interdependence. He is able to trust and let go. He has a gift for bringing people together.

If the professional can meet these criteria, in addition to being eligible for sainthood, he is well-suited to carry forward the message of values-based open adoption.

The leader works hard to bridge the gap between herself and his constituency. It is not an automatic process, because it is the nature of the power he wields, modest or massive, to create anxiety in his constituency. He must earn their trust. For that to occur, he must demonstrate authenticity and dependability.

The leader cannot pretend to be something he is not; he must be authentic. It helps if he has the courage to be vulnerable and imperfect, because imperfect leaders are easier to relate to. He must defeat any movement toward "we-they" thinking and enter, as far as possible, the "we." Henri Nouwen observes in *The Wounded Healer* that a leader "must have the courage to be an explorer of the new territory in himself and to articulate his discoveries as a service to the inward generation." The imaginative leader knows he has much in common with his constituency and is able to comfortably speak to that commonality.

Earlier, I referred to the power of passion. Passion is wonderful but is prone to excess if it stands alone. Excess does not usually generate trust. Passion is most constructive in tandem with stability. "Stable passion" is simultaneously safe and exciting.

One of the great moments in my career occurred at one of the national conferences we hold in Traverse City, Michigan. Open adoption advocate Sharon Kaplan-Roszia gave me a beautiful fossilized rock and offered the high praise of calling me a "rock." Her comment reminded me of a quotation from internationally acclaimed author Frederick Buechner, who, of course, had someone significantly more deserving in mind when he penned this description in *Peculiar Treasures:*

> A rock isn't the prettiest thing in creation or the fanciest or the smartest, and if it gets rolling in the wrong direction watch out, but there's no nonsense about a rock, and once it settles down, it's pretty much there to stay. There's not a lot you can do to change a rock or crack it or get under its skin, and, barring earthquakes, you can depend on it about as much as anything you can depend on.

All of us who work in adoption must be rocks. When chaos and anxiety surges through the system, it is a great comfort to participants to know there is a rock nearby to cling to. "Rockish" behavior does not require the denial of feelings. On the contrary, it is the ability to fully experience the anxieties of the moment and respond to them in unhysterical fashion.

Leaders Stir Capabilities

A leader must have faith. At some point, she must pass the torch to the participants and hope the preparations have been sufficient. In adoption, one of the better ways to understand the phenomenon popularly called *empowerment* is to view it as the cessation of disempowerment. It is frequently a matter of getting out of the way, but there is, of course, more to it than that. The great work of a leader is to create a climate in which people can function with unusual courage and compassion, a culture of excellence and greatness. It is an atmosphere in which thorough and unhurried decisions can be made and where participants understand that it is in their best interest to transcend self-interest. This culture stirs in participants a positive mindset that looks for the best in others. This constructive environment is founded on three factors: a well-designed system, education, and affirmation.

Creative leaders design and fine tune a system that meets the needs of its constituency in a reasonable and respectful fashion. If participants work within its framework, they can reasonably anticipate that their hopes will be realized. The feedback of those who have used the system is crucial, as it provides information necessary to adjust the system. When the system is working optimally, it features opportunity, safety, and community.

If a constituency is to realize its potential, it needs information. A great leader is invariably a great teacher. She has substantial information to share and is skilled at presenting it so that participants can understand and use it. She describes the routine course of events, if there is such a thing, and the roles typically assumed by each participant. Just as important, the leader works hard to prepare participants for less-pleasant possibilities. If the program's educational program is effective and thorough, participants should be confident and prepared for most of the challenges that await them.

Operating within an effective system, and equipped with relevant information, participants are positioned for success. The last piece is affirmation. The leader must make a clear distinction between excellence and perfection. Excellence is an important and inspiring goal, but it does not have much to do with perfection. If participants misunderstand and think they are supposed to be perfect, they will end up either as failures or phonies. Our most spectacular birthparents and adoptive parents are gloriously imperfect. They have learned to transform their shortcomings into strengths, and they are at peace with their imperfections.

Most participants struggle with doubt. They feel prepared but wonder whether they have strength and imagination to carry out the plan. Some think that open adoption is only suitable for highly educated people brimming with confidence, but our experience shows that it works for people from very diverse backgrounds who take the Golden Rule seriously. One of the leader's most joyful roles is to affirm and support her constituency. Although participants may doubt themselves, the leader finds it easy to identify their strengths and capabilities and enjoys the happy task of pointing out and celebrating their otherwise unheralded greatness.

Affirming is as simple as reminding participants of what they already know. It is a matter of respectfully and lovingly reactivating in them ideals and aspirations that have gone dormant. It is a loving nudge. Affirmation must be sincere and founded in reality. Jean Vanier, a peerless builder of communities, offers an especially wise comment.

> To love people is to recognize their gifts and help these to unfold; it is also to accept their wounds and be patient and compassionate toward them. If we see only the gifts and beauty, then we expect too much of people; we idealize them. If we see only the wound, then we do too much for them and tend to keep them in submission.

The empowering leader listens intently to her constituency to discern their immediate needs. This ability to listen enables her to be of greater service to them. She uses the information to respond to the pressures of the moment, but also to modify the vision, thereby creating a seamless loop of service in which it is not clear who is leading and who is following.

Leaders Build Community

The leader has one more method to prepare and strengthen his constituency; namely, to bring them together in community. Embodying a novel approach to adoption, participants often feel misunderstood. During their daily activities, they encounter misinformation about open adoption so routinely that they grow weary of explaining themselves. Participants deeply appreciate the opportunity to commune with like-minded persons. Community has a way of normalizing things. It is in community that participants feel safest and most inclined to explore the manifold implications of their decisions.

Participants are eager to find peers. The leader's most vital task in birthing community is establishing a constructive spirit. It is a moment of optimal influence for a leader, and he must be sure that a positive spirit prevails when new participants are first convened. The quality of a participant's adoptive experience will be directly linked to the attitude of the community of which he or she is a part. Participants must feel a sense of common purpose and direction; without it, a spirit of competition may emerge. As familiarity increases and trust builds, community members naturally look to each other to commiserate in times of discouragement and to celebrate in moments of triumph.

Indigenous leadership invariably emerges, and, presuming it is positive, the professional gladly supports this development. When participants demonstrate their own skills of constructive leadership, thereby ensuring that the process will move forward positively, the professional can relax a little, content in the knowledge that most of his job is done.

Leaders Have Authority

The leader can labor ingeniously to lead, but there is no guarantee that the constituency will follow. She can move forward with a brilliant agenda—challenging the process, creating a vision, inspiring excellence, modeling the message, empowering the participants, and building community—but it is not certain she will be heard. To be heard and followed, the leader needs one more quality: authority. Psychologist Randolph Severson speaks to this with characteristic eloquence in *Adoption: Philosophy and Experience:*

> A charismatic, caring person with authority need merely walk into a room and begin to speak about the theme, the subject in which he has authority, and others are instantly alert and conscious of the fact that here is "someone who knows what he's talking about," who, in the old language, "knows whereof

they speak." Rather than status or position, a person with authority may be said to have human stature and charismatic presence.

This authority of integrity, of kindness, of stable passion is not easily secured. A leader of authority has surely paid her dues. She has read nearly everything on the subject and explored several tangential areas as well. Listening to all who have tales to tell, she has absorbed hundreds of "war stories." They are the source and sample from which she draws many of her conclusions. Perhaps she is an adoption triad member herself and, as a result, has extraordinary sensitivity to the consequential nature of the work. If she is not, she has used her imagination to discover the triad "within." She has searched her heart and found the adoptee, birthparent, and adoptive parent who reside there. This effort produces exceptional self-awareness. Her authority is greater if her convictions have been costly; those who championed the cause before general acceptance have more credibility than those who claim it painlessly. No matter how hectic or dramatic the circumstances become, the leader of authority carries forward with unshakable decency. Indisputably sincere, she sets a tone of moral excellence.

The Response to Effective Leadership

Most of the time, assessing a leader's effectiveness is quite simple. His capabilities will be evident in the attitudes and behavior of his constituency; they are his mirrors. Weak leadership will manifest itself in a variety of ways. Some participants will be insecure and need constant reassurance. Others will be angry and frustrated, and still others will be freelancing and doing their own thing. The leader will find himself worried about the participants and wondering if they can be trusted. When the leadership is too authoritative, the constituency will act immaturely. They will be hesitant and seek permission for every minuscule decision they make. Their relationships may be very formal and lack spontaneity. Over time, it is also possible that they may become rebellious, challenging, or sneaky. In such circumstances, the leader feels very burdened. When the leadership is balanced, the constituency will be in good form. They will be appropriately self-determined, flexible, and graceful under pressure. The leader is then freed to focus on innovation.

THE PROFESSIONAL AS ARTIST

Earlier, I made a distinction between the professional as technician and as an artist. A technician mindlessly follows instructions, but the artist fully invests herself in the process. She has a deft touch. Her artistry is apparent in three ways: She is unobtrusive, she manages hope effectively, and she sets a general tone of respect.

The artistic leader somehow knows when to be around and when to be scarce. This knack comes with experience, but it is also a matter of knowing her constituency well and staying in close enough contact to discern their needs. She has a sixth sense for their anxieties. If a situation is foundering and in need of direction, she steps in to help set a course. On the other hand, if an arrangement is developing positively, she steps back and stays in the background as participants appropriately fashion their relationship. The artistic leader needs neither control nor attention.

One of the most difficult tasks for an adoption worker is to manage the dynamic of hope. Participants crave hope and are especially alert for any particularly positive or negative signs. The artful leader is perpetually conscious of hope and is careful to tread a highly appropriate path concerning it. If she veers a little in one direction or the other, ramifications will quickly reverberate through the constituency. Unrealistic hope raises the prospect of crushing disappointment, whereas too little causes despair. Either error saps morale and energy.

The artistic leader creates an infectious atmosphere of respect. In the presence of such a leader, there is no room for "we-they" thinking; the Golden Rule rules. She helps participants stay aware of their interdependence and keeps them on course by gently and irrepressibly reminding them of the paramount goal of serving the child. Respecting their pain and delighting in their honor, she fashions and energizes the affirming spirit of open adoption.

Chapter 12

Adoption Without Fear

We are a fearful people. The more people I come to know and the more I come to know people, the more I am overwhelmed by the negative power of fear. It often seems that fear has invaded every part of our being to such a degree that we no longer know what a life without fear would feel like. There always seems to be something to fear: something within us or around us, something close or far away, something visible or invisible, something in ourselves, in others, or in God. There never seems to be a totally fear-free moment. When we think, talk, act or react, fear always seems to be there: an omnipresent force that we cannot shake off. Often fear has penetrated our inner selves so deeply that it controls, whether we are aware of it or not, most of our choices and decisions.

Henri Nouwen, *Lifesigns*

There is no fear in love, but perfect love casts out fear.

I John 4:18, *Revised Standard Version*

A few years ago, I edited a book entitled, *Adoption Without Fear*—a reasonably catchy title, but technically incorrect. In a spirit of accuracy, it should have been called, *Getting Mostly*

Beyond Fear in Adoption, because there really is no such thing as adoption without fear. Every adoption is a foray into the realm of terror. It cannot be otherwise, because interdependence is at the core of the experience. Adoption would be far less anxious if it could be accomplished without the involvement of others. Some observers take the amusing view that adoption would be pretty great if it weren't for birthparents. The unavoidable truth of adoption, however, is that every participant's future is held in another participant's hands. In a culture that craves self-sufficiency and independence, for many people this is a fact from hell. It is no simple thing to put one's most heartfelt hopes in the hands of strangers—vulnerability of this magnitude is profoundly disturbing.

Fear is present from the earliest moments and poses an early fork in the road for everyone entering the adoption scene. What shall we do with our fear? Either we yield to the fear and install it as the overarching dynamic, or we look it in the eye, confront it, and come to terms with it. This is the watershed decision in adoption; the entire adoption experience hinges on how the participants respond to the specter of fear. If they feel overwhelmed and capitulate to the fear, the adoption will be worked out in terms of power, and the opportunity for intimacy and community will be lost. On the other hand, if they feel equal to the challenge and face the fear directly, they will grow as individuals and enter extraordinary relationships founded on trust and cooperation.

Fear is adoption's greatest enemy, and it cannot be ignored. The temptation to avoid and evade is, nevertheless, powerful. We think that it might go away if we ignore it. The lure of evasion stirs amazing creativity, and we go to great extremes to put it out of our minds. As Jesuit priest Carlos Valles astutely observes in *Let Go of Fear,* "We seek company, we distract the mind, we pray. All that is good, but never as a substitute for facing the fear and working it out."

FEAR AND CLOSED ADOPTIONS

The closed method of adoption makes the choice for participants. Rather than allowing participants to work through their fear and resolve it, the system empowers the fear. Concluding that adoption has highly anxious, perhaps even dangerous dimensions that should not be underestimated, the closed system resolves to keep birthparents and adoptive parents apart. The hazard of interaction is considered so formidable that a vigorous defense against it has been deemed necessary. Secrecy is the primary mechanism to combat the fear. Birthfamilies and adoptive families are segregated by an imposing barrier of secrecy. If they have no access to each other, the closed system reasons, they will not affect each other. Out of sight, out of mind.

To its chagrin, the closed system's determination to contain the anxiety has not conquered the fear. In fact, its tactics have proved counterproductive. Instead of diminishing the fear, the closed system has unwittingly installed it as the institution's most dominant and enduring factor. The fear has not gone away—it has been merely pushed into the background as an unprocessed dynamic. Secrecy does not diminish fear. On the contrary, secrecy flourishes in a climate of fear, and fear thrives in a climate of secrecy. Fear and secrecy are close cousins.

Casting the discussion in slightly different terms, strategies for coping with fear are either short-term or long-term. A strategy based on secrecy can keep the birthfamily and adoptive family apart in the initial stages of an adoption. For some, this may relieve the immediate anxiety, but the comfort is gained at the price of long-term anxiety. Once a strategy of distance and secrecy is launched, it requires continual maintenance. Dealing with an unfamiliar adversary, one must never let down one's guard. The unknown antagonist looms as an ominous person whose intentions and capabilities are limited only by the boundaries of imagination. Worse yet, the faceless rival is anybody and everybody. Is that her? Do you think he is looking for us? Did we give her too much information? Can he put two and two together and figure us out? She wouldn't sneak up and take the baby, would she? Shall we stay home to make sure nobody spots us? Should we move?

Once fear is fully empowered and takes root, it is tenacious and enduring. Recently, I made a presentation at a small chapter of the Adoption Identity Movement. There were eight or nine people present, and I was astounded to learn that three of the ladies— one in her 30s, one in her 40s, and another in her 50s—had told their families they were somewhere else. According to their cover stories, they were grocery shopping. Decades after achieving adulthood, they were still coping with the burden of fear.

Fear has extracted an enormous toll through the years. Reworking the scriptural axiom that introduces this chapter, it appears that in fear, there is no love. Because of fear, adoptees have been denied fundamental information about themselves, birthparents have been deprived the reassurance and gratitude that might have brought them peace of mind, and adoptive parents have lived in dread of the fated knock on the door. The closed system's capitulation to fear has transformed birthparents and adoptive parents—natural allies sharing a common purpose—into adversaries. Short-term comfort has been gained at the cost of long-term anxiety, anxiety that can only be resolved by dramatic intervention.

HANDLING THE FEAR

Open adoption handles the fear in a very different manner. It "front loads" the fear. The terrifying possibility of rejection is confronted very early in the process; if the test is passed, the fear largely dissipates. Once the fear is confronted and diminished, the adoption adventure becomes far more relaxed and enjoyable. It is not uncommon for those who burst the fear barrier to enter an unexpected state of serenity. With fear put in its place, adoption feels liberating and healthy.

The obvious challenge, then, is to find the most effective methods to successfully confront the fear and cope with it. We are not helpless in response to fear. Since it is an ancient enemy, most remedies for fear are similarly timeless. Here is a portion of our repertoire of tools to tackle fear.

Welcoming fear. It is not our nature to appreciate fear or consider it a vital dimension of our humanness; we perceive it as oppressive and inherently undesirable. Actually, it is positive in many ways. Obviously, fear has the power to motivate, but its value goes much further. Fear is a remarkable instructor. Again, Valles offers an insightful observation in *Let Go of Fear:*

> If we want to grow in spirit, in courage, in faith, in understanding, we can consult our fears and observe where they point....Our fears have shown us our weak points, our deficiencies, our shortcomings, and so to improve our characters, brighten the future, and enlarge our boundaries, we thank our fears for their

valuable information....The frontiers of fear are the frontiers of growth.

It is interesting to consider how time affects our appraisal of fear. Prospectively, for example, we eye a roller coaster with wary but positive anticipation. Retrospectively, safely beyond the threat, we look back on our trepidation with pleasure and humor. Anyone who has survived an encounter with a bear in the woods has, at the very least, a lively story to tell. As we joust with fear in life's various predicaments, our character grows in color, texture, and confidence.

Identifying and verbalizing fears. Some of our fears are entirely justified, and we do well to respond to them sensibly. Much that we dread, however, is imaginary. Unidentified and unspeakable fears are always larger than life. Many fear dragons are slain by simply identifying them and speaking their names aloud. We must recognize that fear is an interior experience, not exterior. Fear is in our own minds and hearts; ultimately, that is where we must search if we wish to understand it. We do well to think less about fear located out there somewhere and more about the insecurity that resides in our hearts.

Reliance on experts. The worker sets the tone for the experience and models appropriate behavior. If he exudes confidence, participants will likely grow in poise. It is not fearlessness that the worker needs to exhibit, but rather the willingness to confront the fear. A competent guide inspires a sense of security in those who follow. An effective leader creates a culture in which clients can operate in optimal fashion. He perceives an anxious circumstance as an especially fruitful opportunity for learning. In a strange way, he welcomes fear, befriends it, and transforms it into an asset.

The power of information. When we gather information, we gain perspective. Fear is integral to the adoption experience, but it is not the complete story. The risks that generate anxiety also lead to very appealing benefits, and most well-informed people conclude that the risks are worth taking. Good information gives participants greater control over their circumstances, an impression that produces a measure of comfort.

Eliminating we-they thinking. Fear makes us intensely self-centered. In the grip of fear, no one else matters. In this fashion, fear squelches compassion. Consumed with fear, we fail to identify with the needs of others, and we overlook all that we have in common with them.

Much of the isolation that accompanies fear can be relieved by recognizing that adoption is best understood as a system. Participants are in the adoption experience together, and everyone's well-being is indisputably interrelated. If the system is to thrive, there must be a balancing of the risks, or, phrasing the idea in different terms, a balance of trust. If this balance is missing, comfort for one participant is gained only at the discomfort of another. Mutual understanding and identification with each other allays many fears. Activist Jim Wallis helps us understand how this process takes place in *The Soul of Politics:*

> Getting close enough to see, hear, touch, smell, and taste the reality of others is what always makes the difference. In listening to the stories of those so seemingly different from us, we find similar but unexpressed voices inside of ourselves. Hearing one another's stories is the beginning of new understanding and the foundation of compassionate action.

Those who listen with interest and sincerity invariably find that, except for some quirks of time, money, and biology, birthparents and adoptive parents are cut from the same cloth. They usually have far more in common than they initially presume.

Hope. False hope is very draining, but appropriate hope is very sustaining. Quality programs provide appropriate hope because they offer a system that produces many pleasing outcomes. Satisfaction does not hinge on a singular event, because the system will provide other opportunities. If a particular situation does not work out, there is reasonable hope for another day.

Truth. Secrecy conceals the truth and works hard to protect the truth from discovery. It lives with the fear of disclosure. That approach stands in stark contrast to the simple wisdom that the truth will set us free. Thinking about secrecy's questionable ability to protect, a friend once commented, "The best form of protection is truth."

Courage. After all the social, mental, and spiritual work is done, there remains the terrifying moment of action, the leap of faith. At some point we are confronted with a moment of decision. At that moment, there is no substitute for courage.

Faith. In *Legacy of the Heart*, therapist and Harvard Divinity School graduate Wayne Muller points out that

...as we grow older we discover that the hazards and discomforts that threaten us never totally disappear from our lives. We begin to see that true safety is not the absence of danger but rather the presence of something else—the presence of a sense of faith, born in the heart and sustained by a spirit of serenity, trust, and courage.

There are many layers of faith, and each has great potential.

- **Faith in self.** Everyone has problem-solving capabilities. Staying calm and focused, people can usually achieve good results.

- **Faith in spouse.** Many couples have complementary skills. Melding their skills and instincts, they will likely be equal to most challenges.

- **Faith in support systems.** Few people go through the adoption journey completely alone. If a couple cannot find the strength they need in themselves, they can lean on the important people in their lives who are following their experience with great interest and who are pleased to be involved and lend support.

- **Faith in ideals.** Many people place their confidence in ideals. They have faith that great ideals ultimately prevail over lesser rivals. It occurs to them that the pursuit of great ideals, even if they go unfulfilled, brings its own rewards. They keep in mind that, ultimately, it is not the ideals themselves that matter but their beneficial impact on people.

- **Faith in God.** Genuine spiritual faith is a tremendous asset for participants as they cope with the anxieties of adoption. Spiritual faith provides uncanny comfort at moments when things feel completely out of control. People of faith do not waste their energies trying to push the river. In deep faith, the only outcome that matters is acquiescence with God's will. Henri Nouwen writes in *Our Greatest Gift,*

    When we can reach beyond our fears to the One who loves us with a love that was there before we were born and will be there after we die, then oppression, persecution, and even death will be unable to take our freedom.

Rooted in faith, we feel an amazing sort of safety that defies reason.

Love. A fascinating remedy for fear surfaces in the scriptural epigraph that opens this chapter: "There is no fear in love, but perfect love casts out fear." What is the meaning of this surprising observation?

Love surely transcends selfishness, for it focuses on respecting, affirming, and serving others. It is the nature of love to give. This is a crucial insight. If facilitators are concerned about the constricting effects of fear and are interested in equipping their constituencies to effectively address this debilitating dynamic, they must engagingly remind them of the power of love and describe the means by which this power can be applied. The most significant task for the professional is to reframe the adoption experience from a process of getting or obtaining to one of giving.

In optimal form, the emotional progression moves from getting to receiving to giving. Participants enter the experience understandably distressed and determined to get what they need. Prospective adoptive parents hope to "get" a child, and prospective birthparents hope to "get" relief. Since their agendas are far from assured, those who are in adoption to "get" are vulnerable to the prospect of shattering disappointment. Challenged to focus more on the process than the outcome, most participants grow to trust the process and are able rise above their initial panic. As trust grows, they are able to open themselves and receive the care and influence of others. Hopefully, a program's system of preparation moves participants one step further. If it successfully reminds them of their most vital values and stirs their compassion, it will enable them to shift into a service mode. Those who learn to view adoption as an opportunity to give need not worry about disappointment, for they will no doubt have their opportunity to love. This perspective organizes them and gives them purpose and direction. The beauty of this approach is that those who are determined to give are sure to succeed. They cannot lose. Consequently, they have nothing to fear.

Love is a truly remarkable response to fear. It is, obviously, easier to talk about than to carry out. No one is fully capable of selfless love. Furthermore, giving must be done carefully and intelligently to avoid the inadvertent reinforcing of another's irresponsibility. Nevertheless, to the extent that participants operate in a spirit of affirming love, the bitterness of fear will be replaced by the sweetness of mutual trust. In one of life's most reliable paradoxes, one's personal needs are met most fully in the process of caring respectfully for others.

FEAR OF DEPENDENCE

Earlier, I noted that there is no way around fear in adoption because interdependence is the heart of the process. As terrifying as that fear may be, there is an even greater source of fear. German philosopher Immanuel Kant, who argued for ethics based on principle, once observed that a man fears nothing more than to find himself on self-examination to be worthless and contemptible in his own eyes. Inept handling of the fear of dependence has enormous potential to generate self-contempt and shame. If Kant is correct, it is possible that the fear of shame is sufficient to move us to face our exaggerated fear of dependence.

What about this fear of dependence? Is dependence the ogre we think it is? Usually not. In fact, if interdependence is worked through with intelligence and respect, it becomes extraordinarily gratifying. Open adoptions of quality produce many pleasing transformations, but none are more important than this. It is exciting to see participants move from fearing interdependence to reveling in it. With the fear of interdependence successfully overcome, participants are free to enjoy the delights of community.

We have seen, then, that as we struggle to come to terms with fear, we are not helpless. We have powerful tools to use in our struggle with this timeless enemy. Among others, we have faith, hope, and love; and the greatest of these is love.

Chapter 13

Adoption Without Shame

There is a nice irony in shame: our feelings of inferiority are a sure sign of our superiority, and our feelings of unworthiness testify to our great worth. Only a very noble being can feel shame. The reason is simple: a creature meant to be a little less than God is likely to feel a deep dissatisfaction with herself if she falls a notch below the splendid human being she is meant to be.

We are destined to feel frustrated at times because we have the power to imagine that we can defy our limits. In our imagination we may enjoy the illusion that we have no limits, but we reach them sooner or later, and when we do, we chafe. To be frustrated by our limits is our destiny and our discomfort; it is our challenge to reach beyond them. But it is our glory, not our shame.

Lewis Smedes, *Shame and Grace*

A few years ago, I was on a national talk show to debate the virtues of open adoption. I was accompanied by a delightful birthparent, Amy Smith, and Michael Spry, the adoptive father she chose to adopt her son. The proponents of closed adoption were deployed in similar fashion, although, of course, their birthmother and adoptive father did not have a child in common. Despite Amy and Michael's warm description of the adoption they were fashioning along with Michael's wife, Jean, the discussion became predictably fruitless as the others injected their cynicism. Almost lost in the ratings-enhancing heat was the fact that the face of the birthmother, given the pseudonym Anne, was disguised from the television audience. When asked about the disguise, she explained, "The reason I've disguised my face is because I've gone on with my life."

People do not disguise themselves as a declaration of general satisfaction and pride. Her claim of contentment rang hollow, completely canceled by her decision to hide her face. When the dust settled that day, words did not especially matter. I am sure they were soon forgotten. What more likely lingered in the minds of the television viewers were the images of two birthmothers claiming contentment but advocating diametrically opposed methods of achieving this peace of mind. One was fully identified, and the other was disguised; one had wrestled with shame and had come to terms with it, whereas the other lives in its clutches as a fact of everyday life. The birthmothers stood as vivid symbols of adoption's contrasting ways of handling the dynamic of shame.

UNDERSTANDING SHAME

For years, shame was a forgotten subject in the social sciences. Lately rediscovered, it is drawing the attention of people from a variety of fields, and the literature is growing rapidly. Michael Lewis, a professor of pediatrics, psychiatry, and psychology at the Robert Woods Johnson Medical School, describes it clearly in *Shame: The Exposed Self:*

> Shame can be defined simply as the feeling we have when we evaluate our actions, feelings, or behavior, and conclude that we have done wrong. It encompasses the whole of ourselves; it generates a wish to hide, to disappear or even to die.

This definition brings attention to four fundamental aspects of shame: It is a feeling, a judgment, a perception of self, and a desire to hide.

The initial feeling of shame is intensely negative. We describe shameful situations as "mortifying," revealing the extent of our discomfort by linking it to death. Once the initial intensity fades, shame settles into an enduring sensation that compassionate theologian Lewis Smedes describes in picturesque language in *Shame and Grace:*

> Shame is a very heavy feeling. It is a feeling that we do not measure up and maybe never will measure up to the sort of persons we were meant to be. The feeling, when we are conscious of it, gives us a vague disgust with ourselves, which in turn feels like a hunk of lead on our hearts...like an invisible load that weighs our spirits down and crushes our joy.

Shame is rooted in a negative judgment. It can be our own conclusion or that of others. Whatever its source, we believe it is deserved and take the judgment into our souls. In *No Place to Hide,* Michael Nichols, professor of psychiatry at Albany Medical College, describes shame as "a painful discrepancy between our image of who we'd like to be and our perception of an ugly reality." Our susceptibility to shame is clearly linked to our commitment to standards; if we had no standards, we would have no shame.

Shame is an issue of identity, a matter of self. The best way to illustrate this is to contrast it with guilt. Guilt occurs when a good person does a bad thing. There is a distinction between the person and the bad thing that has happened. Shame reaches a very different conclusion. It concludes that the person who did the bad thing is bad. Shame is understood in terms of the basic person; it fuses the person and the unacceptable act.

Shame generates a powerful desire to hide. Its fruits are avoidance, secrecy, and isolation. In his book, *The Psychology of Shame,* Gershen Kaufman, a leading authority in the field, says shame "breaks the interpersonal bridge." In the throes of shame, we feel entirely alone. The isolation is exacerbated by the defenses frequently employed to deal with shame—defenses like rage, contempt, striving for perfection, striving for power, and blame. These reactions typically add to the tension and estrangement, thereby launching a depleting spiral of shame.

Shame is often associated with exposure. In an experience of shame, we are defenseless as our unacceptability is uncovered and our hideous flaws of character are shouted from the rooftops. For some theorists, exposure is a critical factor; as they see it, the shame is in the disclosure. Others believe it can be entirely internal. For them, the exposure is to oneself. It appears that there is truth in each view and that shame can be activated externally or internally.

Although shame is considered a decidedly undesirable emotion, a sense of shame is very desirable. In the quotation leading into this chapter, Smedes highlights the paradox that "our feelings of inferiority are a sure sign of our superiority." He is right. In contrast to shamelessness, shame indicates the presence of standards and concern for others. In *Shame, Exposure, and Privacy*, ordained minister Carl Schneider, an observer with an unusual eye for the positive aspects of shame, underscores this observation: "The immediate awareness in shame is often the sting of self-negation; a more sustained look reveals an underlying core of positive beliefs and self-evaluation.... Shame implies that a person cares." The person without shame does not care what others think, suggesting to his discredit an absent sense of community. Shame can also be a healthy response to indignity; we properly cringe at the shame of someone unjustly berated in public.

In general terms, shame is usually linked to one or more of five related factors that provide a framework for understanding the shame that permeates adoption as we have known it through the years:

- **Defectiveness.** When we feel deeply flawed and unacceptable, we feel defective. It is the feeling that the original equipment—our givens, the very stuff of which we are made—is ruined. Even small anomalies, real or imagined, can lead us to this conclusion.

- **Powerlessness.** Shame can result from the inability to control a situation reasonably. It is helplessness and humiliation, a spirit-crushing confrontation with the limits of our capabilities.

- **Dirtiness.** At times, we may feel repugnant or repulsive. We may feel self-contempt as well as the disgust of others. Causing others to wrinkle up their noses, shudder, and reflexively step back, we instinctively feel ashamed.

- **Rejection.** When we feel undesirable, pushed away, and abandoned—in a word, unlovable—we are seized with shame. Shame results when one is disowned and "put out of the pack."

- **Depersonalization.** We cannot stand being treated like nonpersons, as if we do not exist. We suffer deeply when we are treated like we are not there, reduced to numbers or nobodies In *Shame and Grace,* Smedes notes, "When another person looks us up and down the way a shopper inspects a chest of drawers, and then scorns us, he shames us because he makes us feel like nonpersons."

In addition to these five basic shame factors, special instances merit brief mention because they are common in the realm of adoption:

The shame of a victim. It is human to pity those who have experienced particular misfortune, yet we dislike being pitied because it leaves us feeling uncomfortably self-conscious and discounted. We hate to have our vulnerability as mortals exposed. As illogical as this shame seems—it is, after all, completely undeserved—it is very real.

The shame of hypocrisy. In her book, *On Shame and the Search for Identity,* psychoanalyst Helen Merrill Lynd comments, "There is a particularly deep shame in deceiving other persons into believing something about oneself that is not true."

The shame of betrayal. A double dose of shame often results from situations where trust has been mishandled. It is humiliating to be betrayed, and it is especially inexcusable and shameful to betray someone made vulnerable through trust. Special instances of betrayal include the traitor or someone who has sold out.

Shame felt in connection to our loved ones. Because of our close identification with the people we love, we often borrow their shame and take their humiliation into our hearts as our own.

The shame of failing to protect those whom we love. A particularly devastating form of torture is the powerlessness to prevent or interrupt misfortune directed to loved ones. It is humiliating and deeply shameful.

The shame of taking advantage of the disadvantaged. There is something repugnant connected to cashing in on someone's tragedy or gratifying our needs at the expense of another's dignity.

The toll of shame is enormous. Almost every aspect of it is exceptionally debilitating. It is a spiral of diminishment. The initial feelings, the lingering responses, and the coping defenses all tend toward negativity. An incident of shame often causes a person to review previous experiences with shame, a response that compounds and magnifies the original pain. It is the nature of shame to produce hiding and isolation—actions that, in turn, undermine self-esteem. As one's sense of unworthiness grows, prospects for additional problems grow rapidly. Furthermore, shame not only injures the person who experiences it, shame often spills over and contaminates others who are near to that person.

If we do not somehow come to terms with shame, it exists as a hidden factor that we cannot predict or control. It lingers in the background, like Smede's "hunk of lead weighing down our spirits." Unprocessed shame affects, among other things, our ability to trust. We gauge others too high or too low, thinking that we are not worthy of relating closely to others or reasoning, "If I have failed so pitifully, others probably will also." When one loses the capacity to trust, they also lose the ability to enjoy relationships.

Shame feels like a dead end, a quagmire of self-loathing. How does one fix something as major as oneself? Where does one begin? In *Facing Shame*, authors Merle Fossum and Marilyn Mason demonstrate an understanding of the magnitude of this question:

> The possibility for repair seems foreclosed to the shameful person because shame is a matter of identity.... There is nothing to be learned from it and no growth is opened by the experience because it only confirms one's negative feeling about one's self.

This depressing line of thought completes shame as a self-contained system of emotional debilitation. Shame begins with a negative self-appraisal, is nourished by psychic defenses that generate additional isolation, and is forever perpetuated by a determined distrust in the prospect of relief.

The devastation of shame should never be underestimated. It is intense, deep, insidious, enduring, tenacious, and consuming.

THE SHAME OF ADOPTION

As the introduction to this book says, shame resides in the heart of closed adoption. It is lodged there because the closed system is comfortable with it and welcomes it. In fact, the closed system is founded on it. Closed adoption makes two major assumptions about shame. First, it presumes that it is natural and inevitable for birthparents to experience shame. Second, it assumes that the best way for birthparents to deal with shame and move on with their lives is to go into hiding. It is a superficial strategy of denial that sometimes produces the illusion of resolution; but in their souls, birthfamilies feel ashamed and irreparably flawed. With shame as its foundation, the closed system of adoption has lost its capacity for health. With devastating symptoms like secrecy, withdrawal, and isolation, shame is no one's usual description of a satisfying and desirable outcome.

Shame is the ally of closed adoption. It is not surprising, then, that the closed system has never been very interested in finding remedies. In fact, the closed system has significant disincentives to relieve shame, for shame has been helpful to that form of adoption in at least five ways:

- Shame has been a fundamental motivator prompting birthparents to consider adoption. Trying to avoid exposing one's out-of-wedlock pregnancy, birthparents have welcomed the secrecy of the closed system.

- Shame makes the professionals involved especially useful. Defending against the prospect of discovery is the most important task for the practitioners of closed adoption. If damaging information is to be contained, a trusted middle man is required to keep the secrets. If that task were jettisoned, what would remain for the service provider to do?

- A shame-confirming system produces clients who do not feel worthy of respectful treatment. They are, as a result, very compliant and easy to work with.

- Shame-based adoption produces short-term, cost-effective clients. Shame-filled clients desperately want to avoid attention. They just want to get through their ordeals as quickly as possible and go into hiding. The alternative response to shame—painstakingly working through the issues—is extremely difficult, time-consuming, and costly.

- Shame creates circumstances that allow professionals to speak for clients. With birthparents and adoptees driven into hiding, the primary voices in adoption are those of adoptive parents and professionals. This has allowed practitioners to perpetuate their own ideas and interests for years without challenge.

The fact that shame and fear each generate hiding behavior suggests they may be related. Clearly, they are. Hiding in adoption originated as a response to shame and was rooted in the fear of discovery and the desire to avoid the sanctions that would follow exposure. As the stigma of illegitimacy has lessened through the years, the need for hiding should have diminished; but the closed system has not reach that conclusion. Why? As the birthfamily was gradually viewed less negatively, they were perceived as more effective rivals and therefore more frightening. As a result, the reason for secrecy has shifted from birthparents dodging shame to adoptive parents avoiding birthparents because they misperceive them as adversaries.

As symbolized by the television birthmother claiming health while hiding her identity, closed adoption is uncomfortably based on contradictory messages. It claims to appreciate birthparents, yet the endorsement of hiding implicitly conveys the message, "You really are unacceptable." Something does not add up between the messages, "You did a good and brave thing" and "We will help you hide from being detected." Many eye this inconsistency and conclude that the first message is in error. I believe it is the second message that merits reconsideration.

Adoption desperately wants to be viewed positively, but that is not possible as long as it is rooted in shame. Shame seriously detracts from the vitality of the institution. Adapting Kaufman's observation in *The Psychology of Shame* that shame is a "sickness of the soul," we might observe that shame is a sickness in the soul of the institution. It sullies the experience of all the players. It must be addressed and relieved. Adoption's only hope for health is to jettison its alliance with shame and embrace the dynamic of honor.

The Shame of Birthparents

Shame strikes deepest in the ranks of birthparents. It helps explain the pregnant woman somehow denying the intermittent soccer practices occurring in her belly. It explains the young man suddenly disowning his girlfriend of two years. As one birthmother recalled, "He broke up with me when he learned I was pregnant. He said he 'always wanted to marry a virgin.'"

Let's consider the shame of birthparents from the perspective of the five basic factors. As we identify the many sources of shame, we must remember that all the factors need not apply; it only takes one shaming dynamic to color the entire experience.

- **Defectiveness.** Pregnancy is exposure. The expectant mother is acutely conscious of her lost body shape and feels that she is on display. She may also feel defective because she managed her sexuality ineffectively.

- **Powerlessness.** The birthmother is in an unfavorable circumstance that she is unable to fix. Although every cell in her body cries out to stay attached to her baby, she cannot find a way to satisfactorily carry out that craving, so she feels a great sense of failure. Birthfathers often feel a vague masculine responsibility to make things work and, as a result, may feel the shame of powerlessness intensely. Birthparents may also feel shame related to the sensation of being stuck and going nowhere in life.

- **Dirtiness.** Depending on the standards of her family and community, a birthmother may feel sinful and unacceptable in the sight of "good" people. She may feel that her relationship with the birthfather was too short to justify sexual involvement. Some feel the contempt of those who view her as a potential welfare mother.

- **Rejection.** Many birthmothers feel abandoned by the significant people in their lives. She may wonder, "Where is the baby's father? Where are my family and friends? How can God let this happen?" Although it is far less common than was previously the case, some birthparents are banished from their families and sent to remote locations. Not only does the typical birthmother feel rejected, she also feels rejecting. Virtually every birthmother fears that her child will interpret the adoption as an act of rejection and chose some day to reject her in turn.

- **Depersonalization.** Some birthmothers feel reduced to baby machines or incubators. One family with a penchant for anatomically correct language referred to their child's birthmother as the "uterus mother." Many birthparents are made to feel important only as long as their adoption decision is pending, but they feel dropped and discarded once the legal work has been accomplished.

Part of the problem is societal. We expect a great deal from mothers—and, of course, we need to. The dedication of mothers is so vital to the social order that it is frightening to in any manner lighten the expectation. In a demand that approaches taboo status, we forbid mothers from setting aside their parental responsibilities. The accepted societal script insists that a "good" mother will stick with her child no matter what. This requirement is considered more important than any other factor, including the crucial question of what is good for the child. In divorce proceedings, for example, a mother may recognize that the husband is the better caregiver, yet fight him for custody lest she appear to be a bad person. Her image is at stake, and it may be less painful to actually fail as a parent and possibly avoid detection than to be responsible and appear to be a failure.

Sadly, in comparison to our lofty expectations of mothers, our expectations of fathers are terribly modest. We have come to expect virtually nothing from them and are pleasantly surprised when they contribute in some way. Because expectations are so low, he may feel less pressure to take on the parental role, and his image is far less affected by the decision to set aside parental responsibilities. The judgment he feels is more internal and less societal.

Although we must appreciate and support the dedication of mothers and encourage the involvement of fathers, we also need an acceptable script for the reasonable transfer of parental responsibilities when that course best serves the child. The new script must not be a finding of failure or a disowning of interest. It should be understood as a gentle transfer of responsibility based on careful consideration, love, foresight, and personal conscience. On that basis, an adoption decision deserves to be supported, not second-guessed. Can we imagine a day when we unambivalently celebrate the entrustment decision as an extraordinary act of love?

Although societal attitudes have changed dramatically, many birthmothers still feel shame linked to the circumstances of conception. The pregnancy may be attributed to poor moral judgment, poor impulse control, or contraceptive failure. Those possibilities leave her feeling fallen, foolish, or feckless. Shame may also be related to the procreative partner. In that regard, the options are similarly unflattering. Perhaps she made a poor choice of companion. Maybe she "can't hold her man." Was the relationship sufficiently substantial, we wonder, to justify sexual involvement?

In the minds of many, the birthparent decision is controversial and subject to various interpretations. Either it is a shame-generating decision:

- She did not care (rejection).
- She gave up too easily (rejection, powerlessness).
- She was more concerned with herself (rejection, defectiveness).
- She couldn't find another way (powerlessness).
- She was forced (powerlessness, depersonalization).
- She was tricked (powerlessness, defectiveness).
- She was unsupported (rejection, defectiveness).
- She was ineffective in the parental role; she was in over her head (defectiveness).
- She was paralyzed by fear (powerlessness).
- She took the easy path or shirked responsibility (defectiveness).

Or it is an honor-based decision:

- It was the sensible thing to do (smart, competent).
- It was the most loving and tender thing to do (respectful, sacrificial).
- It was a response to conscience, "the right thing to do" (moral conviction).
- The child will fare better (sacrificial).
- It was damage control; raising the child herself would have been more difficult on the child than the separation (practical, intelligent).
- It was a genuinely better choice for the child, offering more love, more stability, more joy, more health, and more opportunity (competent, affirming).
- It was a reduction of the role but not of the love (loving, responsible).

Some people rank shamefulness according to their own life views. For instance, it may be less shameful to be forced, tricked, or unsupported than to freely chose adoption. Or choosing adoption may feel to the birthparent like the vacating of responsibility and rejection of the child. This may explain why some parents are not able to carry out their adoption plans, even when they are convinced it is best. They could possibly endure the loss if it were imposed on them, but they cannot carry out the choice of their own volition. I noted earlier that shame can lead birthparents to adoption. Shame can also prohibit it.

Shame can be activated by a variety of people in the birthparent's circle. Family members are especially powerful. The father who responds to the news of pregnancy with, "I love you, but I'll never think of you the same way," stirs immense feelings of shame. The mother who has faced reproductive decisions of her own is an important figure in the shame equation, as are grandmothers. Their compassion or lack of understanding makes a vast difference to the birthmother. Shame can be generated by encounters with heroic mothers who found ways against all odds to keep their families together. Struggling single parents can also evoke this shame. Judgmental professionals can convey society's disapproval with a sigh, a look of contempt, or chilly indifference.

Shame is stirred for birthparents in a variety of circumstances. Mother's Day, with its annual cascade of accolades for the special love of mothers, is invariably difficult for them. Songs, movies, and television programs that celebrate heroic overcoming are often hard on birthparents. The common but damning praise, "Your decision was wonderful—I could never do that," is often understood to mean, "How could you do such a thing?"

The Shame of Adoptive Parents

Adoptive parent shame usually originates from three sources: infertility, the experience of gaining at another's expense, and a profound sense of powerlessness that leaves them feeling like beggars.

- **Defectiveness.** Because of infertility, adoptive parents are unable to accomplish what most people appear to do naturally and effortlessly. The defect is embedded in the aspect of human experience that is most vulnerable to shame—sexuality. One adoptive father commented that he wanted to put a paper bag over his head when went he went for his infertility checkups. The emphasis on pathology that was launched by the infertility specialists is often sustained by a suspicious adoption system.

- **Powerlessness.** Infertility leaves prospective adoptive parents dependent on the system. They are required to prove themselves to others who may, in many ways, be less capable than they. They feel like they need to set aside their dignity and sell themselves.

- **Dirtiness.** When a couple's sex life is ruled by the calendar and thermometer, romance and tenderness become elusive. They begin to wonder if money might accomplish what love could not. Families feel like vultures when it sinks in that their dreams can only be realized as a consequence of devastating loss experienced by others.

- **Rejection.** Many infertile couples feel cosmic abandonment. In more practical terms, they fear that they may not appeal to birthparents. Even very self-confident and extroverted families feel anxiety that they may not be chosen. Some resent the need to prove themselves to birthparents whom they privately view as youthful, inexperienced, and unaccomplished.

- **Depersonalization.** As adoptive father Dan Wolf puts it, pursuers of fertility are "herded through an industry of stainless steel, stirrups, and petri dishes."[*] In the adoption arena, the cold trappings of medicine are replaced with social work's chilly forms, computer checks, and relentless meetings that invariably begin with clumsy personal introductions.

Sometimes, it seems that the adoption system deliberately seeks to destroy what little dignity the medical world leaves intact. Prospective parents are required to prove their worth to bureaucrats with yellow pads. It is as though they are guilty until they prove themselves innocent. Where the medical process requires extraordinary physical exposure, the adoptive process insists on emotional exposure. Participants are asked to share their private thoughts and feelings. It is unnerving, for the system is hard to read. Prospective parents feel pressure to be simultaneously honest and perfect. Given these incompatible expectations, something has to give. If trust in the system is low, this dilemma is especially disconcerting.

---

[*] *From undated personal correspondence.*

Adoptive parents must come to terms with the fact that their joy comes at the expense of the birthfamily's anguish. Decades ago, when the stigma of illegitimacy was far greater than now, adoption was framed as a favor that adoptive parents did for birthparents. That day has passed, and it is now obvious that the adoptive parents are the beneficiaries of adoption. Although some try to ignore this reality, it cannot be avoided for long. If they acknowledge the grief of birthparents, how can they respond? How does one deal with indebtedness of this scale? How does one begin to balance the scales and achieve a measure of interpersonal comfort? How does one avoid the taint of exploitation?

The newest potential source of shame for adoptive parents is, to use a word from the newly revised Michigan adoption code, "solicitation." Contemporary adoptive parents are expected to solicit the attention and favor of birthparents. It is an ill-chosen but revealing word that, according to *Webster's*, carries such ignoble meanings as "beg," "tempt," "lure," and "deceive." Perhaps one is not surprised by indignities at the hands of professionals conducting their necessary inquiries, but one does not ordinarily expect to be insulted by the law itself.

The Shame of Adoptees

The impact of shame varies greatly among adoptees because their dispositional susceptibility to it differs and because their experiences are so diverse. Some feel its grip acutely, whereas others respond with a shrug of the emotional shoulders. Some view adoption very positively and do not consider shame a factor in their experience. On a rational level at least, most adoptees feel little responsibility for the institution's shortcomings since they were never in a position to make any of the decisions. For many adoptees, shame is an unrecognized dynamic underlying their lives. They may be touchy, for example, about situations in which they do not have control. They may be especially sensitive to the hazards of interpersonal rejection. They may feel vague discomfort when there is too much discussion of stray cats and orphaned children, but they do not usually link these sensations to shame. Recognized or not, however, shame is potentially a powerful dynamic in the lives of adoptees.

Defectiveness. Many adoptees conclude that there must be some personal shortcoming about them that explains their birthmother's decision to release them for adoption. Something about them, they reason, made them unacceptable and difficult to love.

Powerlessness. The chief complaint of many adoptees is that other people—birthparents, adoptive parents, and bureaucrats—make the important decision in their lives.

Dirtiness. Adoptees realize that they were "illegitimate." Some struggle with the idea that they are the fruit of unstable relationships or the products of unwanted pregnancies. Secrecy suggests to them that there is some very dark reality that must be covered up.

Rejection. Many adoptees feel abandoned. They may feel like orphans and objects of pity. They know that before they gained a family, they lost a family. They are tempted by the interpretation of events that suggests they were inconvenient and expendable.

Depersonalization. Barred access to their original names, and lacking detailed information about their origins, many adoptees feel disconnected from the generational process. It feels to them that an important part of themselves is not acknowledged and does not even exist in the eyes of others. There is no more powerful symbol of identity than one's name. People who know their name and the history of their naming process take its power for granted and are unable to identify with the depth of despair felt by those who lack this basic information. Denied rights automatically afforded to others, adoptees feel devalued. When they learn that an important aspect of their becoming part of an adoptive family was money, they may feel like commodities with price tags.

Occasionally, adoptees borrow shame from others. They may feel shame for "causing" the shame of the birthparents, or they may feel ashamed of their birthparents' shameful circumstances. Lynd writes about shame borrowed from parents:

> Shame for one's parents can pierce deeper than shame for oneself.... No matter how disgusted I am with myself, in some respects I can perhaps change. But the fact that these are my parents, that I am fruit of their loins, is unchangeable.

Other adoptees feel shame that they cannot measure up to the fantasy child desired by their adoptive parents.

Adoptees are especially vulnerable to shame. For them, adoption is not a set of behaviors; it is a matter of the self, a question of identity. If there is an unhealthy quality to the adoption process, it is incorporated into their beings, their souls—and that is where shame prefers to seek residence.

REMEDIES FOR SHAME

We have seen that shame is rooted in our most fundamental appraisals of ourselves. It is an insidious dynamic. We are so sensitive to the intense discomfort of shame, that we actively resist any careful consideration of the theme in our lives, thereby shutting down the prospect of relief. It is never a simple matter to address issues of shame. It may be a simple matter to list possible avenues of relief, but it is decidedly difficult to do the actual hard work of healing shame.

Awareness

There is no possibility to overcome shame if it is denied. The first step is to interrupt the hiding process and replace it with an effort to recognize and confront the shame. This small but vital step requires great emotional strength and courage. We need to distinguish between a healthy sense of shame and un-healthy shame. We need to take responsibility for our actions, because this not only offers the prospect of correcting the original error, it goes some distance toward restoring our sense of being appropriate and effective persons.

Ownership

One reason we are pessimistic about relieving shame is our impression that its source is in the contemptuous hearts of the people around us. In *The Culture of Shame*, psychiatrist Andrew Morrison writes,

> Only when we realize and accept that it is *our own judgment* about ourselves that is so painful and de-structive—far more painful than such judgment by another—are we able to contain and alter it. To the degree that shame becomes experienced as a *product of our own doing* can we free ourselves from its domination.

Recognizing that shame is within our own domain, we gain a little optimism that it may be possible to make repairs.

Expectations

Shame can completely disorient us. Much of the shame in adoption is irrational. Morrison attributes much shame to our insistence on imposing impossible standards on ourselves. He suggests,

> I find it helpful to try to articulate the ideals that cause us to feel imperfect or inadequate....When these underlying ideals have been expressed, we can experience them dispassionately, holding them up to the light of scrutiny and judgment.

He goes on to argue for reasonable personal standards.

If shame is to be relieved, we need to rework our "self-talk," the attributions we assign to ourselves. Those who are in the grip of shame need to suspend their inclination to condemn themselves summarily and irrevocably and conduct dispassionate and thorough reviews of the experience, particularly in the light of freshly reviewed personal standards. They may discover that their behavior and decisions are more acceptable than they had previously concluded. Perhaps they will discover that the shame is deserved, but there is an even greater chance they will find it is unfounded.

Guilt

As I asked before, how do we fix a person? It is too large a project. If possible, it is very useful to reframe a circumstance of shame from shame to guilt. That is not to say, of course, that guilt is a great state of mind, but it is far more amenable to amelioration than is shame. The guilty person usually has more avenues leading to peace of mind.

Forgiveness

To confess our failures is to face them. That is the first advantage of forgiveness. When forgiveness occurs, the sting of the offense is diminished. We cannot erase our memories of painful failings or the damage that was done, but we can gain a more realistic understanding of ourselves that features greater acceptance of our imperfections. The intertwined experiences of forgiving and being forgiven are exquisite markers along the path of healing.

Small Dignities

Even in overwhelming, devastating, and mortifying circumstances, there are often small beachheads of personal dignity to be savored. These small victories take endless forms—a small act defying a repressive power, something done more thoroughly than necessary, a gesture of tenderness accomplished in the context of tremendous stress—and give the recovering person a place to begin. Shame recedes in the presence of dignity.

Courage and Community

Genuine community is an obvious remedy for isolation, but it is a form of relief that goes against the alienating current of shame. It is easy to forget that everybody experiences shame, so we think that our horror is unprecedented. In the aftermath of an experience of shame, it takes great courage to counter the urge to hide and reenter community. This is especially true when significant people reinforce the shame and encourage hiding. It is worth the effort, however, because, as Smedes puts it in *Shame and Grace*, "The experience of being accepted is the beginning of healing for the feeling of being unacceptable." In *No Place to Hide*, Michael Nichols astutely observes, "The self gains strength from becoming part of a web of relationships, not by accumulating power and not by becoming self sufficient."

Those who have been touched by the shame of adoption have found particular healing in support groups. There they have found the understanding and acceptance they needed to move beyond isolation. In the company of peers, they are able to reinterpret their stories and rediscover their honor. They grow from having friends believe in them.

Humor

An important but initially difficult remedy for shame is laughter. In the midst of our shameful circumstances, we have no inclination to laugh; but sometimes it comes with the passage of time. When it does, it magically changes our perspective on the gravity of the situation and lightens the heaviness of the shame. Through humor, we stand a chance to escape our self-consciousness and look at the situation as an outsider might.

When I share my ideas with professionals about desirable qualities in adoptive parents, I suggest that humor is frosting on the cake. They invariably mount a campaign to promote it to the *indispensable* category. They do not build a particularly strong rationale for this elevated status, they "just know it's really important." Their reaction reflects their intuitive response to shame. Mary Jo Rillera, an especially insightful adoption reformer, has collected the humor of adoption—cartoons, jokes and comical stories—for years, no doubt because of the same intuition.

Celebration

Pride, honor, delight, progress, health, and joy are all antithetical to shame and are worth pursuing as a remedy to shame. It is not, of course, the shameful event that we celebrate—that is not honest, desirable or even possible—but we can celebrate our redemption from our moments of anguish. We can find joy in our movement beyond personal tragedy, and, if we choose, we can share this joyful capacity to overcome with the people we love. Perhaps, in the middle of celebration—and, of all things, drawing attention to the movement from despair to triumph—our heart begins to entertain the idea that the abhorrent event is perhaps not as shameful as we previously believed.

Grace

Spiritual persons know that ultimate healing is always a matter of grace. Lewis Smedes writes in *Shame and Grace*, "Grace heals our shame...by removing the one thing all our shame makes us fear the most: rejection." There is inexpressible comfort in the realization that, even in the throes of relentless self-loathing, we are held in God's amazing grace.

VALUES-BASED OPEN ADOPTION AND SHAME

The best way to deal with shame, of course, is to prevent it. This means learning from past errors and correcting them to the best of our ability. The values-based system is organized to keep participants within the bounds of their value systems. That is important, because shame enters the process through the violation of standards. Open adoption in optimal form brings some remedy to each of the five factors of shame.

Defectiveness. Values-based open adoption has a healing quality. It detoxifies imperfection and transforms it into a potential source of personal strength and a basis for mutual understanding with others.

Powerlessness. Open adoption encourages autonomy and provides opportunities for participants to make the major decisive that affect their futures. It transforms the interdependence that exists at the core of adoption from a source of fear to a source of delight.

Dirtiness. The luminescence of candor is very contrary to dirtiness. The idealism and optimism of values-based open adoption creates an aura that is anything but dirty. Hiding implies the existence of something repulsive, but availability expresses normalcy.

Rejection. The children of open adoption are not abandoned to unknown facts; they are entrusted to carefully selected adoptive families. There is a commitment to inclusion, which means families are brought together rather than separated.

Depersonalization. In well-implemented values-based open adoption, everyone is acknowledged and affirmed. In a healthy community, everyone counts.

Privacy

Secrecy is linked to shame, but so is exposure. Is open adoption a form of exposure? Does open adoption produce its own version of shame? Perhaps the best way to approach the question is to consider the issue of privacy, the primary defense against exposure. Privacy is a subject of great interest to supporters of open adoption as well as detractors. It is an important ingredient in healthy open adoption, but it is also a potential impediment. This dual nature makes it is vital for us to understand it and know how to work with it.

Privacy is an important aspect of personal mental health. It is essential for autonomy, individuality, and maturity. Privacy is often confused with secrecy. Not everyone wanting privacy desires secrecy, but most people wanting secrecy will claim privacy because it has a more respectable aura. Privacy is best understood as voluntary restriction of two factors: personal disclosure and sociability. The following series of simple graphs will help make the variations and implications of privacy as conspicuous as possible.

Let's consider the element of disclosure first. Each extreme of disclosure—secrecy and exposure—is related to shame. Secrecy is the lead symptom of shame, and exposure is an

Figure 1

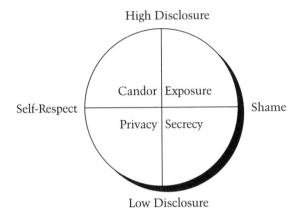

important precipitant of shame. Graphing the relationship between shame and disclosure, the first dimension of privacy, is helpful.

Figure 1 suggests four styles of disclosure: secrecy, privacy, candor, and exposure. Chapter 4 addressed secrecy and candor, so we will limit this discussion to exposure and privacy.

Exposure is disclosure that is beyond our control. It is the loss of control that distinguishes exposure from candor, which is volitional. When personal control is lost, the cost is high. We lose our boundaries, the standards that organize us and make us unique. Significantly, we lose that aspect of ourselves referred to as personal. Exposure violates our dignity and diminishes our personhood. We become less free and less human.

Privacy protects us from soul-shriveling exposure. In *Shame, Exposure, and Privacy*, Carl Schneider states the case for privacy well: "When society does not provide for privacy, being apart can only take the form of hiding." His point is illustrated by the reclusive lifestyles led by celebrities trying to escape the burden of relentless public attention. Indisputably, we all need time apart. In the privacy of our inner circle we can relax and let down our guard. In moments of solitude, we recover our strength and explore our greatest depth. Privacy allows us to make decisions that are not tainted by the whims and pressures of public opinion. And, of course, much of the good we accomplish is better done privately than publicly.

So we see from Figure 1 that the options for healthy disclosure are privacy and candor. Does this mean they are equally

Figure 2

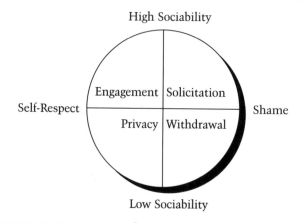

positive in the realm of adoption? To address that question we need to consider the second aspect of privacy, *sociability*, which I define as receptivity to interaction with others.

Private people choose to limit their sociability. As a matter of personal style, they prefer to interact with a limited number of people and elect to restrict their availability to others. The sociability factor can also be graphed relative to shame, as in Figure 2.

When sociability is distributed across a continuum of shame, we discover four styles of interaction: withdrawal, privacy, engagement, and solicitation. The healthy alternatives relative to sociability are privacy and engagement, whereas withdrawal and solicitation are related to shame. I mentioned solicitation earlier as an uncomfortable new activity expected of prospective adoptive parents. A solicitous person is so eager to interact with others that she may set aside her usual independence. Whereas exposure threatened personal boundaries involuntarily, the solicitous seeking of acceptance threatens them voluntarily. The shamelessness of the beggar, the brownnoser, and the ambitious social climber all come to mind. We cringe as we see them trade their personal dignity for conditional and temporary favor. As adoption becomes increasingly commercial, the shame of solicitation grows more common. As I write this chapter, an adoptive family is advertising in the local newspaper. Their advertisement, which oddly features their affection for chickadees, is uncomfortably lodged between ads for septic tank cleaning and a one-way ticket to Phoenix.

In each figure, privacy shows up in the healthy region. In Figure 1, it is the alternative to candor; in Figure 2, it is the

Figure 3

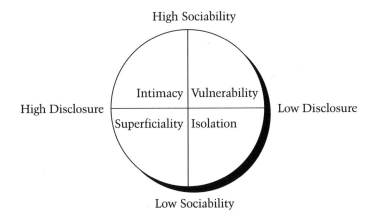

alternative to engagement. How does it hold up when we graph the relationship between disclosure and sociability? Figure 3 suggests four options for involvement: isolation, superficiality, vulnerability, and intimacy. Privacy appears less pleasing when its two elements are considered together. It produces the options of isolation, superficiality, or vulnerability. Obviously, intimacy, the alternative based on high disclosure and high sociability, has the greatest potential. Intimacy is available to those who have the courage to meaningfully share themselves with others.

A person may choose to be private and mysterious, but in doing so he is likely choosing to not relate fully; making that choice brings predictable losses. Prospective adoptive parents who expect to be chosen to receive a child without any disclosure or availability are saying to birthparents, "You'll just have to trust us," without providing any basis for that massive trust. On the other hand, the adoptive parent who exposes too much too soon may regret it and make a subsequent overcorrection toward isolation. Similarly, the birthparent who shares too little withholds vital information from the child and all who would serve her, whereas the birthparent who shares all may feel too exposed and vulnerable. She may need to retreat to regain her sense of privacy. Personal privacy must be artfully weighed against the reasonable need that others have for information.

Everyone involved in adoption has a great need to know about the others involved. If this need to know is put into the language of rights, the situation can easily become a struggle for power. More promisingly, if the tension between the need for privacy and the need for information can be put into the context of a meaningful relationship, and everyone is helped to understand the reasons for privacy and the basis for the other's need to know, resolution is usually not a problem. Unilateral disclosure can be unnerving, but a gradual process of mutual disclosure feels safer. If the disclosure of information is organized as a mutual process, the vulnerability is lessened. Ideally, everyone involved is eager to accommodate the need of others for information, insofar as decency allows. They want to be known so they can be more fully loved and appreciated. Those who accommodate will do well in adoption. Those who assert their desire for privacy may find themselves retaining their rights but not participating in adoption.

Not only must participants be willing to accommodate the needs of others, they must appreciate and respect the accommodation of others. Accommodation and respect are important dimensions of working out a mutually satisfying plan. If these factors are absent and participants find it difficult to work out details, it may signal that the families are not well-suited for each other.

Accommodation and respect lead naturally to candor and engagement, the key factors that allow for intimacy. For intimacy to emerge in a relationship, the people involved must set aside some personal privacy while protecting collective privacy. The intimacy of an open adoption relationship requires privacy. Respectful adoptive parents do not tell the private stories of the birthparents and their children to everybody they meet. Many details are important for them to know as parents, but no one else needs to know. Similarly, birthparents may learn details about the adoptive parents that are best kept within the adoption triad. Respectful adoptive parents and birthparents are careful about whom they bring into each other's lives.

Strangely, open adoption participants sometimes afford each other too much respect and find themselves in "courtesy standoffs." Typically in these situations, the birthmother subdues her intense curiosity because she does not want to intrude on the adoptive parents' need for private time with the baby. Meanwhile, the adoptive parents are besides themselves with the desire to know how the birthmother is doing, but they choose to not contact her because they do not want to interrupt her grieving process. Obviously, one or the other of them needs to delicately reach out to the other. It takes time, effort, and sensitivity to work out the degrees of trust and intimacy.

Adoption practitioners must be alert to situations in which the process can inadvertently generate shame:

- **Profound intimacy.** The most emotionally intense moment in the adoption drama occurs when the birthparents separate from the baby. We try to arrange for the moment to occur in privacy, away from spectators and gawkers. We have also learned that the worker may initially be a central figure in the relationship between birthparents and adoptive parents but will quickly work his way to the sidelines. As their relationship becomes primary, the worker's connection becomes secondary. Although he may remain an honorary member of the clan, he becomes an outsider, and there may be intensely intimate moments in the experience when outsiders do not belong. Some moments of joy and pain are so intimate that the worker is present only by invitation.

- **Inappropriate gathering and handling of information.** Thoroughness in getting to know people requires inquiry into areas that are usually considered private. If practitioners ask questions tactlessly, respondents may feel uncomfortably exposed.

- **Putting people on display.** In the escalating competition to garner the attention of potential birthparents, promoters are continually devising new methods for "displaying their wares." They look for clever ways to draw attention to prospective adoptive families. Some families have greater tolerance for this than others. For some, it feels like shameful exposure.

- **Expectations of perfection.** Although it is important for practitioners to set high standards for their constituency, distinguishing these expectations from perfection is crucial. Judged by standards of perfection, we are all—workers included—candidates for shame. To the extent they explicitly or implicitly expect perfection, whatever that is, adoption systems will generate shame. Our expectations need to be reworked so we are more interested in the way people handle their failures than we are in their particular errors.

Sensitive professionals can make a great difference. Some privacy can be comfortably sacrificed in the context of a respectful program carried out by a trustworthy worker.

Professionals build trust and rapport when they take time to find some common ground with participants. Appropriate self-disclosure helps the information-gathering process feel more like a conversation than an interrogation. Playfulness adds a lightness to the process and keeps it from taking on a judgmental tone.

Because it generates high expectations, and because its outcomes are visible for all to see, open adoption may generate opportunities for guilt and shame that were not possible in the closed system. Some birthparents may discover that spending time with the baby stimulates their sense of shame. Participants may feel shabby about commitments and relationships they fail to nurture. Each open adoption relationship is begun on the basis of very positive regard for one another, and participants may feel embarrassed if they are not able to live up to the lofty images held by the others. In an open adoption community, comparisons are inevitable, and they are another potent source of shame. An adoptee, for example, may feel ashamed of her birthmother who is less involved than her brother's birthmother.

The new frontiers of shame in adoption are solicitation and exploitation, and it is entirely possible that the commercial system will generate as much shame as the secretive system that preceded it. The remedy for any shame-based system of adoption—secretive or commercially exploitative—is honor. If we are serious about transforming adoption into a healthy institution, we will learn to respect and affirm the best in each other. We will learn to honor and uphold the people on whom we depend.

Chapter 14

Adoption Without Haste

The action of those whose lives are given to the Spirit has in it something of the leisure of eternity; and because of this, they achieve far more than those whose lives are enslaved by the rush and hurry, the unceasing tick-tick of the world.

Evelyn Underhill, *The Spiritual Life*

He who is in a hurry delays the things of God.

St. Vincent de Paul*

When it comes to adoption, it is never well for it to be done too quickly.

Randolph Severson, *Adoption: Charms and Rituals for Healing*

Adoption these days is preoccupied with speed. It wants to be fast. Adoptive parents want it, birthparents want it, and adoption professionals appear to want it as well. Programs advertise that they "specialize in the rapid placement of healthy newborns." With books catching attention with the promise to help accomplish an adoption within a year, adoption's first million seller will no doubt herald the prospect of adopting "the child you want" by sundown. Why this fascination with speed?

---

* *Quoted by Evelyn Underhill in* The Spiritual Life, *Oxford: Oneworld, 1993.*

Speed, a child of time, is a relative thing. Its desirability often depends on one's vantage point. Some adoptive parents, for example, take a very long time deciding to trust adoption as a way to build their families but want birthparents to settle on adoption very speedily. When it comes to speed, the Golden Rule is often set aside. Many people gloating about their speedy adoptions seem oblivious to the impact of their behavior on others. Is the person who flies past a two-mile line of creeping traffic, puts on his turn signal, and capitalizes on the good nature and kindness of some patient motorist to be saluted for his cleverness? Much of the emphasis on speed is little more than an effort to bypass orderly process. Sadly, the success of the speedy usually comes at the expense of those with fewer resources.

There are times for speed and times to go slow. Examples of each circumstance abound. Speed is desirable, for example, when ripping off a bandage, responding to a heart attack, fleeing disaster, or approaching a great book sale. When excitement is high, we are inclined to go fast. Deliberation and patience, on the other hand, are wise when contemplating marriage, making a major purchase, producing fine wine, or training aircraft mechanics. When the stakes are high, our usual impulse is to go slow.

THE PRESSURE FOR SPEED

The emphasis on speedy adoption is at least partially understandable. It is consistent with life as we know it. In a world of fast food and on-the-spot credit, we are so accustomed to seeing things happen quickly that we are not quite sure how to handle projects that take time. Delayed gratification is a conceptual artifact from a quaint, long-ago era. Furthermore, we are all familiar with genuine longing. We know what it means to want something so badly we can hardly stand it, and chances are we have all driven the people around us crazy with our impatience. There is more, however, to the pressure for speed in adoption than normal longing. Many factors are involved.

Relief from fear. In *Let Go of Fear*, Carlos Valles clearly describes the relationship between fear and haste:

> Fear makes us feel insecure, and in our insecurity we readily turn to whatever can make us feel safe again.

We are impatient with insecurity, we cannot bear being long in a state of uncertainty, and we rush to protection and clarity at whatever cost.... Fear makes us shake, in our minds more than in our bodies, and so we grab at the first prop that may steady our faltering stand. In our weakness we fall an easy prey to any dispenser of certainty.

Relief from shame. In Chapter 13, we noted that adoption is prone to shame. Shame is intolerably painful, and we want it over as quickly as possible. Discomfort with shame is a major source of the urgency felt by birthparents.

Urgency. The institution of adoption inherits problems generated by an infertility industry that often holds people too long. Having tarried in the pursuit of fertility, couples are acutely conscious of a window of opportunity to adopt that appears to narrow with each passing day. Birthparents also feed the urgency dynamic. When a pregnancy is denied, the opportunity for leisurely adoptive preparations is lost and the arrangements take on an eleventh hour flavor of flurry and frenzy.

Promotion. Adoption promoters dislike deliberation because it has the potential to undo adoption plans. To avoid the costly possibility of a change of heart, they encourage a brisk pace in the decision-making process.

Convenience. Sometimes, adoptions happen rapidly for the simple reason that the law allows it. Adoption statues may prohibit, for example, the taking of a relinquishment signature for 48 hours after a child is born. There is not much emotional difference between 47 hours and 49 hours; but because decisions are permitted at that point, they are sought. The need to relieve uncertainty is apparently more important than careful, clearheaded decision making. Occasionally, adoption decisions are made quickly because geographic distance makes delay impractical.

Bonding and attachment. The most compelling rationale for moving briskly is the attraction of situating a child in his permanent home promptly. This goal must be balanced with the equally important goal of arranging a gentle transition. Because bonding and attachment is the most acceptable rationale for expeditious movement, it is often used to justify swift placement procedures actually based on other motives.

Efficiency. A fast-moving process is potentially efficient, a quality that can contain costs and increase profits.

THE DOWNSIDE OF SPEED

So we see that the pressure for speed is formidable. It is fueled by a powerful combination of attraction and fear—a tandem that is difficult to resist. As we examine the current fascination with speed, however, we must keep in mind the extraordinary negative potential of speed. Let's consider the darker side of this cavalier emphasis on speed.

Mistakes. There are reasons we associate the expression *living dangerously* with speed. Fast-moving processes are prone to oversight and error. When one cuts corners and suspends usual precautions, tragic results are possible.

Pressure. Speed builds momentum and generates pressure. Many people find that pressure impairs their ability to think. They lose composure and settle for the first possible solution to emerge. In pressured circumstances, prospects for regret grow exponentially. Chapter 6, on the blessing of choice, pointed out that open adoptions satisfy in direct correlation to the extent of the birthparents' blessing. If birthparents feel pressured and disgruntled, all members of the triad may pay an excruciating price in the years that follow.

Circular process. Impatient prospective adoptive parents are busy these days beating the bushes in hopes of discovering potential birthparents. The intensity of this effort is not lost on families dealing with untimely pregnancies. As they feel the growing pressure to choose adoption, they become increasingly guarded and reluctant to reveal any potential interest in adoption for fear someone will twist their arm. Often, this means that potential birthparents emerge late in the pregnancy, thereby setting a rushed process into motion.

Isolation. If speed is everything, other families interested in adoption are competitors. If everyone is a competitor, where is community to be found?

Superficiality. In our hurry to arrange adoptions, we often fail to see birthparents as multidimensional persons. We overlook their hurts and capabilities, and we fail to understand them as symptom bearers. The energy that could be directed toward helping them in a time of incomparable stress is instead focused on garnering their early commitment so that everyone else involved will feel comfortable.

Changed tone. Optimal adoption has an aura of dignity. Hasty adoption does not. It is better if words like *restless, impetuous, hectic, rushed,* or *hurried* are not linked to adoption. They are words seldom associated with quality.

SPEED AS A SYMPTOM

Fascination with speed in adoption is revealing. Where speed is featured, a commercial approach to adoption is in effect. In the commercial approach to adoption, which I discuss in Chapter 15, speed makes sense. If adoption is organized as a service for prospective adoptive parents, an emphasis on speed is understandable. They are, after all, incredibly eager to try out their parental wings, and a good outfit does not keep customers waiting. The emphasis on speed also makes sense when adoption is approached as a transaction. If adoption is considered a mechanical process—a matter of acquiring desired goods—there is no reason for hesitation or deliberation. If adoption is viewed as a simple problem-solving process, it is desirable to solve the problems rapidly and move on.

On the other hand, if adoption is understood as a service to children, speed is not so interesting. From the perspective of children, compatibility and stability are the vital issues, not speed. If adoption is approached as the building of a permanent relationship, it makes sense to proceed at a sensible pace. We expedite transactions but nurture relationships.

The fascination with speed is a symptom of self-gratification. Speed is not about giving, it is about getting. When adoption is framed as an opportunity to care sacrificially for others, speed is irrelevant. In fact, in a child-focused open adoption program, speed is most likely a source of concern. When an adoption comes together with accidental speed, conscientious professionals experience it more as a source of worry than of pleasure.

Preoccupation with speed is often a symptom of doubt, desperation, and lost hope. Desperation is an enemy of quality adoption, not a friend. It is based in emotion and leaves little room for reason. Desperate people lose their usual multidimensional perspective; they focus narrowly on the goal without considering the broader view. This makes them erratic and unpredictable. They are so focused on their goal that they are inclined to lock onto immediate solutions with little regard for long-term consequences. If we are interested in adoptions of enduring quality, we must not capitulate to and empower desperation. We must take the time to understand desperation, relieve it, and calm it down. Adoptions of quality are built on convictions, not personal doubts.

The desperation that prospective adoptive families feel is rooted in a powerful conglomeration of confusing factors—urgency, woundedness, deprivation, anger, and fear—each of which needs attention. It begins with a sense of urgency. Prospective adoptive parents are acutely conscious of the passage of time. They typically leave the infertility treadmill feeling wounded and exhausted, their arms aching with emptiness. This emptiness dominates their consciousness. Somehow, fate has denied them something that the rest of the world appears to take for granted, and they are incensed with the unfairness of it all. The situation feels out of control, and they are afraid their dreams will never be realized. They want action. Anything, they reason, even if it is inherently unstable, is better than nothing.

Although birthparents are familiar with most of these feelings, many have only one thing on their mind—RELIEF. Their circumstances generate tremendous pressure, which they hope will somehow magically end. They are often desperate for relief and resolution. Like a toothache, the emotional discomfort of birthparents is typically so great that it dominates; relief is all that matters.

A quality program does not simply pat desperate people on the back, wish them well, and send them out to find and negotiate with potential partners for adoption. Operating from a state of single-minded desperation, their efforts may be counterproductive to their long-term goals. A quality program works wholeheartedly to relieve their driving sense of urgency. It calms their desperation by establishing a pace that allows time for necessary and productive recuperation and healing. It relieves urgency with the balm of reasonable hope and gently reminds good people of their usual standards of kindness and consideration for others.

THE CASE FOR PACE

The challenge is getting people beyond short-range thinking. It is not an easy matter. In a crisis, relief is all we ask. We are willing to pay a big price later for a little relief at the moment. When the time comes to pay, however, we predictably resent it. Driven by a short-term perspective, people think they want a child on any terms. From a long-term perspective, what they really want is a child on positive terms. They want a healthy circumstance and a full sense of entitlement. When prospective adoptive parents pause for a moment of reflection, they realize that long-term peace of mind is their ultimate goal. If a sense of urgency is fueled and allowed to dominate, the long-term goal is easily overlooked.

Adoption is best accomplished with a dignified and reasonable sense of pace—a pace found somewhere between a runaway freight train and mindless dawdling. The optimal pace will neither be too fast nor too slow; it acknowledges the enormity of the circumstances and allows each participant to function with respect and concern for the others involved. Adoptions with healthy pace offer several advantages over hasty procedures:

Foresight. Deliberation is the best defense against future regret and resentment. Foresight brings long-term contentment.

Confidence. The birthparent blessing is the key to satisfying open adoption. Without this blessing, adoptive parents will live with persistent anxiety about the birthparents, an anxiety that is sure to be transmitted to the adoptee.

Decency. Birthparent Brenda Romanchik recalls the days following her son's birth as a "hormonal hurricane," hardly an appropriate time to make a life-altering decision. Adoptions that are respectful and gentle produce good consciences.

Joy in the journey. A process with reasonable pace allows for preparation and anticipation. When the focus is exclusively on the destination, the beauty of the journey is lost.

Many people treat the time of waiting as an awful, wasteful time to be endured. Henri Nouwen takes a different view: "Patient living means to live actively in the present and wait there. Waiting, then, is not passive. It involves nurturing the moment."[*] The time of expectancy is to be nurtured. In *Time and*

---

[*] *Henri Nouwen. "Advent: Waiting." In* Seeds of Hope: A Henri Nouwen Reader. Robert Durback. (Ed.). New York: Bantam, 1989.

the Art of Living, Professor Robert Grudin, who has been hailed as a modern-day Emerson adds an important perspective on expectancy:

> Do not be impatient about the future when you know it contains good things. Instead, enjoy these as future things, as often and lingeringly as possible. Events can be enjoyed in all three dimensions of time: as future, present, and past. Impatience robs you of the first of these three enjoyments; and this is the sadder because the enjoyment of the future is by no means the least extensive of the three and contains qualities—a simplicity and a pure willingness—possessed by neither of the others.

The time of waiting can be a time of reflection and delicious anticipation. It is a time to savor the joys that already exist.

In *When the Heart Waits,* writer Sue Monk Kidd observes, "All lines must be kept moving. That's one of the primary rules of modernity. Movement is a kind of diversion from our inner misery." She goes on to share a profound insight: "When we keep the line moving forward at the expense of inward motion, something deep within us 'walks backwards.'" The more we narrow the contradiction between whom we are and who we hope to be, the greater our peace of mind. Well understood, patience is not self-denial; it is a matter of affirming and staying close to the best that exists within us. Ultimately, patience is a statement of faith.

A healthy sense of anticipation and expectancy is neither impatience nor complacency. In the words of Yale's Margaret Farley, it is a "relaxation of heart." She describes this state of being very clearly in *Personal Commitments:*

> "Relaxation" can be found in the center of "patience" when patience is strong enough to trust and wait for what "takes time." Relaxation of heart is the opposite of foolish patience (the tolerance of injustices or stupidities that can and ought to be changed here and now). Rather it is part of that patience which—while it is impatient for wholeness, for reason, for an end to irresponsibility—nevertheless refuses to close off in tightening bitterness. This kind of "relaxation" is not a "giving up" in premature surrender, not a

sterile or cowardly resignation. It does not fear to name nonsense or the unfairness that it must resist. Still, it waits even as it challenges; desires, even as it trusts.... Irritation and impatience are such "small" emotions, but without a certain relaxation of heart they can defeat our greatest passions.

We need this relaxation of heart to function in optimal fashion. It emphasizes being rather than doing. In adoption, the way of haste is preoccupied with the speedy discovery of relief. The way of relaxation, on the other hand, is concerned with carefully crafted connections that celebrate "goodness of fit." It aspires to relationships that serve children because they feature enduring compatibility between the families. Relaxation of heart allows a spirit of openness to emerge, a spirit of exceptional willingness to learn from the moment.

The trouble with speed is that it draws the attention that should be reserved for quality. Is adoption's priority speed or is it quality? They are not easily blended. If speed is the priority, quality is not. Since quality is fundamental, since it is in the fabric of the process, it is not something that can be tacked onto a hasty process as an afterthought. Quality takes time.

Why does quality take time? Part of the answer is that addressing the difficult aspects of adoption takes time. Shame, for example, is overcome only through very substantial and time-consuming work. That patient, painstaking work contrasts to the shortcut approach to shame—namely, denial. Denial is a quick defense, but it has very enduring effects. Instead of healing the negative dynamics, the hasty defense of denial drives them deep and installs them as continuing detractions, siphoning away all prospects for deep contentment. This is also true in dealing with fear and with the pain of loss. There is no way around the fact that healing requires time. Since the losses associated with adoption are great, the time necessary for healing is correspondingly great. Participants show respect for each other by being patient with each other's healing processes.

Developing the positive aspects of adoption also takes time. Clarity of mind, so crucial to effective decision making, requires deliberation. Relationships need time to mature and rise above superficiality. Learning from mistakes and triumphs takes hard work and time. Covenantal relationships seldom occur suddenly; they only emerge as trust grows. Communities also need seasoning if they are to become meaningful and enduring. When the emphasis is on speed, there is little opportunity for excellence to emerge.

Our children deserve something better than haste. As they grow older, it is doubtful they will be impressed with speed. Few will ask, "Was it fast, Dad? Was my adoption really fast?" Some day, though, they will surely ask about the quality of the process. "How did you find each other? Did you care for each other right away, or did it take a while? How did you know you were right for each other? How did you learn to trust each other? Was it a happy time?"

A week before his death, in *I Asked for Wonder,* Rabbi Abraham Heschel challenged the young to "above all, remember that the meaning of life is to build a life as if it were a work of art." He proposed that we live with an eye toward enduring beauty. We know that the artist of distinction attends to every detail with great intimacy, while keeping in mind its relation to the whole. In art, speed can be the difference between a masterpiece and a trinket. This is also true in adoption.

Chapter 15

Commercialism and Related Worries

Where there is no prophecy, the people will cast off restraint.

Proverbs 29:18 *(New Revised Standard Version)*

The poor are always prophetic. As true prophets always point out, they reveal God's design. That is why we should take time to listen to them. And that means staying near them, because they lack confidence in themselves because they have been broken and oppressed. But if we listen to them, they will bring us back to the things that are essential.

Jean Vanier, *Community and Growth*

We have failed to fight *for* right, *for* justice, *for* goodness; as a result we must fight *against* wrong, *against* injustice, *against* evil.

Abraham Heschel, *I Asked for Wonder*

The foremost challenge to quality adoption is no longer closed adoption. Rooted and wrapped in shame, the closed approach is hopelessly out of sync with contemporary birthfamilies and holds little appeal for them. The present and future enemy of thoughtful adoption is commercialization, a glitzy trend that suits the instant gratification mood of the age. It is a trend that may prove even more destructive than secrecy was in its day.

The transition from highly restrictive closed adoption to "anything goes" commercial adoption has been swift. One day, a program practices closed adoption, officially detesting open adoption. The next, it seems, they have prospective adoptive parents advertising and tracking down pregnant women, by-passing the reasonable alternative of classic, nonaggressive open adoption. The institution is swiftly shifting from a professional model, in which service providers hang their shingles and aspire to suspended self-interest, to a business model that aggressively recruits consumers on a buyer-beware basis. An age of commercialism is upon us.

Although I am convinced that adoption should not become a business, I do not mean this as an assault on the business world. Certainly, there is much to be learned from the business community. With its emphasis on practicality, research, ethics, and generosity, business at its best sets an impressive tone that adoption practitioners do well to emulate. To its great credit, the business world is exceptionally sensitive to the interests of its constituency. All that excellence notwithstanding, adoption is not meant to be a business.

THE COMMERCIAL APPROACH

The commercial approach to adoption is difficult to define because it has many variations and degrees of sophistication, but it includes the following factors:

- **Advertising.** The cornerstone of the commercial approach to adoption is personal advertising. It is considered a desirable mechanism for locating potential birthparents and drawing their interest. The commercial system views prospective adoptive families as products in need of clever packaging.

- **Adoptive-parent driven.** Since adoptive parents are paying customers, it is not unreasonable to expect they will be the priority clients. They present reasonable needs, and the commercial approach sets out to meet those needs. The unmistakable motivation of the commercial system is to satisfy the desires of infertile families—their needs come first.

- **Emphasis on money.** As promoters arrange placements for profit, adoption obviously becomes a business. One does not get far in the world of business without capital. It takes capital to advertise and solicit birthparent interest. If the wheels of commerce stop, more capital will usually get things moving again. In the commercial system, emotion is a nuisance; adoption is best understood as a no-nonsense business transaction.

- **Deregulation.** The foundation of commercial adoption is free enterprise, the great American way. The commercial system views adoption as a competitive marketplace driven by supply and demand. It assumes that the unencumbered natural laws of economics will appropriately govern the process. The fewer regulations, the better.

- **Short-term focus.** The commercial approach treats adoption as a point-in-time transaction; it is considered an event, not a process. There are immediate needs to meet, and the purpose of adoption is to meet those needs.

- **Self-serving.** Commercial adoption fuels the engines of self-interest and encourages the use of unilateral power. It is goal-oriented and unabashedly competitive. In an every-man-for-himself system, concern for others is an unaffordable luxury. The commercial approach to adoption values and rewards initiative, cleverness, and determination. Success is measured in terms of quantity and speed.

- **Euphoric perspective.** The commercial perspective views adoption in completely positive terms. It energetically highlights the gains of adoption, while it denies, minimizes, or sugarcoats the pain.

Concerns Related to Personal Advertising

Let's consider these factors, starting with the cornerstone of commercial adoption, personal advertising. People vary in their tolerance for it, but many find it inherently unattractive and demeaning. Personal advertising stirs many noteworthy concerns

First of all, many people find personal advertising intrinsically tacky. It feels like displaying and selling oneself to unknown buyers. It is an odd mixture of lost privacy on one hand and imposition into the privacy of others on the other. Personal advertising often has a desperate, "what do we have to lose" flavor about it. "Nothing else has worked," it reasons, "so we might as well try this." Curiously, it begs and boasts in the same statement: "Please pick us because we are wonderful."

In many locations, classified advertisements of this sort are not allowed. Where they are allowed, they are only available for prospective adoptive parents. Potential birthparents are usually not permitted to advertise because, apparently, this practice has the potential to degenerate into baby selling. It seems our indignation is greater on one end of the commercial transaction than the other.

Advertising too often emphasizes image over substance. A whimsical three-sentence description of an enterprising couple reveals nothing of substance about them other than their eagerness to adopt. Certainly there are no liabilities described in their declaration of availability. On a positive note, it is good to know that Ozzie and Harriet are alive, well, and plentiful.

To its great discredit, advertising pays little attention to issues of compatibility. Its goal is to catch someone's—perhaps anyone's—attention. It is availability that matters, not compatibility. Since compatibility is instrumental to adopted children feeling like they fit in with the adoptive family, this is a very serious shortcoming. If, when the placement dust settles, adoptive families and birthfamilies find they have only canaries and spring storms in common, prospects for a meaningful relationship are slim.

Personal advertising seems to work best when there is no middle man. Because this type of advertising is unmonitored, it exposes people to risks they never imagined. In the unaccountable realm of anonymity, all things are possible. The door is open to calls of sick humor, emotional manipulation, and financial extortion. When advertising bypasses the dispassionate filtering of experienced intermediaries, prospects for nonsense and exploitation escalate significantly.

Personal advertising can be very expensive. When linkage between birthfamilies and adoptive families depends on expensive tactics, wealthy families are advantaged.

Advertising tarnishes public perception of adoption. Instead of presenting itself as a well-reasoned, well-organized institution, it is reduced to a mad scramble of desperate families clamoring for attention. With prospective families casting their lot with lonely hearts and lost kittens, the dignity of the institution is not advanced.

Adoptive Parents as Primary Clients

Although it seems innocuous for commercial agents to proclaim the right of infertile families to have their needs met, it is important to realize that, in defining adoptive parents as the primary clients, they fundamentally redesign the institution of adoption. The commercial approach demotes the longstanding prior priority, service to children, to an afterthought. Instead of providing children with needed families, this form of adoption provides couples with needed children. Something is seriously awry when children are considered resources to met the needs of adults.

In advocating for adoptive parents, the commercial approach makes the most powerful members of the triad even more powerful. To some, it may seem odd to refer to prospective adoptive parents as powerful, since the futile pursuit of fertility often leaves them feeling spent and helpless. Although it is true that they lack the power to overcome the quirks and vagaries of biology, in the interpersonal world they remain resourceful and potent. With few exceptions, they enjoy educational, material, and financial advantages over the birthparents. Although the basic decency of prospective adoptive parents usually calms this uncomfortable contrast, a system that is tilted toward adoptive parents is not likely to produce balanced adoptive relationships.

The Deleterious Effect of Money

An emphasis on money seriously changes the emotional tone of adoption. Even when it is motivated by love and sacrifice, adoption overflows with pain and guilt. As money becomes a motivating factor, prospects for guilt multiply. Whereas sacrificial love potentially ennobles, money usually cheapens. Birthfamilies are ostensibly given money to make their experience more tolerable, but the "relief" they receive may soon feel like blood money, ultimately producing unspeakable guilt and misery. For the child, there is no consolation for the thought that one has been sold and purchased. The gratitude and warmth that adoptive families feel toward birthfamilies, an indispensable dynamic in building satisfying open adoption relationships, is inversely related to the amount of money they spend on the adoption process. Since gratitude is the dynamic that gives open adoption its warmth and endurance, its erosion is a profound threat to the quality of open adoption relationships.

Money adds to the sense of expectation and obligation that participants feel. When a prospective adoptive family "invests" in a prospective birthparent, they expect a return on their investment. It is a rare family that can calmly watch a few thousand dollars slip through their fingers as a change of heart emerges. Many will guard their investments with occasional discrete reminders of the financial sacrifices they are making. In complementary fashion, birthparents can easily feel indebted and trapped by their financial dependence on the prospective adoptive parents. The financial support may add to their reluctance to change their course, even if they feel that the right thing is to set aside the adoption intentions. Predictably, the cessation of support when the adoptive arrangements are complete can also add to the birthparent's feeling of being used and dropped. Another worrisome possibility is that expectant birthparents may exploit the desperation of prospective adoptive parents by misleading them about their intentions. Unfortunately, when substantial sums of money are involved, everyone worries that they may be taken advantage of, and trust is significantly more difficult to achieve.

Adoption as a Business

The commercial approach to adoption introduces a profound paradigm shift. It moves the institution from a professional, service-oriented model to a business model focused on results. When adoptive parents pay $25,000 for 10 hours of service, it is difficult to pretend that they are paying for services rendered. They are obviously buying an outcome. They are buying a product.

Free enterprise has proven its greatness in the international arena, but it has its limits in the interpersonal realm. It does not acknowledge that the commodity of adoption is a child—a fact that makes the commercial approach inherently dehumanizing and shameful. On this basis alone, the commercial approach to adoption merits summary dismissal, but there is more to it. The commercial approach does not recognize that the pursuit of this "product" is extraordinarily emotional. This emotionality adds enormously to the vulnerability of the participants. Making matters worse, there is a striking disequilibrium between the number of couples wanting to adopt infants and the number of infants needing adoptive families. This supply-and-demand disparity creates desperation and intense competition, a circumstance ripe for exploitation. If any practice in the country merits regulation, it is adoption. That is not to glorify the merits of regulation—it is difficult for auditors to get beyond the scrutiny of a program's mechanical process and measure its heart and spirit—but some form of toothy accountability is necessary to protect consumers.

Adoption Lasts Forever

The commercial approach focuses on arranging adoptions and has little interest in the long haul. Since the big money is connected to the drama of arranging placements, most profit-conscious service providers concentrate on the front end of the process and discourage long-term involvements. A short-term perspective keeps costs down and profits up. To no one's surprise, there is no sense of continuing obligation to participants. Problems that persist beyond the placement phase are promptly referred to other professionals.

Adoption entrepreneurs provide a cheerful message. They tell people what they want to hear—namely, that adoption is benign and carries little meaning over the long term. They suggest to prospective adoptive parents that adoption is virtually identical to having children biologically, and they lead prospective birthparents to think that they will quickly get over their loss. Ignoring numerous studies suggesting that adopted people may be prone to greater psychological distress than the general population, they eagerly direct attention to other studies that describe their adjustment in positive terms.

A short-term perspective denies the obvious truth that adoption lasts a lifetime, and it seriously underestimates the significance of the adoption theme in the lives of the participants. By spreading the impression that there is nothing out of the ordinary about adoption, it leads those who are conscious of their pain to question their feelings. It has the cruel effect of making those who speak of their pain seem peculiar and pathological. The myth that adoption is insignificant interferes with participants' opportunities to prepare themselves for issues that will predictably surface over time. Furthermore, a short-term perspective does not gather the feedback that is necessary to improve services, and it does not in any way contribute to the profession's body of knowledge.

Unrestrained Self-Interest: The Edge of Exploitation

At its worst, adoption is a process of people using others for selfish gain. Sometimes, the using is unilateral; other times it is mutual. In the commercial system, participants act as independent agents pursuing their individual needs primarily and attending to the needs of others incidentally, if at all. Kindness shown to others is, at times, calculated and ulterior—in forlorn contrast to a relational perspective that views participants as members of a coherent, interdependent system. When self-interest reigns, compassion is scarce. On these terms, adoption is a chilly transaction. To the degree that adoption is energized by unrestrained self-interest and is organized to meet individual needs without enduring regard for others, it is exploitative. Who can delight in a process that cashes in on the brokenness of others for selfish gain?

There is no sense of community for those who practice a selfish version of adoption. Others holding similar dreams are considered competitors, not supportive peers. Adoption becomes a lonely experience. Competition between participants or service providers is a dynamic that produces mixed outcomes, some desirable and others undesirable. Something about human nature responds powerfully to competition. Competition fires the creative juices and generates innovation. By adding to the range of alternatives, it empowers people. It also heightens awareness of the differences between alternate systems. On the other hand, competition causes wasteful duplication of effort and funnels scarce resources into marketing rather than product—that is, service—development. It leads organizations to hoard information to gain competitive advantage, rather than disseminate it for the public good.

Candy-Coated Adoption

As it sentimentally portrays adoption as a wonderful thing, the commercial approach glosses over the pain of adoption. This saccharine, air-brushed version of adoption generates misleading expectations. In the depths of subsequent soul-crushing pain, participants—especially birthparents—gasp, "I had no idea how much I would hurt. No one ever told me it would be like this. I feel betrayed." It is true that there is beauty in adoption, but it is never gained painlessly. Sugarcoated adoption is shallow and unable to tap into the authentic joy of those who have sacrificed and endured the pain.

Some commentators ask that positive language be developed to describe adoption. They rightly hope to escape linguistic references to adoption that imply pathology. Although I appreciate their intentions, I believe the goal is better understood as developing accurate language. Accurate descriptions of adoption are sometimes very positive—ecstatic, actually. Other times, however, accurate descriptions of adoption are drenched with pain. Inaccurate descriptions—unduly negative or positive—undermine our ability to understand each other and damage the credibility of the institution.

DIVERTED CREATIVITY

In the new competitive reality, it is important to look good. There is nothing wrong about that. The ultimate goal, of course, is to look good and be good too; but that requires tremendous energy. The commercial slant holds that, if you can manage only one of the two, it is sufficient to look good. Since many consumers have not yet learned to approach service providers with caution, looking good is considered far more important than being good. There is not much return business among birthparents—it is usually a "one time sale"—so long-term satisfaction is not especially important. Adoption, an experience with profound lifelong consequences, now hinges on little more than the ability of an individual or organization to gain and capitalize on a lingering moment of birthparent consideration.

How sad that the creative energy of adoption in an age of commercialization is seldom directed toward improving the institution. The issue of exclusive interest for many adoption handlers these days is marketing. So many resources are spent getting to potential birthparents before competitors that there is little interest in making the process serve children more effectively. The research and development effort in adoption has long been skimpy. In the future, it may be nonexistent as whatever resources and creativity an organization can muster will be channeled into marketing. I am reminded of a sad observation shared by artists who have adopted through our program. When they gather with other artists to relax at the end of an art show, they do not talk about creative technique; they discuss marketing. They are describing the new reality of adoption; presentation and image are more important than substance.

The commercial approach to adoption is orchestrated by very bright, often very likable people who are expert in making their product appealing. They know their product must attract potential birthparents, so they disguise the process to make it appear as though it prioritizes birthparents. It can be difficult to distinguish between a business approach to adoption and a professional approach, and the lines are increasingly blurred as each system borrows from the other. Perhaps the distinctions will become more clear as the commercial system becomes bolder and more aggressive in response to increasing competition. The point is this: Consumers must approach adoption services carefully, because things are frequently not what they seem.

Unhappily, commercialism splits the open adoption community. Proponents of open adoption agree about many issues, but commercialism is not one of them. To no one's credit, this schism is seldom addressed openly. It is usually politely ignored, but the tension is real, and it interferes with cooperation. Some adoption workers reside in the commercial camp enthusiastically. Placing all the action in the hands of participants, they are glad to shed responsibility for outcomes. Some associate with commercial practitioners in the hope of influencing them for the better. It is a worrisome strategy. They warn their children, "Don't hang out with trouble," but set aside the injunction's wisdom when it comes to their own associations. Often, their logic is little more than rationalization for their compromised behavior. For others, association with commercialism is an unfortunate imperative imposed by superiors in their organization. In stark terms, their need for employment requires them to suspend and sacrifice many of their personal and professional convictions. Sadly, they either lack the stature in their organization or the personal courage to effectively make the case for the enduring and ethical appeal of values-based open adoption.

Those who support the commercial approach to adoption innocently refer to their activity as "promotion." It is, they suggest, little more than an effort to get the word out. Although I agree that there is an important need to inform the public, the commercial approach to adoption does not strike me as innocent. It falls short on all eight values of values-based open adoption. It focuses on the needs of infertile families, not children. Candor is set aside in favor of more palatable, "adoption positive" messages. Certainly, there is no need to talk about the pain—it might discourage birthparents from choosing adoption. Birthparent choice is replaced with an adoptive parent-driven process of discovery and capture. In the commercial approach to adoption, commitments are considered cumbersome and are avoided whenever possible. There is no need for transformation or learning. Adaptability is unimportant because, once the legal work is done, issues can be handled based on authority and power. The pleasures of community are not available to competitors.

ADDITIONAL WORRIES

There are several additional worrisome issues, many of which spin off from the trend toward the commercialization of adoption.

Interstate Detours

One worrisome manifestation of the commercial approach is interstate adoption. With few exceptions, this practice, because it severely restricts the potential for relationships to grow between the families, runs contrary to the spirit of open adoption as we define it. Since many interstate adoptions come together based on far flung advertising, a fact that usually means selection is made from limited information about an extremely narrow pool of prospects, the likelihood of significant compatibility between the birthfamily and adoptive family is severely reduced. Even more to the point, the geographic distance largely forecloses the possibility of any meaningful connection beyond that of pen pals.

Interstate adoption is conspicuously inefficient. At a minimum, it requires a variety of extra expenses related to travel. Because the statutes of different states are invoked, it generates extra layers of bureaucracy and extra opportunities for fundamental confusion and misunderstanding. It may require extra work and extra expense to iron out those details. While prospective adoptive families from state x recruit in state y, families from y recruit in x. What is gained? Inefficiency is a luxury that favors the wealthy.

What motivates interstate adoption? Occasionally, it is necessary to cast the net broadly to find appropriate families in response to very exotic circumstances in the birthfamily, but that helpful process is only a small part of the interstate scene. In rare situations, where birthparents are temporarily dislocated, it may be wise to make an interstate connection back to their permanent location. Sometimes, it is necessary to cross state lines because the type of service wanted is not available locally. Open adoption from a distance, for example, is more attractive than closed adoption nearby. Most of the time, however, interstate adoption is motivated by two homely factors: intrusion and evasion.

Many interstate efforts are an intrusion of aggressive commercial tactics into less commercial territory. Commercial adoption works best when it first enters regions where indigenous adoption services are offered according to longstanding professional standards that frown on advertising and solicitation for clients. Glamorous and daring, personal advertisers from far away seem an interesting alternative to the local reality that has perhaps grown too familiar and tame. A taste for the exotic momentarily overrules the importance of accountability and continuing contact.

If it is not a matter of intrusion, interstate adoption is likely a matter of evasion. It is a repackaging of the old shameful energy of avoidance that characterizes the closed system. In closed adoption, emotional distance between the adoptive family and birthfamily is treasured. It helps to contain secrets and keep people apart. Geographic distance is a new way to keep people apart and enable them to avoid having to deal with each other. This new form of evasion is often very intentional. I once heard an adoptive father on a conference panel explain that he was pleased to be involved in a program that did open adoption on a national basis because "you could claim this very contemporary thing called open adoption; but, with any luck, you find birthparents from across the country, and you end up not having any significant interaction with them."

In open adoption, as in all friendships, geographic distance is decidedly undesirable. Distance interferes with the building and sustaining of relationships. If a visit—including the travel to and from—cannot occur in one day, the distance is too great for comfortable open adoption. Visits from inconvenient distances never feel normal. They are major events, and, as a result, everyone behaves in unusual fashion.

A Value-Free System

There has always been tension between the anything-goes perspective and the view that the old ways are best. In his book *Shame*, author Salman Rushdie suggests that history is best understood as a struggle between "the epicure" and "the puritan."* This description certainly fits the current adoption scene. The pendulum swings wildly between the excesses of prejudicial restraint and hazardous permission. The high road of steady and sensible progress is difficult to locate and sustain. Presently, the winds blow lustily toward unimpeded permission.

There are growing pressures to remove professional discretion from the process of adoption. Adoption is increasingly considered a matter of right. If you are an adult American, you have a right to adopt. This line of thought rests on two observations. First, our society believes people have an unchallengeable right to procreate as they see fit. No one has to prove themselves to take on parental responsibility in the biologic arena, the reasoning goes, so why should adoptive parents have to prove themselves? The second premise is that professional screening is so flawed that it has no value. This perspective holds that screening is a hopelessly subjective process with no verifiable predictive relevance.

The biological argument is interesting. Since it appeals to the court of basic fairness, it is quite alluring. After all, many would say, parenting is parenting—what's the big deal about adoption? Adoptive parents are very interested in biologic parenting. There is, after all, much about biological parenting that looks good to adoptive parents. They like the ordinariness

---

* *Rushdie is cited by Phillip Yancey in* The Jesus I Never Knew. *Grand Rapids, MI: Zondervan Publishing House, 1995.*

and presumptiveness of it. They like the fact it is not subject to anyone's challenge, and they envy the generational connectedness and the "stuck-togetherness" that biological families take for granted. Biological families enjoy an extensive heritage—genes, ancestry, ethnicity, and history—which gives them a deep and unerasable extra dimension of commonality that endures through the years. Tempting as the comparison is, biologic parenting and adoptive parenting are not identical. Adoption is not an automatic process; it is volitional. It hinges on decisions, not hormones, and the thinking that goes into it is subject to reasonable review. As Canadian sociologist and adoption researcher, David Kirk pointed out decades ago in his groundbreaking book *Shared Fate*, there are significant differences in the two experiences. Although he made a convincing case for "acknowledgment-of-difference" as the most promising approach to adoption, it is clear that the "rejection-of-difference" strategy remains persistent and seductive.

Furthermore, if we are honest, we will admit we are not entirely happy about the absolute procreative rights afforded the general population. Certainly not all persons who head down the biological parenting trail are suited for the challenge. Although we are rightly reluctant to set aside the assumption of parental fitness, there surely are times when protective service workers wish they had more authority to act on their predictions. Whenever they fail to defend children from obviously deficient parenting, they are criticized for clinging too long to the naive notion of family preservation. It is almost as though some of the voices for deregulation would like to invert the usual assumptions. They would like to require biological parents to prove themselves while affording prospective adoptive parents a presumption of fitness.

The second line of argument is less charming but more substantive. Those who wish to abolish all standards for prospective adoptive parents point out that these standards have long been subjective and capricious. Additionally, they question the predictive validity of our assessment efforts. Their criticisms have some merit and are difficult to refute.

Adoption is losing its discretionary prerogatives because professionals have failed to establish and articulate a consensus on standard expectations for participating in the adoption drama. This was, in many ways, inevitable. It is unlawful to discriminate; but that was, uncomfortably, the adoption worker's job for years. No doubt, most screening decisions were and are subject to judicial reversal. Agencies exacerbated this problem by insisting on provincial, ideological, and irrelevant requirements. For too long, the core question in the home study was whether the couple was good enough—that is, were they sufficiently conventional to adopt—when it should have been, whether they were able and ready to handle the unique challenges of a particular form of adoption.

We must address this oversight forthrightly. The fact that our work is not scientific does not mean that we do not know anything or that our work is without value. As professionals, we must end our confusion about standards of readiness to adopt. If not, all that we have learned from decades of practice about factors that enhance or detract from effective and satisfying participation in the adoption experience will be wasted.

It is not unreasonable to insist on standards as long as they are fair and clearly stated. Institutions routinely discriminate based on ability or readiness to meet the requirements unique to a particular field. Medical schools, for example, find prestige in the rate at which they reject taxpaying applicants. Organ transplant programs make excruciating discriminations according to carefully developed standards. Although there are occasional controversies, these practices enjoy broad acceptance. Without these standards, perhaps we would see potential recipients soliciting donors through personal advertising: "Cheerful, professional 35 year-old woman with three stray cats and a golden retriever seeks healthy, young kidney. Please call Mary at...."

The value-free trend reduces adoption to a legal and mechanical process. The home study of the 21st century will be brief: "Are you actively involved in any criminal activity? Will your doctor certify that you will live through the year? Okay, who's next?" Inappropriate professional decision making over the years has surely been a problem, but the absence of professional judgment will only make things worse.

Lawmakers may wink at common sense and pretend not to notice, but clear thinkers recognize that there will always be a need for discretionary thinking in the practice of adoption. If social workers who are well-versed in the complex issues of adoption are not trusted to provide discretionary thinking early in the process, judges will supply the necessary discretion later in the experience. By the time a court exercises official judgment, the situation almost certainly will have degenerated into a destructive win-lose struggle, the sort of tug of war in which children invariably suffer the most.

Adoption must not become a permissive system where anything goes and every interested person is considered suitable. On that basis, adoption has no credibility. It stands to reason that if "anything goes" for prospective adoptive parents, anything goes for birthfamilies as well. If every form of adoptive family is acceptable, every form of birthfamily is equally acceptable. In a values-cleansed, all-things-are-permissible version of adoption, there are no reasonable grounds to assume an adoption will produce psychological upward mobility for the child; consequently, there is little reason for birthfamilies to consider adoption.

If the value-free trend continues and professional screening is disallowed, openness in adoption will become more crucial than ever. By virtue of their indisputable right to choose, birthparents will have the only legally defendable opportunity to determine suitability for adoption. That is to say, birthparents will be the only persons involved in the adoption process with any right to use discretion and common sense. One wonders, though, if the judgment of this youthful population is sufficient protection for children?

Over-Simplification

Cleansed of the mystique associated with secrecy, adoption has the awkward look of a puppy that has just had a bath and does not quite know what to do with itself. As it shuffles around forlornly, exposed for all the world to see, the casual onlooker thinks, "Well, there's not much to it without the fluff." That impression stirs the temptation to oversimplify and streamline, a manner of thinking that prompts amateurs to roll up their sleeves and have a go at it. It enables virtually everyone to provide an opinion on how it should work: "I know someone who is adopted, and my opinion is that...." With the mystique expunged, we live with expert opinion based on a sample of one. The life-altering institution of adoption is being trivialized and taken lightly.

Sometimes, simplistic thinking takes the sophisticated form of research, contemporary society's most revered gateway to truth. Our faith in social research is interesting because, as every graduate student quickly discovers in the required research class, there are countless opportunities for error to enter the process. Furthermore, whatever "facts" research generates are clearly subject to various interpretations. Amazingly, competing schools of thought sometimes stake their positions on the same research. And, of course, we all know that research is not especially enlightening or consoling when you happen to be the exception to the norm.

One of our adoptive parents tells an amusing story about research: She recalls a survey about drug usage, which she filled out as a high-school freshman. The surveyors stressed that no one would know who was answering particular surveys, so it was safe for students to share the truth. As this mother—who never even touched alcohol in high school—tells the story, the confidentiality also made it safe to play with the research tool. She and a few of her rural scholastic cronies decided to have some fun. Chortling over their preposterous responses, they reported that they were loading up with heroin at least three times a day. Because of the research finding that their school had one of the worst hard-drug problems in the state, they spent the next three years getting to know the undercover officer who was shortly thereafter assigned to their school. A few years later, the policeman married one of the seniors, and they lived happily ever after. The storyteller concludes with the observation that the episode taught her to take research with a grain of salt.

Some things are self-apparent. Do we need research to confirm the Golden Rule? Do we need research to appreciate the assumption of innocence until guilt is proven, or the beauty of an oriole's song?

There are many paths to understanding, and each requires faith. Research-with-a-grain-of-salt is a very useful tool to help us grow in knowledge, but research-as-the-absolute-truth calls for faith that I do not have. There are many other important avenues to comprehension that have proven fruitful for leading figures in the field. Psychologist Randolph Severson, for example, draws insight from the classic masters of philosophy and literature, whose wisdom endures through the centuries. Open adoption advocate Sharon Kaplan-Roszia uses an impressive combination of experience, social-science knowledge, and spirituality. In my own search for direction, I look mostly to contemporary moral and spiritual authorities. The point is, understanding is found in many sources, one of which is research.

Professional Turf Wars

Although the trend toward deregulation is growing, some service providers will always be regulated. Agencies with 100 years of tradition, well-organized supervisory processes, interested constituencies, boards of directors, and accountability to funding sources remain heavily monitored. Meanwhile, the legal profession proceeds with self-regulation. Their extraregulatory presence in adoption happens, I suppose, because of all the child development courses they take in law school. In my experience, the typical adoption is 5% legal work and 95% socio-psychological. Unfortunately, when attorneys take the lead role, there is a tendency to invert the distribution of energy. With an eye toward irony, I propose we watch closely to see which system generates the most legal problems. In a perverse and predictable correlation, it is likely that the more that unregulated practitioners err, the more that social workers will be regulated, because, if nothing else, social workers are "regulatable." The playing field in this competition between professions is oddly tilted in favor of the less-experienced players. The golden age for attorneys in adoption, though, may be more fleeting than many expect. They fit the commercial mold better than social workers but less well than professional marketers and advertising agents. In a thriving commercial climate, attorneys will eventually give way to public relations firms as the real experts in adoption.

Why should social workers be good-natured about the encroachment of other professions into their historic sphere of practice? Any profession of substance will fight for the opportunity to serve its constituency without interference. Is adoption natural territory for lawyers? If so, why were they uninterested for so many decades? Is it accidental that their interest coincides with an emerging awareness of the supply-and-demand pressures associated with infant adoption? If their motivation were altruistic, they would be jockeying with equal vigor for a presence in the special-needs arena.

There are, of course, outstanding attorneys who practice open adoption with great competence and integrity. Conversely, there are agencies that have been and continue to be incompetent and duplicitous. It is a shameful truth that many agencies operate with diffidence and arrogance. These errors are seldom acknowledged, and forgiveness is rarely sought. Furthermore, agencies are frequently plagued by an immobilizing gap between progressive professionals working every day to serve clients, and administrators who alternately defend the status quo or sell out to the pressures of fiscal expediency. Despite these serious demerits, I believe agencies offer the greatest potential for quality adoption services. Adoption is about children and families, and so is social work. It is a good fit.

The agency system offers some important advantages over alternate approaches:

- **Sponsorship.** Most agencies have a sponsoring constituency that provides vision, values, and material support.

- **Accountability.** Consumers have established, easily accessed avenues of recourse in the event they are treated unreasonably.

- **Minimized socioeconomic factors.** Money is an inevitable factor in every service delivery system, but most agencies conscientiously seek to include participants with modest incomes and afford them opportunities identical to those offered families that are well off.

- **Long-term availability and follow-up.** Although it is a perpetual struggle, agencies usually manage to persevere. This allows continuity of service and the possibility of well-informed follow up services.

- **Systems perspective.** There is a conscious effort to balance the interests of all the parties involved. Social work agencies do not operate on an adversarial model; their instinct and training are to work toward collaboration and consensus. It does not make sense to a systems thinker to advocate for the advantage of any participant at the possible expense of others.

- **Quality control.** Regular staff meetings and supervisory sessions to review cases and improve services are standard practice. Difficult decisions are seldom in the hands of individual practitioners.

• **Collectivity.** Effective agency programs usually provide opportunities for participants to meet peers and enjoy their support. Participants do not have to go through anxious experiences alone; hazards and breakthroughs can be shared. Very importantly, birthparents have several families to choose from and significant amounts of material to review regarding each prospective adoptive family.

• **Auxiliary services.** If specialized or remedial social services are needed, chances are they will be readily available within the same system.

• **Training.** Agencies provide opportunities for young workers to practice their skills under supervised conditions. This apprenticeship system provides for continuity of quality service.

• **Community support.** Families who participate in programs that are known and respected find their decisions are accepted and supported in the broader community.

• **Research and development.** Truly effective agencies take the time to think deeply about the issues and are committed to improving the overall practice of adoption.

It is possible to imagine an effective hybrid system that teams the strengths of both professions. A merger of this type can only work, however, if founded on extraordinary mutual respect. If the professionals involved cannot agree on a basic philosophy, conflict is likely. Since contemporary social workers think in terms of family systems, and attorneys think in terms of advocacy for particular clients, it is extremely difficult to reconcile the differences. One model sees participants as prospects for cooperation, whereas the other sees them as likely adversaries. As one system encourages relational power, the other employs unilateral power. From the social work perspective, there is no escape from the premise that quality adoption services must nurture collectivity, not unmitigated self-interest. In moments of calm, the two approaches may look comparable. In times of high anxiety, however, the differences will be conspicuous. A true blending of professional efforts is possible only if the professionals can agree on the ideals of values-based open adoption. On those terms, the relationship savvy and community building of social work could be harnessed with the intelligence and prestige of law. Most efforts like this, however, will not be full partnerships. The most common alliances will function with one profession in the dominant role and the other in an auxiliary role. The few truly effective hybrids that do emerge will be a consequence of unusual dedication to ideals and, quite likely, friendship between principals.

The Impact of the Media

Because adoptive families are built through a series of decisions rather than biological processes, adoption serves as a convenient laboratory to test our societal ideas about acceptable variations on the family theme. As various participants assert their rights in a very complex emotional, social, and legal arena, conflicts are inevitable. Adoption custody disputes hold sufficient intrigue and drama to provide steady fodder for prime time "news" shows. These media minidramas paint adoption as a very unstable institution.

At my house—and I think it is true in family rooms around the nation—these so-called news pieces turn into popularity contests. The family quickly takes sides: "I like that person." "No way! That other person is nicer!" The media is developing a new, extralegal standard for custody: Who is more likable, who is nicer, or who is closer to the mythical American Dream? For the media to pose this "beauty contest" version of custody determination while the forces of deregulation seek to abolish standards puts the institution of adoption into a very schizophrenic mode.

The bad guys in these media dramas are usually birthparents, particularly birthfathers. This vilification puts these men in an obvious double bind. We are disgusted when fathers bail out on their responsibilities, but, as far as adoption is concerned, we are even more indignant when they show interest.

This sensationalized media attention has sad consequences. It feeds insecurity in adoptive parents, an anxiety that lurks in every adoption unless the participants take adequate time to carefully build and nurture the open adoption relationship. This fear has become so exaggerated that some families have given up on their intentions for adoption for the sake of emotional safety. Tragically, this creates an adversarial atmosphere be-tween birthparents and adoptive parents, a wretched energy that complicates efforts to build the broader community of adoption. Media sensationalism creates public distaste for adoption. The public is impatient with foolishness and insists on a more sensible system of adoption. Astonishingly, the typical political response to this public outcry is to streamline the process. In other words, the political response is to reduce standards but talk a lot about progress.

Family Preservation at All Cost

One predictable reaction to the commercialization and overpromotion of adoption is condemnation of the entire institution by frustrated members of the adoption reform community. This is partially understandable—we are all frustrated—but the message that adoption should be abolished is unhelpful. Overstatement of this position works against reformers. They end up written off as extremists, and their urgently needed call for reform is lost. If reformers hope to influence future developments, they cannot only be against things; they need to determine what variations on the theme they can support. As astute and invested observers, reformers must learn to distinguish between quality and commerce. Once they are clear about the differences, they can help the next generation of consumers understand the distinctions.

Weary Workers

I worry that I will go into to work some Monday morning and learn that the 50 best adoption workers in the country have decided in independent decisions to leave the field. Their consciences will have driven them out. Although the world slaps them on the back and salutes the "happy work" they do, they are more impressed with the pain of adoption. This awareness makes them effective, but it consumes them. Even when the work goes well, it is anxious and strangely depleting.

These days, adoption professionals must also find ways to deal with the aggravations of the commercial system. It is not pleasing to be lumped together with entrepreneurs who profit from the uprooting of children for the benefit of adults. Perhaps even more depleting is our own dissension. For some inexplicable reason, open adoption proponents are inclined to overlook common beliefs and prefer to focus on areas of disagreement. We must keep in mind a division of labor within the cause. Some are philosophical, whereas others are practical. Some set standards and point out distinctions; others stress commonality and build bridges. We must close ranks. And when we disagree—as we must, if we hope to grow—we must spar with civility and respect.

What happens if the commercial system drives off all the artists? Who will nurture this institution? Who will make it hospitable—not the utilitarian hospitality of those who want something, but the hospitality of care from one human to another? What if adoption is only carried out by technicians? Who will take the time to improve it and make it better? Universities with their million-dollar research projects can help, but it is often difficult to translate their findings into practice. Therapists making repairs accumulate important impressions, but who will take the time to listen to them? Shall we look to marketers to produce a more substantive institution?

We grow weary of endless controversy, but we must remember that the moment we let up in our struggle against the commercial treatment of children, we drift into resembling that system.

FINDING HOPE

Where do we find the strength to persevere? It is an important question. I believe there are two answers: First, we must draw from our love for the work. In Chapter 11, I quoted philosopher Robert Grudin from *The Grace of Great Things* to define this love as a matter of "insight...justice...frankness...humor...[and] precise expression." These variables are sources of strength. One must have faith in the common sense idea that work well done is appreciated. The second source of hope resides in the hearts of the participants. In one of the quotes leading into this chapter, Jean Vanier reminds us to stay close to the poor. In the contemporary adoption arena, I define the wide-eyed child, the hurried birthparent, and the bewildered adoptive parent of modest means as the poor. We must stay close to them and draw from their innocence. The fight for quality in adoption will be fought for them and with them.

HALLMARKS OF EXCELLENCE

There is hope in excellence. Outstanding adoption programs pose a stunning contrast to the commercial system. The robust values-based open adoption program diverges from the lackluster offerings of the business model on a number of variables.

It is oriented to birthparents. Excellent programs organize their efforts around the goal of serving families who are working through the issues of an untimely pregnancy. It seems so simple, but this perspective makes an extraordinary difference. It guards against the exploitative potential of adoption by supporting the most vulnerable participants. As a result, it is the perspective that produces the least conflict and the greatest sense of security.

It is conscious of pain. Outstanding programs do not deny the pain of adoption. Among other things, this honesty keeps them credible. Pain-conscious programs are authentic, not saccharine. They do not get carried away with the potential of adoption because they know that the emotional costs are high. The quality of an adoption program is directly correlated to its capacity to face the pain that is inherent in the experience. Those who address the sadness stand a chance to find the profound joy that exists on the other side of pain.

It has a forthright style. Participants always know where they stand in the context of a quality program. There are no games or hidden agendas. As a result, the level of trust runs high.

It stresses collectivity. Excellent programs work hard to minimize the dynamic of narrow self-interest. They work hard to overcome we-they thinking, which undermines cooperation. Participants in quality programs learn to share the fears and risks they face. They learn to wait and hope together. They reinforce each other's strengths and hold each other accountable to principled behavior.

It is healthy and healing. Great adoption programs do not focus on pathology. They are not clinical, and they are not stuffy. They use the language of learning and basic decency. With their emphasis on respectful interdependence and cooperation, they are healing in an almost incidental manner. The effective program briefly accepts the dependence of its constituency and, while it has their undivided attention, reminds them of their ideals. It works the temporary dependence to the advantage of the participants.

It handles financial issues responsibly and openly. Money is not a predominant issue in a first-class program. Finances are handled prudently and with complete transparency. It puts value on service, not on an outcome or product. Excellent programs find creative ways to reduce their dependence on fees charged to adoptive participants.

It is not productivity-driven. Because high-quality adoption programs are clear about their purpose and direction, they tend to be reasonably efficient. They are not, however, driven to be quantifiably productive, and they are not fascinated with numbers. They promote clear thinking, and respect the fact that some people who use the program take longer than others to achieve that capacity. Exceptional programs are committed to building relationships. As a result, they refuse to take an assembly-line approach. Quality programs are interested in research and development. They encourage staff to take some time to sit and think. The best programs are always searching for better ways to serve participants; they are always learning.

It has champions for the ideals of open adoption. Strong programs invariably have committed advocates for openness. These champions—not necessarily the persons in charge—are completely in sync with the values and ideals of open adoption and are able to articulate them with exceptional sincerity and conviction. This depth of belief is very compelling and sustaining. The most outstanding programs have nothing but champions.

It expects excellence. Exemplary programs have great respect for their constituency and their capabilities. This appreciation leads very naturally to high expectations. Participants appreciate this affirmation and usually rise to the challenge.

It is playful. The adoptive journey is emotionally draining. Because the stakes are high, because numerous moral issues are raised, and because it is rooted in loss, adoption has long been a serious and humorless process. It does not have to be that way. Great programs sparkle with fun and provide many lighthearted moments along the way. They are not always completely orthodox. When professionals get out of their offices and spend time with participants in less sterile environments, the experience has much greater texture and color.

It works for community education. Excellent programs proactively help the public understand the complexity of adoption and the difference between commercial and professional systems of adoption. They keep public attention on the needs of children.

HOPE FOR ADOPTION

A variety of emotions go into a book like this. Concern, delight, pride, exasperation, and gratitude are all involved. I am aware of writing much of this chapter from frustration—frustration with politicians who, rhetoric not withstanding, set a statutory course that disregards children and caters to would-be adopters with wherewithal, with status quo agencies whose stubbornness has devastated the once-proud agency service delivery system, and with snake oil adoption promoters who poison the atmosphere of the entire institution. I am frustrated with triad members who generalize too broadly, with media that treat anguished custody disputes like beauty contests, with a consuming public that prepares itself poorly before plunging into the adoption process, and with lackadaisical social workers who do not take time to read or think.

Rabbi Abraham Heschel, in *I Asked for Wonder,* warned years ago, "The conscience of the world was destroyed by those who were wont to blame others rather than themselves.... We have bartered holiness for convenience, loyalty for success, love for power, wisdom for information, tradition for fashion." Recognizing the truth of his observation, I am mostly frustrated with myself. Until I have done all that I can, my frustration with others is of little importance.

The hope for adoption resides in each of us with an interest in this institution. We must not for a moment think that it is up to the other guy to straighten things out. Each caring person has power. Birthparents have the power to choose wisely. Adoptive parents have the marvelous power to honor commitments. Social workers have the power to establish and articulate standards of excellence. Everyone has the power to honor children.

Those of us who work in adoption must examine our consciences. Have we been responsible stewards of the institution? Do we stand for anything? Or, putting it more pointedly, is there any form of adoption we will not join? Are we willing to be part of adoptions built on enticement, pressure, or deception? Do we think adoption is always better than the alternative? Are we so impressed with adoptive parents and so distrustful of birthparents that we think a bad adoption is better than no adoption? Our responsibility is to remain true to our clearest understanding of those practices that genuinely serve children and are, as best we can determine, right in the eyes of God. If we are to know peace of mind, we must stand tall for the sake of children.

Although they seldom feel powerful, birthparents are positioned to control the way adoption occurs. They want the best for their children, and if they become informed about the issues, they will insist on quality. For that to happen, the important people in their lives need to encourage them to proceed slowly and carefully. The siren call of the speedy, short-term solution must be resisted. It is exciting to see a new generation of birthparents, open adoption birthparents, emerge as spokespersons for quality. They will provide an important and welcomed perspective.

I believe the best hope for the future of adoption is the good-heartedness of prospective adoptive parents. As the most powerful participants in the institution, they are the ultimate jury. They are, of course, distracted and tempted by their feelings of desperation as they first enter the arena; but once they are fully informed, they prefer, with rare exception, to pursue the most ethical course available to them. We must help them understand that quality in adoption is important to them and to the children they hope to adopt. If they can be persuaded to think through the issues carefully, they will chose to honor the children. Given a bit of reasonable hope, they will surely choose dignity over desperation.

The commercial system may flourish for some time. With its appeal to short-term thinking, it taps into a powerful vein of human nature. Ultimately, though, it carries the seeds of its own destruction. The early-bird advertiser will soon be joined by a flock of competitors. Overeagerness and deception will produce resistance. Every adoption born from enticement and pressure will reverberate with enduring insecurity. Every under-the-table dollar spent early invites the expenditure of another 10 in subsequent years. Commercial adoption is an unreflective industry that will not easily correct itself. Instead, it will be altered by painful retribution sought through the legal system by its victims.

Adoption promoters do not really promote adoption; they systematically destroy it. They promote themselves. As they sugarcoat the process and tinker with truth, they create suspicion. As they turn educational and health care professionals into adoption recruiters, they drive prospective birthparents into cover. Steamrolling the "barriers to adoption," they set into motion a reckless system. As they process adoptions at the speed of light, they create time bombs of anguish. They are adoption's greedy merchants of shame.

If adoption is to be promoted—if that is the word for it—it will happen paradoxically. Those who approach adoption cautiously and warn of its pain, who are conscious of shame and its destructive potential, who focus on compatibility and choice rather than marketing, are the ones who will preserve the institution as a decent and reasonable alternative.

We do not have to careen from one shame-generating system to another. We do not have to choose between a secretive system founded on judgment and a commercial system that lacks it. We can choose a course based on values tested by the centuries, a path of honor. We can choose to honor children as astonishing gifts from God. We can shine with the luminescence of candor. We can find beauty, resolve, and each other in the mysterious and cleansing pool of shared pain. We can create positive cultures for choice. We can create order and freedom through our commitments and covenants. We can remain dynamic through our willingness to adapt and remain open to the adventure of meaningful relationships. We can support each other on the journey with compassion and celebration.

We must resist from the bottom of our hearts any trend that reduces children to commodities. If there are adoptions to be done, let them be done with beauty and grace. Let them be done in a spirit of honor.

Chapter 16

Adoption with Reverence

It's spiritual. It's always spiritual. A matter of heart
and soul.

Randolph Severson, *Adoption: Charms and Rituals for Healing*

There are three things that are too amazing for me,
four that I do not understand:
the way of an eagle in the sky,
the way of a snake on a rock,
the way of a ship on the high seas,
and the way of a man with a maiden.

Proverbs 30:18–19, *New International Version*

Surely no one can state the case for wonder more beautifully
than the sage of Proverbs. For all his wisdom, though, he seems
a little unsure of his numbers. Is it three or four? Since there
appears to be a little leeway here, I am inclined to add a fifth
item to the list: the deep and mysterious way of adoption.

Mystery is in the fabric of adoption. It was unhappily mysterious in the days of secrecy, but it remains spiritually
mysterious even in the age of candor. There is something about
adoption that is too big to get one's arms around. It strangely
fascinates and stirs in each of us a sense of awe and wonder. In
fact, if we are honest with ourselves, we will admit there is
something about adoption that makes us a little nervous. It
has a way of pulling people in, of drawing a crowd, of gathering

spectators. Whatever else adoption may or may not be, it is certainly dramatic. Some say the work of adoption is Godlike, as though the hand of God were reaching in to rearrange the order of things. Less cheerful observers might characterize it is a method of second-guessing God.

About Spirituality

In the quote opening this chapter, psychologist Randolph Severson makes the point that adoption is essentially a spiritual matter. I find myself reacting powerfully to this observation and to this word, feeling an ambivalent mixture of wariness and excitement. My guard instinctively goes up, yet I lean into it. It is an important lead that could take us in countless directions. Might spirituality lead us into strange territory? Is it the end of rational inquiry? Or could this insight be the gateway to the extraordinary?

A colleague in our program, Audrey Juola, does not see it in ambivalent terms. Reflecting on her experience with open adoption as she approached retirement, she summarized her impressions with these observations:

> From pain to blessing—it's clearly spiritual. Our culture does not support sacrificial love, and when it happens, it stands out. The gift of great value changes the giver and the receiver.... Ultimately, the coming together is a creative act. Our work is a ministry, helping people stay organized when pain renders them unable to think. We are like the Holy Spirit at people's side in times of anxiety.*

Although spirituality is appealing, it can spin off in some dubious directions. A measure of skepticism is desirable because some versions of spirituality lead to peculiarity, exploitation, or even oppression. These aberrations have been especially damaging in the field of adoption. Under the guise of religious help, participants have been judged, manipulated, and sometimes deceived into preformulated outcomes. Sadly, many participants have encountered more shame than grace from professional conveyors of compassion.

---

* *From an undated personal conversation.*

Four worrisome and common distortions of this theme come quickly to mind. They are the ideas that spirituality is

- centered on the searcher rather than the source,

- impractical,

- beyond accountability, and

- a means of capturing the truth.

Let's consider these concerns briefly.

First, self-awareness is not the goal of our spiritual search. Rather, it is a tool for the journey. Although introspection enables us to detect spiritual subtleties that might otherwise elude our awareness, lingering self-centeredness fails to recognize that authentic spirituality seeks that which is greater—namely, God. Expanded awareness of God invariably minimizes our self-centeredness.

Second, in moving us from preoccupation with ourselves to concern for others, spirituality becomes immensely practical. It is concerned with the whole person, and the whole person has a way of presenting multidimensional challenges that go far beyond abstraction. As we grow spiritually, we grow in our capacity to serve.

Third, although spirituality does not lend itself to scientific measurement, it is exceptionally conscious of accountability. By nature, it generates ideals and is concerned with our ability to approach those ideals. Spiritually mature persons do not ask to be measured by different standards than others.

Finally, spirituality is alive with the breath of life—inhaling new potential and exhaling that which is stagnant. It seeks to approach the truth without trying to contain it. Those who believe they have captured the truth are candidates for arrogance. Worse yet, they are at risk—in the name of spirituality, of all things—to impose their personal or political views on emotionally and morally insecure people they encounter. On the other hand, those who fully respect the enormity of truth are pleased to simply approach it. They are characterized by humility. The humility or lack of humility contained in a voice will reveal much about its spirituality.

A spiritual approach to adoption is essential. If we seek to understand the depth and fullness of adoption, we need a spiritual perspective. It is not overstatement to point out that our ability to talk about adoption depends on it. Consider the language of adoption: *sacrifice, gift, surrender, reunion, honor, chosen, reconciliation, search, destiny, grateful, decision, joy, blessing, service, grace, forgiveness, hope, faith, fear, trust, claiming, mystery.* The great themes in adoption are clearly spiritual. The strength of these glorious words is that they are well-suited to convey both practicality and abstraction. Some also carry psychological meaning, but it is their spiritual applications that participants understand best. If we ignore the spiritual dimensions of adoption, we lose a major portion of our capacity to address the subject, and we will have access to only a slender fraction of the reality of the experience.

The alternative to a spiritual perspective is not attractive. An unspiritual understanding of adoption is mechanical, random, self-centered, self-reliant, and possessive. It is a cold and homely piece of thinking. Spirituality offers a sumptuous alternative to that drab conception of adoption. When I refer to the spirituality of adoption, I am referring to a spirit of awe, providential faith, sacrifice, surrender, search, hope, and gratitude.

In *The Spiritual Life,* Evelyn Underhill, a turn-of-the-century interpreter of the mystic, acquaints us with the potential of a spiritual perspective:

> When, for one reason or another, we begin to wake up a little bit, to lift the nose from the ground and notice that spiritual light and that spiritual atmosphere as real constituents of our human world, then the whole situation is changed. Our horizon is widened, our experience is enormously enriched, and at the same time our responsibilities are enlarged. For now we get an entirely new idea of what human beings are for, and what they can achieve; and as a result, first our notions about life, our scale of values begin to change, and then we do.

Our best hope for a deep understanding of adoption depends on our willingness to develop our spiritual senses.

MECHANICAL OR AWE-FILLED?

Adoption is often approached as a problem-solving process. It solves the triple ills of untimely pregnancy, infertility, and parentlessness. It is further simplified into a supply-and-demand challenge involving the transfer of a child from one environment to another—a modest matter of practicality, little more. From a legal perspective, it is usually a straightforward circumstance that can be accomplished without much fuss. A few forms to fill out, a few signatures to collect—there really is not much to it.

For many people, adoption really does appear to be a simple matter. Once, I overheard a pair of adoption workers with a few years of open adoption experience comment that they were not interested in attending a national conference because they "already knew all that stuff." This was the same conference that the presenters, the leading people in the field, called "formative" in their growing comprehension of open adoption. Many adoption practitioners are impatient with abstraction. They want flashy tools and the tricks of the trade without the labor of deep thought. They are adoption's technicians, and they want the wiring kept simple. They have roles to play, but they seldom tap into the elegance and wonder of adoption.

A mechanical approach points adoption down a trail of low potential. It leaves the soul of adoption unnourished. A more promising approach to adoption is characterized by reverence and awe. In *I Asked for Wonder,* Rabbi Abraham Heschel described awe with exceptional insight and authority:

> Awe is an intuition for the dignity of all things...a sense for the transcendence, for the reference to the mystery beyond all things. It enables us to perceive in the world intimations of the divine...to sense the ultimate in the common and simple; to feel in the rush of the passing the stillness of the eternal.

Even when participants take occasional glory in their irreverence—as earthy people of humor are thankfully wont to do in their efforts to keep our feet on the ground—the adoption experience remains profound. Surrounded by creativity, sacrifice, and transformation, anything less than a response of awe seems evasive and profane. Front-row witnesses to the workings of destiny, we are, if we are paying attention, irresistibly moved toward reverence. That does not mean we forever tiptoe around humorlessly, whispering and weeping—just some of the time.

According to Albert Einstein, "The most beautiful thing we can experience is the mysterious. It is the source of all true art and science."* Note that Einstein does not contrast the beauty of art and the precision of science; he couples them. An awe-based perspective enjoys the astounding information gathered by science, but it also makes room for something beyond. Awe allows for and encourages an extra-scientific way of thinking about things.

Gerald May, a psychiatrist who has written extensively about spirituality, makes a helpful distinction between appreciation and comprehension. He suggests appreciation is as important as comprehension. Our 20th century training drives us to capture and dissect the truth, and in this fashion we often do violence to it. We must be careful about comprehension; it can add to appreciation, but it can also detract from it. Sometimes, it is best for us to hush our overwrought minds, resist the urge to analyze, and simply savor with reverence the surpassing wonder and mystery of adoption.

Awe welcomes another way of knowing. As Rabbi Heschel puts it in *I Asked for Wonder*, "What we cannot comprehend by analysis we become aware of in awe." It legitimizes intuition, a process that Gerald May defines as "the state of apprehending that occurs *before* any thinking takes place." That definition explains why people who trust and act on their intuition often are a step ahead of the pack. Intuition is a valuable, often underrated means to comprehension and appreciation. When open adoption proponents speak of people who "get it" and people who do not, they are referring to their intuitive response to the fundamental concepts. Intuition can provide a valuable shortcut to understanding. Unfortunately, as an essentially preverbal process, intuition has obvious limits. When we pour intuitive insights into the constraining mold of words, those insights lose much of their power. Knowing about things has the sorry tendency of reducing them to less than they are.

A spirit of reverence is unusually comfortable with paradox and hospitable to what may appear as contradictory truths. It appreciates, for example, that there is strength through weakness, and that there is a significant relationship between pain and joy. It is in the domain of paradox that we will learn the most, and I am convinced that new discoveries lurk somewhere in the tension between apparently irreconcilable truths.

---

* *Albert Einstein. "What I Believe." Forum, October 1930.*

CHANCE OR PROVIDENCE?

Adoption is especially frightening when it feels accidental or random. It is difficult for an adoptee to gain a sense of personal dignity if the first chapter of his life has the imprint of chaos and chance. Is his life a matter of people coming together in haphazard fashion, or does it have a "meant to be" quality? When we reduce adoption to a roll of the dice for everyone involved, peace of mind is hard to find.

I have learned from my work that adoption is in many ways inexplicable, yet unaccidental. Most of the time, our standard processes work well and produce satisfying results. At times, however, things will not come together despite our best efforts. We may labor mightily to accomplish a plan that appears desirable and reasonable, but it may not happen. Although I yield with reluctance, these situations have taught me that the original plan was not meant to work because a different and better plan awaited the end of our stubbornness. On other occasions, things suddenly take shape out of a context of disorganization. Truthfully, the workings of adoption are beyond me, and I believe most experienced adoption workers will verify my impression that there is more to adoption than we are conscious of and able to explain.

What do we do with the inexplicable? Naturally, we continually do our best to understand, but on some level we realize full comprehension will forever elude us. Our limitations confront us, and it is clear that we need an extra dimension to our considerations. This is typically the moment when we must decide, as insightful and understandable psychiatrist Scott Peck says in *A World Waiting to Be Born,* whether "God belongs in the system or does not." I believe there is a providential quality to open adoption as I have witnessed it; I have seen astounding coincidences and have heard "This was meant to be" too often to think otherwise. This is not a variation of fatalism, nor is it grounds to forfeit professional responsibility. Everyone involved must fully apply themselves and take personal responsibility for their actions, but I am convinced we do well to develop our spiritual senses so we can be receptive to the leading of the Spirit. There is a strange comfort in all this. Two thousand years ago, the Apostle Paul told us that "all things work together for good to them that love God."* A few hundred years ago, Protestant theologian and reformer John Calvin observed, "If you pay attention, you will easily perceive that ignorance of providence is the ultimate of all miseries; the highest blessedness lies in the knowledge of it."

An important aspect of spirituality is the search for meaning. It is variously expressed as a quest for wholeness, integration, togetherness, unity, connection, peace, or contentment. Two things stand out about this search. First of all, it is invariably understood in integrative terms. It is the nature of spirituality to seek harmony. Against a several-decade backdrop of adoption dedicated to separating people as thoroughly and as permanently as possible, a spiritual perspective clearly has much to teach us. It is the nature of spirituality to search restlessly for more meaningful ways to bring people together. Second, the search is active. As Scott Peck says in *Further Along the Road Less Traveled*, "To really seek the truth, one cannot carve out a safe niche and hole up in it. One must blunder out there into the unknown, the mysterious." There are limits to the seeking—ultimately, we must be found—but the effort is indispensable and to our credit.

SELF-SERVING OR SACRIFICIAL?

Adoption can easily be a selfish matter. There is, after all, only so much deprivation, emptiness, and desperation that a person can put up with. It is hardly surprising to see participants barreling down the road of self-interest, and it is easy to understand the ease with which they build a case to justify their actions.

Self-interest is such a dominant aspect of life that it is tempting to consider it the only motivational factor of consequence. Certainly, self-interest is a useful and necessary, but it cannot be the entire story. If adoption does not rise above self-interest, it teeters on the edge of exploitation—people using each other, sometimes subtly and other times blatantly. The premise of spiritually tuned adoption is that people long to be part of something bigger, better, and more excellent than self-interest. The challenge is to invite and call participants to make this choice, and it is a rare privilege to watch this spirit overtake them.

---

* *Romans 8:28* (King James Version).

Spirituality seeks consistency between the process and the outcome, the how and what of adoption. It provides direction regarding the way adoption should be accomplished and what it should lead to. Hopefully, both the how and the what will be characterized by grace and beauty. Again, from *The Spiritual Life*, Evelyn Underhill provides wisdom:

> That choice, cause, or action which is least tainted by self-interest, which makes for the increase of happiness, health, beauty and peace, which cleanses and harmonizes life, must always be in accordance with the will of the Spirit that is drawing life towards perfection.

Adoption happens best when it is "least tainted by self interest." It happens best when it is rises above the "what's in it for me" currents of our culture. Our hearts know this is true. We know that our contentment largely depends on our ability to interact respectfully with others. That is the attraction and potential of relational power. In *A World Split Apart*, Russian author and dissident Alexander Solzhenitsyn calls us beyond narrow and self-protective thinking and invites us to extend ourselves with trust:

> A society based on the letter of the law and never reaching any higher fails to take advantage of the full range of human possibilities. The letter of the law is too cold and formal to have a beneficial influence on society. Whenever the tissue of life is woven of legalistic relationships, this creates an atmosphere of spiritual mediocrity that paralyzes men's noblest impulses.

The opposite of selfishness is sacrifice, an act of self-denial and courage that we prefer to avoid. We enjoy prescribing it for others but doubt that it holds much potential for ourselves. We have much to learn from Episcopal priest Alan Jones, who puts the importance of sacrifice in bold terms in *Exploring Spiritual Direction:* "Human life is meaningless without some sort of sacrifice at its heart." He goes on to describe it as a creative force that is nurturing and transforming. Sacrifice makes our values and beliefs costly; it makes them real and credible. Because of the cost, sacrifice commands respect.

SELF-DEPENDENCE OR SURRENDER?

There are times when we reach our limits. There are times when nothing is clear and times when things are clear but subverted and unavailable. We do our best to act responsibly and address the peculiarities of which we are a part, but we know that solutions are well beyond our sphere of influence. Eventually, we are confronted with our helplessness. When that happens, the choices are limited; either we enter the futility of personal competence more fully, or we surrender to the necessity of faith.

Spiritual growth, or "soul making," as Alan Jones puts it in his book of that title, "requires a move away from the need and desire to control to a waiting on the mystery at the heart of things." This is consistent with the move from knowing to appreciating. To grow spiritually, we must let go of control. Surrender is an act of trust; and although our pride resists the possibility with phenomenal vigor, it is seldom the tragedy we predict. In fact, there is tremendous relief in surrendering the illusion of competence, independence, and perfection; and there is joy in rejoining the ranks of mere mortals.

Surrender is healing. It not only liberates us from the tyranny of competence, it also moves us into a gratifying style of life. In *Leadership Is an Art*, Max DePree speaks of the "living edge." This edge is found in the act of risk, in the acceptance of uncertainty, and in the activating of faith. In this state of being, we are fully alive to ourselves and to those around us. Perhaps the most powerful version of surrender is forgiveness. As we release our impulse to avenge injury and hurt, we discover peace of mind and heart.

DESPERATION OR HOPE?

Many people approach adoption impatiently. Nothing else has worked, and adoption is the card they have kept up their sleeve. When the time comes to play it, they expect results, and they expect them quickly. If things do not promptly fall into place the way they imagined, desperation makes an early appearance. Desperate people are seldom at their best; they are unpredictable and prone to flawed judgment.

The ultimate remedy for desperation is hope. James Krouze and Barry Posner, authorities on leadership in the business world, provide an especially clear description of hope in their book, *Credibility:*

> Hope is an attitude in action. It enables people to mobilize their healing and their achieving powers. It helps them to transcend the difficulties of today and envision the potentialities of tomorrow. Hope enables people to find the will and the way to aspire to greatness. Hope is testimony to the power of the human spirit.

The great beauty of hope is its ability to sustain us and keep us hanging in there.

In *How Can It Be All Right When Everything Is All Wrong,* Ethicist Lewis Smedes suggests that hope is a matter of desire, belief, and doubt. The fervor of the hope is correlated to the depth of the desire. Something of importance merits greater hope than something minor. There is no prospect for hope without some basis to believe that the hope can be realized. Interestingly, doubt is also a necessary dimension of hope. There is no need to hope for things that are certain; hope emerges as compensation for the anguish of doubt.

Hope is well-regarded, but it has a darker side. It can distract and lead to the squandering of unmeasurable resources. When hope is detached from all that appears reasonable, it is either miraculous or destructive. The mischief of hope is that it sustains the pursuit of both the absurd and the sublime. For some, false hope leads to devastation; but for others, false hope is better than none at all. Hope is a friend to turn to with some caution.

Spiritual people are never desperate; they are expectant. They wait expectantly for the moment of consummation. They are keenly aware of the current state of imperfection and wholeheartedly long for a better day. That is not to say, of course, that the present moment is lost on them—that is hardly the case—but it is their nature to look forward to a day of correction, integration, and completion. They have the strange and wonderful calm of the confidently hopeful.

CAN *GRATITUDE* BE REDEEMED?

One of the most tragic aspects of the last generation of adoption practice is the way it has poisoned the dynamic of gratitude.

In the adoption community, *gratitude* is a word that makes people cringe, as it brings to mind the specter of the "grateful adoptee." We know the script well. Spared, in a harrowing close call of destiny, the woeful fate of life with a hopelessly inadequate birthfamily, and fortuitously inserted into a proper and thriving family environment, the adoptee was surely compelled to respond with heartfelt gratitude. The preferred expression of this gratitude was perfect behavior and unfaltering allegiance to the rescuing parents.

Adding to the sadness of the gratitude theme as practiced in adoption over the decades is the fact that a large portion of the healthy gratitude generated by the experience is intercepted. In closed adoptions, babies do not come from birthfamilies. Babies come from agencies, and workers gladly bask in the excited gratitude of adoptive parents. Because the closed system erases the birthfamily from the equation, they are not around to receive anyone's respect or appreciation. It is an unfortunate interception because the reception of the gratitude they deserve might accelerate their healing and bolster their standing in the institution.

So we are reminded that gratitude, ordinarily well-reputed, is subject to grotesque distortion. When gratitude is mishandled, it generates great resentment. This is true in the nonadopted world also, but the mishandling has been especially damaging for members of the adoption triad. For many of them, the word *gratitude* is so saturated with pain that it cannot be salvaged; nevertheless, I believe gratitude has so much potential that we must do our best to reclaim it.

In *Life of the Beloved*, Henri Nouwen reminds us that gratitude is a matter of choice: "Where there is reason for gratitude there can always be found a reason for bitterness. It is here that we are faced with the freedom to make a decision. We can decide to be grateful or bitter." This is an important observation. We need to appreciate that the choice is often surprisingly difficult, but we must encourage the choice of healthy gratitude because it makes an extraordinary difference.

We usually paint gratitude with the broad brush of familiarity. We think we have a solid grasp of the idea and give it little thought. We are mistaken. Gratitude is far more powerful and complex than we realize. Clearly, there are significant variations on the theme, and it is helpful to distinguish between them. At least three distinct types of gratitude can be identified: *perfunctory, obligating,* and *profound.*

Perfunctory gratitude is a matter of etiquette and civility. It is the most common form of gratitude and is in the usual range of reasonable expectations. Sincere or not, it is regarded as a good habit. Occasionally, an expression of perfunctory gratitude rings with unusual sincerity. When that happens, we are apt to notice and enjoy it. Although perfunctory gratitude is a helpful aspect of everyday interaction, it tends to dull our sensitivity to the potential of gratitude.

The notion of *obligating gratitude* is actually an oxymoron. Genuine gratitude does not obligate; it liberates. At heart, gratitude is a matter of personal volition; it only exists if it is voluntary. When "gratitude" is somehow compelled, we observe something that superficially resembles gratitude—most likely acquiescence or compliance—but we do not witness true thankfulness. Forced gratitude fails much in the fashion of a bouquet of flowers sent because the wife demanded them.

It is hard to imagine words that destroy joy more quickly than "you should be grateful." Once the words are issued, the prospect of genuine gratitude evaporates. The words actually mean "You have failed to acknowledge all that you have been given, and, as a result, it is clear that you are an inferior person." It is a controlling message that urges acquiescence. It manipulates behavior much like the strategic mentioning of a prospective inheritance, although in the case of obligating gratitude, the leverage is a legacy from the past rather than a prospect for the future. The "should be grateful" message creates an inescapable indebtedness. This indebtedness is the antithesis of gratitude, and, if it is pushed, eventually it requires a choice. Either one capitulates and offers the gratitude tarnished by obligation, or one rejects the gift and all the strings attached. It is an unhappy choice that is painfully familiar to too many adoptees.

Profound gratitude is the opposite of obligating gratitude. It is so powerful and amazing that it approaches the mystical. It is alluring, yet many of us resist it because it requires humility and courage. There is no gratitude without the admission of dependence on another for the gift, and this admission is often a painful blow to our conceit. In *The Listening Heart,* Brother David Steindl-Rast, a priest who has written extensively and exquisitely about gratitude, muses, "Is not gratitude a passage from proud isolation to a humble give and take, from enslavement to false independence to self-acceptance in that dependence which liberates?" Gratitude requires courage. In *Gratefulness: The Heart of Prayer,* Steindl-Rast observes, "No one can say 'Thank you' for a gift and mean it without trust in the giver; and to trust always takes courage." In Chapter 7, we described commitment as a mechanism that enables us to shift from unilateral power, which manipulates, to relational power, which welcomes the influence of others. In pointing out that gratitude requires the courage of dependency, Steindl-Rast is describing another way to make this rewarding transition.

The fruits of profound gratitude are incomparable; they are nothing less than the fullness of life. Profound gratitude generates acceptance; belonging; wholeness; a "spiral of joy," as Steindl-Rast puts it in *The Listening Heart;* and a spirit of generosity. These aspects of gratitude merit some consideration.

Acceptance is a most challenging concept. It is a lifelong project and perhaps is an ideal that is ultimately out of reach. Even so, most of us aspire to acceptance. Each person's journey to acceptance begins with a measure of respect and appreciation for himself. Next, it recognizes that each person is the product of his or her experiences. If she thinks well of herself, she must accept the totality of her experiences, even those that were terribly painful, because they were formative. In this manner, acceptance can defend us from dwelling on the past and from endless speculations on what might have been.

Speaking of the limitations of hindsight, Robert Grudin supplies a major assault on the foolishness of "could have been" thinking in *Time and the Art of Living:*

> After an event, we normally know at most what has happened; not what *might* have happened, had one or more of its innumerable circumstances been altered. What we "understand," in other words, is the result of a single configuration of variables, rather than the sum of what those variable were capable of producing. And we understand each circumstance only in the sense in which, conjoined with others, it produced the happening, rather than in terms of its full potentialities. Moreover, deluged in details, we miss the nobler and simpler view of forms and purposes

we had when looking into the future. Finally, the fact that retrospective analysis, as opposed to prior strategies and predictions, hold little danger (they need only be plausible) often renders us more careless and self-indulgent in making them.

If we make the choice for gratitude, we will not be stuck in time, and we will not be forever looking over our shoulders.

Profound gratitude produces a sense of belonging. In Steindl-Rast's words in *Gratefulness: The Heart of Prayer,* "One who says 'Thank you' to another really says 'We belong together.' Giver and thanksgiver belong together." He goes on to wonder, "Does our society suffer from so much alienation because we find it difficult to cultivate gratitude?"

Gratitude can lead to wholeness. In an inspired passage in *The Listening Heart,* Steindl-Rast states,

> The whole man is involved when he gives thanks from his heart.... The intellect recognizes the gift as gift; the will acknowledges my dependence; the emotions, like a sounding board, give fullness to the melody of this experience.... The intellect recognizes: yes, it is true, this joy is a free gift; the will acknowledges: yes, it is good to accept my dependence; the emotions resound in gratitude, celebrating the beauty of this experience. Thus, the grateful heart experiences in truth, goodness, and beauty the fullness of being, finds through gratitude its own fulfillment.

There is more. Profound gratitude produces a spirit of generosity. Gratitude flows naturally, perhaps inevitably, into generosity. Generosity is an attitude of great beauty. In *The Ways of the Spirit,* Evelyn Underhill puts it this way:

> There is nothing harsh, rigorous, or intense about the invitation to generosity. It puts us in line with all the noble aspects of creation: the generous output of sunshine, the uncalculated fertility of the earth, and the great life-giving mantle of air.... We are reminded that the attitude of clutching, however spiritual, is never Christian and that the attitude of giving is always religious because it is an imitation of God.

She stretches us even further with this observation:

Generosity means that longing to bring joy, peace, and salvation, not to the lovable, but to the unlovable, and at one's own cost. It is to bring all this to the people whose views and beliefs we dislike or whose conduct we disapprove. It is to bring it to those who are tiresome, embattled, selfish, degraded, and whose whole being seems twisted out of shape.

Profound gratitude sets into motion a pattern of interaction that Steindl-Rast, in *The Listening Heart*, calls a "spiral of joy." The gift of beauty naturally elicits a reaction of profound gratitude and generosity. The spontaneous gift of profound gratitude affirms the original giver and stirs a response of warmth and appreciation. The gift of warmth and appreciation prompts an echo of still greater trust, and the spiral is well-launched.

So we have caught at least a glimpse of the constructive potential of gratitude. It seems almost too good to be true, but it has the potential to fill our lives with great beauty. It also has the potential to relieve us from a trio of debilitating possibilities—fear, unwholesome indebtedness, and shame—which loom as woeful alternatives to gratitude.

We are often approached by birthparents from the closed era of adoption who ask us to contact the adoptive parents in the hope of finding out how things turned out. We have learned to approach the adoptive parents delicately, because they are predictably fearful. Many are gracious, but fear drives others to snarl with hostility. In a heart dominated by fear, there is no room for gratitude. Fortunately, the inverse is also true. A heart full of gratitude has little room for fear. Everything in adoption changes when adoptive parents view birthparents with gratitude instead of fear. Interestingly, those who give of themselves generously know much more about gratitude than those who are focused on receiving.

Everything also changes when profound gratitude replaces obligating gratitude. The atmosphere is lighter and more joyful. Adoptive parents often mention a feeling that resembles "survivor guilt." Like the soldier in the trenches spared an ugly death by the heroic covering of a grenade by a buddy, adoptive parents are sometimes haunted by the awesome sacrifice of the birthfamilies. It is a thoroughly unnerving experience to dramatically benefit at another's excruciating expense. They are bothered by their inability to balance the scales, and they feel trapped and drained by their impressions that they are forever beholden to their benefactors. They may try to somehow pay off their debts, but their efforts are futile.

This haunting guilt is a version of obligating gratitude. If not corrected, it breeds resentment. When beneficiaries become aware of their resentment, they feel even more guilt. As the Roman orator, historian, and politician Tacitus observed long ago, "Benefits are agreeable as long as we hope to be able to repay them. If they greatly exceed this point, gratitude is changed into hate."* The remedy to this distressing burden of indebtedness will not be found in efforts to diminish the magnificence of the gift or in efforts to reduce the gift to an exchange by offering substitutions; relief is only found in recognizing that the gift is an expression of grace, undeserved and unearned. When obligating gratitude is replaced by profound gratitude, the burden of indebtedness is lifted and a spirit of mutuality takes hold. Gratitude becomes spontaneous, heartfelt, and deeply pleasing.

Gratitude is also an important alternative to shame. Lewis Smedes captures this insight with these words from *Shame and Grace:*

> The feeling called joy is the ultimate alternative to the feeling of shame. Joy, not shame, is our destiny. We know, don't we, by a kind of intuition, what joy is. Is it not the ecstasy of gratitude? Not cheerfulness, not humor, not drugged highs, but plain and simple thankfulness, deeply felt, down to the bone: is this not what joy is?

The healthy choice is obviously gratitude, but it is not as simple as it seems. The challenge is to sustain the spirit of gratitude and generosity and make a lifestyle of it. In one of life's more interesting twists, we are more conscious of gratitude in hard times than in good. Often, the greatest threats to gratitude are the tiny aggravations that are part of everyday life. Nuisances have the power to derail the momentum of gratitude.

Adoptees benefit when birthfamilies and adoptive families are able to launch a joyful spiral of profound gratitude. In the process, though, we must be extremely careful not to place an expectation of gratitude on adoptees, or we will foul the prospect.

---

* *Cornelius Tacitus*, Annals, *4.18.*

Although we cannot demand it, there is a strong likelihood that, in an atmosphere of healthy gratitude, the adoptee will catch the spirit. It is a spirit better caught than taught.

THE ADOPTEE AS THE "GIFT"

So how about for the adoptee? All this discussion of gratitude is fine for adoptive parents, birthparents and others, but what does it mean if you are the gift? For the gift, there are no easy answers, but I believe there are some possibilities worth pondering.

Let's consider the gift. To begin with, what is the gift? One birthmother very astutely pointed out that she did not give her child as a gift to a family, she gave her child the gift of a loving family. It is a vital distinction. For some, the gift is a granting of trust, a rare and exquisite act. Trust is the gift of ourselves. In loving relationships, for example, we speak of giving ourselves over to the other. Even if we conclude that the child is given as a gift, is it not worth something to be greeted as a gift rather than endured as a bane? And aren't we all, adopted or not adopted, gifts to our families and to all who love us?

There is still more to consider. In *Life of the Beloved*, Henri Nouwen suggests, "Gratitude is the most fruitful way of deepening our consciousness that you are not an accident, but a divine choice." It is comforting to know that we fit into a larger plan. Perhaps the good news is that the gift is the gift—it doesn't owe anyone anything. The gift is not indebted.

The problem for adoptees is not so much in being a gift as in having been given. The having-been-given frustrates in two ways: It can feel like rejection, and it is an affront to self-determination. Each factor deserves consideration.

We cannot speak lightly of the pain associated with rejection. For many adoptees, it is primal and relentless. Perhaps, though, there is a measure of relief to be found in a careful understanding of gifts. We need to search our own gift-giving histories. When we give a gift to a loved friend, are we in any way rejecting the gift? I think we are inclined to reach a contrary conclusion. When we give a gift in love—a distinctly different action than the careless giving with which we are more familiar—we are, in fact, valuing the gift. Perhaps we have reached yet another important distinction, the difference between the gift given carelessly and the gift given carefully. If there is offense in all this, it is in the carelessness, not in the giving. There is reasonable hope that a gentle, caring adoption experience leads to a sense of belonging to a loving, extended open adoption clan. Belonging is the ultimate remedy to alienation and rejection.

The having-been-given is an affront to self-determination. In America, self-determination approaches religious importance. For many people, it is the ultimate value and is not subject to debate. Adoption, which drastically redirects the adoptee's life circumstances without his assent, stands in stark and unsettling contrast to our belief that each person has a right to determine his or her own life course.

I believe an important part of every adoptee's journey involves finding some peace of mind related to the issue of self-determination. It is interesting to hear the report of adoptees who have searched and reconnected to their birthfamilies. Many of them discover something they did not expect—they discover that they are finally willing to fully accept their adoptive families. Perhaps adoption is only complete when adoptees reclaim themselves and then willingly give themselves as renewed gifts to all who have sacrificially given to them. When birthparents, adoptive parents, and adoptees all taste the sweetness of shared profound gratitude, they will know the rich, joyous potential of adoption.

Chapter 17

The Spirit of Open Adoption

> All who are guided by the Spirit of God are sons [and daughters] of God: for what you received was not the spirit of slavery to bring you back into fear; you have received the spirit of adoption...
>
> Romans 8:14–15 *(New Jerusalem Bible)*

The spirit of adoption is succinctly and beautifully captured in this stunning Scripture, which employs adoption as a metaphor for faith and its rewards. Those who are spiritually attuned, we are instructed, receive a great blessing—nothing less than the "spirit of adoption." As we consider the quotation, we quickly encounter the highly significant word *receive*. Clearly, the spirit of adoption cannot be seized, purchased, or earned. Like most of life's sweetest fruits, it is only available to us as a gift. If we are to fully experience this sustaining spirit, we have no choice but to open ourselves to it with humility and gratitude. We must acknowledge our limits and say, "Yes" to the gift.

It is fascinating to see that the spirit of adoption is contrasted to slavery, a practice that represents so much that is destructive to the human spirit—domination, degradation, and humiliation. The ugliness of slavery is rooted in its abysmal premise that one human can possess another as property. This depersonalizing notion is shameful by any standard of basic decency. So we discover that the spirit of adoption is not a spirit of ownership, possessiveness, or exploitation. It is not a spirit of shame.

The Scripture explicitly adds another important contrast: The spirit of adoption is not grounded in fear; it can never be reduced to a narrow focus on keeping one's psyche safe. Since all adoption journeys begin with pronounced feelings of fear, this observation confronts and profoundly challenges every participant. For the nurturing spirit of adoption to take hold, clearly participants must face and overcome this aboriginal fear. This is axiomatic, because unresolved fear invariably constricts, divides, and hides. It is forlornly aloof, quick to judge, and defensive. In the grip of fear, we cower and retreat rather than embrace with heart and soul each moment and the people in it. As long as this interior fear dominates and persists, we can be sure there is ample room for growth in our lives.

If the spirit of adoption is not possessive, shameful, selfish, or fearful, what is it? The Scripture suggests that the spirit of adoption is a deep and unshakable sense of belonging. There is an extraordinary difference between feeling owned and feeling that one belongs. In the case of ownership, one is valued for one's usefulness in meeting the needs of others. When the dynamic is that of belonging, one is valued for his or her very being. Each circumstance features unequivocal claiming, but in the case of belonging the claiming is reciprocal. People who belong to each other are comfortably interdependent; they are "in it together." They feel a pronounced sense of feeling at home, of fitting in, of being settled. This connectedness is not a simple matter of sameness. Homogeneity often produces comfort, but it does not guarantee any persevering depth of care. Nor is it in any way a matter of worthiness; one does not achieve belonging. Rather, this state of being is a consequence of intentional, wholehearted, abiding investment and commitment. To belong, then, is to feel that all that I am—my past, present, and future; my quirks, dreams, capabilities and eccentricities; my wild and independent spirit—is fully acceptable and accepted.

Belonging is wondrously unconditional, enduring, and certain. When we know that we belong, we do not hold back. Belonging generates a healthy presumptiveness—not that of presuming too much too soon, but the reasonable and deep confidence that the bonds of our relationships will endure. Emboldened by the security of belonging, we can relate to "our people" with candor and intimacy. As insiders, we can relax and function without pretense. In a simple, exuberant way, we feel the freedom to be ourselves.

The great task confronting birthparents and adoptive parents as they fashion a loving adoption is to create an environment in which the adopted person feels fully at home and at peace with the arrangement. Belonging is not an automatic outcome; it cannot be assumed or imposed. It requires sacrifice, vulnerability, and extraordinary emotional labor. The prospect of belonging begins with the birthfamily's careful selection of a highly compatible adoptive family and that family's decision to reciprocate the trust. This tender relationship sinks its roots into the promising soil of authentic commitment, is nourished by forthright communication, and is maintained by an attitude of endless engagement.

Although we are usually unconscious of our sense of belonging, it occasionally enters our awareness, and we recognize it as an encompassing blessing. And in our best moments, we are generous with this warmth and extend it to others who enter our lives. South African Archbishop Desmond Tutu describes this state of being with great warmth and beauty:

> We Africans speak about a concept difficult to render in English. We speak of *ubuntu* or *botho*. You know when it is there, and it is obvious when it is absent. It has to do with what it means to be truly human, it refers to gentleness, to compassion, to hospitality, to openness to others, to vulnerability, to be available for others, and to know that you are bound up with them in the bundle of life, for a person is only a person through other persons.

Yes, that is it. When all is well, when we know where and how we fit in, we are bound up with each other in the bundle of life.

Once we understand that the spirit of adoption is a matter of belonging, of *ubuntu*, we discover one more important contrast: The spirit of adoption is not apologetic. To the contrary, it is sturdy, confident, and profoundly grateful. It knows well the pain of separation and is humble in the face of that anguish. It knows the vulnerability of belonging and is courageous in coming to terms with those risks. But, thankfully, it also knows the deep joy of genuine belonging that is only available to those who face the pain. It knows the deep joy on the other side of suffering.

But what of the spirit of *open* adoption? How does this little qualifying word affect the course of adoption? It is a difficult word to address, but mostly it speaks to two factors: scope and style. The spirit of open adoption dramatically expands the range of participation. Averting the narrowing temptations of possessive love, it significantly extends the notion of household to incorporate and honor all who love the youngster. In this fashion, it obliterates the we-they thinking that has tormented adoption for decades. *They* becomes *us;* the unknown ominous *other* becomes a supportive member of the clan.

The inclusionary spirit of open adoption completely alters the psychology of the experience. The prior undercurrent of insecurity is transformed into a pleasing sense of solidarity. In the place of wariness, the spirit of open adoption celebrates the wonder of birthfamilies and adoptive families who are joined as kindred spirits in service to children. It is, in essence, a welcoming spirit of respect and invitation.

Since the variations on the open adoption theme are endless, it is nearly impossible to succinctly describe its style. The difficulty of this task brings to mind an observation of writer Annie Dillard:

> The spirit seems to roll along like the mythical hoop snake with its tail in its mouth. There are no hands to shake or edges to untie. It rolls along the mountain ridges like a fireball, shooting off a spray of sparks at random, and will not be trapped, slowed, grasped, fetched, peeled, or aimed.

A few variables, however, beginning with Randolph Severson's "courage, compassion, and common sense" (as cited in Chapter 1) are conspicuous and foundational. In addition to those basic elements, it is clear that open adoption features creativity, candor, and community. Let's look at these factors.

- **Courage.** There is no way around the fact that participation in open adoption requires courage. It is required to face the fear that is woven into the fabric of the experience, and it is necessary if we are to find the strength to sacrifice personal comfort.

- **Common sense.** Although open adoption seems exotic to some observers, those who take a longer look will discover that it is sensible and consistent with everyday ideas about effective living. There is great common sense in direct communication as well as in straightforward, cards-on-the-table problem solving.

- **Creativity.** Every open adoption is the unique creation of those who are involved in it. The vitality and promise of open adoption is its ability to adapt to circumstances that emerge over time.

- **Candor.** Open adoption wholeheartedly embraces candor. As a result, it is full of innocence, kindness, and transparency. This spirit can reasonably be likened to the guileless, inquisitive spirit of a child.

- **Community.** Open adoption does not sell participants short; it believes that well-prepared participants are fully capable of cooperation.

- **Compassion.** The ability to see things from the perspective of others is vital. Compassion is persistently optimistic, respectful, and affirming. It not only takes the time to understand others, it welcomes and values their input.

Because compassion is at the heart of open adoption, it merits more thorough consideration. Some forms of adoption do not promote concern for others. Dominated by fear, they are devoid of compassion. When adoption is considered a process of filling personal emptiness, when it is viewed as an adventure in procuring a desired good, when it is approached as an exercise in cleverness, it is self-serving and full of emotional hazard. The spirit of open adoption, on the other hand, is ultimately the spirit of love. In *The Wisdom of the Desert*, Thomas Merton—quite possibly the most important Christian commentator of the 20th century—comments on this spirit with rare beauty:

> Love means an interior and spiritual identification with one's brother, so he is not regarded as an "object" to "which" one "does good." The fact is that good done to another as an object is of little or no

spiritual value. Love takes one's neighbor as one's other self, and loves him with all the immense humility and discretion and reserve and reverence without which no one can presume to enter into the sanctuary of another's subjectivity. From such love...all exploitation, domineering and condescension must necessarily be absent.

From this perspective, we see clearly that the spirit of open adoption is a spirit of profound honor and deep compassion. We are humbled by the gentleness and respect that is required of us if we "presume to enter into the sanctuary of another's subjectivity." Open adoption comes alive when it is reframed from a process of getting to a process of giving. On these terms, it is a spirit of affirmation and transformation.

In *With Burning Hearts*, Henri Nouwen, with characteristic understanding for our insecurities, points out that the prospect of meaningfully relating to others, despite its instinctual appeal, is often a close call: "Our fear of being completely open and vulnerable is equal to our desire to know and be known." He is frustratingly correct. Even when our intellect clearly determines that the path of promise is that of cooperation, our hearts fill with fear and plead for protection. At the point most adoptive journeys begin, the decision to face the fear or capitulate to it is indeed a close call.

Our response to fear, so often ruled by the emotions, is seldom recognized as pivotal, but it is. Our response has nothing less than a watershed effect leading to wildly divergent end points. All adoptive journeys begin in the same terrifying region of uncertainty; but like rain failing near the Continental Divide, we feel the tug of our nature's gravity. Our faint, early leanings gain subtle momentum, and we trickle, meander, and flow inexorably toward our destination, ultimately joining and blending with the larger, deeper waters of either shame or honor.

For all its complexity, the experience of adoption can be reduced to this single dilemma: Shall we be driven by fear, or shall we put our confidence in love? Our hearts may tremble, but we know the answer. We know what is important, we know the kind of people we want to be, and we know how children deserve to be treated. The power of fear and possession must be defeated, because, as writer Madeleine L'Engle warns in *Walking on Water*, "The refusal to love is the only unbearable thing."

Bibliography

Mortimer Adler. *Six Great Ideas*. New York: McMillan, 1984.

Hannah Arendt. *The Human Condition*. Chicago: University of Chicago Press, 1958.

Suzanne Arms. *Adoption: A Handful of Hope*. Berkeley, CA: Celestial Arts, 1990.

Annette Baran and Reuben Pannor. *Lethal Secrets*. New York: Warner, 1989.

Robert Bellah, Richard Madsen, William Sullivan, Ann Swidler, and Steven Tipton. *Habits of the Heart*. New York: Perennial, 1986.

Warren Bennis and Burt Nanus. *Leaders: The Strategies for Taking Charge*. New York: Harper & Row, 1985.

Jeffrey Blustein. *Care and Commitment*. New York: Oxford University Press, 1991.

Sissela Bok. *Lying: Moral Choice in Public and Private Life*. New York: Vintage, 1978.

Sissela Bok. *Secrets*. New York: Pantheon, 1982.

Richard Bolles. *How to Find Your Mission in Life*. Berkely: Ten Speed Press, 1991.

Antoinette Bosco. *Finding Peace Through Pain*. New York: Ballantine, 1994.

John Bradshaw. *Healing the Shame That Binds You*. Deerfield Beach, FL: Health Communications, 1988.

Paul Brand and Philip Yancey. *Pain: The Gift Nobody Wants*. New York: HarperCollins, 1993.

David Brodzinsky, Marshall Schecter, and Robin Marantz Henig. *Being Adopted: The Lifelong Search for Self*. New York: Doubleday, 1992.

Frederick Buechner. *Wishful Thinking*. New York: HarperCollins, 1973.

Frederick Buechner. *Telling the Truth*. New York: HarperCollins, 1977.

Frederick Buechner. *Peculiar Treasures.* New York: HarperCollins, 1979.

Frederick Buechner. *A Clown in the Belfry.* New York: HarperCollins, 1992.

Barbara Burlingham-Brown. *Why Didn't She Keep Me?* South Bend, IN: Langford Books, 1994.

John Calvin. *The Institutes of the Christian Religion.* Philadelphia: Westminster Press, 1960.

Donald Capps. *The Depleted Self.* Minneapolis: Fortress Press, 1993.

Stephan Covey. *The Seven Habits of Highly Effective People.* New York: Fireside, 1990.

Stephen Covey. *Principle-Centered Leadership.* New York: Summit, 1991.

Stephen Covey. *First Things First.* New York: Simon & Schuster, 1994.

Stanley Davis. *Managing Corporate Culture.* Cambridge, MA: Ballinger Publishing, 1984.

Christopher De Vinck. *The Power of the Powerless.* New York: Image, 1988.

Max DePree. *Leadership Is an Art.* New York: Dell, 1989.

Max DePree. *Leadership Jazz.* New York: Currency, 1992.

Annie Dillard. *Pilgrim at Tinker Creek.* New York: Harper Perennial, 1988.

Michael K. Duffey. *Be Blessed in What You Do.* Mawhah NJ: Paulist Press, 1988.

Robert Durback (Ed.). *Seeds of Hope: A Henri Nouwen Reader.* New York: Bantam, 1989.

Jean Etter and John Chally. *Adoption Mediation Training Manual.* Eugene, OR: Adoption Mediation Seminars, 1988.

Amitai Etzioni. *The Spirit of Community.* New York: Touchstone, 1993.

Margaret Farley. *Personal Commitments.* New York: HarperCollins, 1986.

Merle Fossum and Marilyn Mason. *Facing Shame.* New York: WW. Norton & Company, 1986.

Mohandas K. Gandhi. *An Autobiography: The Story of My Experiments with Truth.* Boston: Beacon Press, 1993.

Carl Goldberg. *Understanding Shame.* Northvale, NJ: Jason Aronson Inc, 1991.

Robert Greenleaf. *Servant Leadership.* Mahwah, NJ: Paulist Press, 1991.

James Gritter (Ed.). *Adoption Without Fear.* San Antonio, TX: Corona, 1989.

Robert Grudin. *Time and the Art of Living.* New York: Ticknor & Fields, 1988.

Robert Grudin. *The Grace of Great Things.* New York: Ticknor & Fields, 1990.

Gay Hendricks and Kathlyn Hendricks. *Concious Loving: The Journey to Co-Commitment.* New York: Bantam Books, 1990.

Abraham Heschel. *Between God and Man.* New York: The Free Press, 1959.

Abraham Heschel. *I Asked for Wonder.* New York: Crossroad, 1993.

Susan Jeffers. *Feel the Fear and Do It Anyway.* New York: Fawcett Columbine, 1987.

Charles W. Joiner Jr. *Leadership for Change.* Cambridge, MA: Ballinger Publishing, 1987.

Alan Jones. *Exploring Spiritual Direction.* New York: HarperCollins: 1982.

Alan Jones. *Soul Making.* New York: Harper & Row, 1985.

Alan Jones. *Passion for Pilgrimage.* New York: HarperCollins, 1995.

Gershen Kaufman. *Shame: The Power of Caring.* Rochester, VT: Schenkman Books, 1980.

Gershen Kaufman. *The Psychology of Shame.* New York: Springer Publishing Company, 1989.

Thomas Kelly. *A Testament of Devotion.* New York: Harper Collins, 1992.

Sue Monk Kidd. *When the Heart Waits.* New York: HarperCollins, 1992.

David Kirk. *Shared Fate.* New York: The Free Press, 1964.

David Kirk. *Adoptive Kinship.* Toronto: Butterworths, 1981.

James M. Kouzes and Barry Posner. *The Leadership Challenge.* San Francisco: Jossey-Bass, 1987.

James M. Kouzes and Barry Posner. *Credibility.* San Francisco: Jossey-Bass, 1993.

Peter Kreeft. *Making Sense Out of Suffering.* Ann Arbor: Servant Books, 1986.

Peter Kreeft. *Making Choices.* Ann Arbor: Servant Books, 1990.

Jill Kremitz. *How It Feels To Be Adopted.* New York: Knopf, 1982.

Earnest Kurtz and Katherine Ketcham. *The Spirituality of Imperfection.* New York: Bantam, 1992.

Madeleine L'Engle. *A Circle of Quiet.* New York: HarperCollins, 1972.

Madeleine L'Engle. *The Irrational Season.* New York: HarperCollins, 1977.

Madeleine L'Engle. *Walking on Water.* Wheaton, Illinois: Harold Shaw Publishers, 1980.

Carol Land and Sharon Kaplan-Roszia. (Producers). *Open Adoption: The Experts Speak Out.* (1989). Video available from Parenting Resources, 250 El Camino Real, Suite 216, Tustin, CA 92680.

Denise Lang. *How to Stop Your Relatives from Driving You Crazy.* New York: Fireside, 1990.

Penelope Leach. *Children First.* New York: Knopf, 1994.

C.S. Lewis. *The Problem with Pain.* New York: Macmillan, 1962.

C. S. Lewis. *A Grief Observed.* New York: Bantam, 1976.

Hunter Lewis. *A Question of Values.* New York: HarperCollins, 1990.

Michael Lewis. *Shame: The Exposed Self.* New York, The Free Press, 1992.

Betty Jean Lifton. *Lost and Found.* New York: Perennial, 1988.

Betty Jean Lifton. *Journey of the Adopted Self.* New York: Basic Books, 1994.

Anne Morrow Lindberg. *A Gift from the Sea.* New York: Vintage, 1991.

Jeanne Lindsey. *Open Adoption: A Caring Option.* Buena Park, CA: Morning Glory Press, 1987.

Helen Merrill Lynd. *On Shame and the Search for Identity.* New York: Science Editions, 1961.

Michael Maccoby. *The Leader.* New York: Simon and Schuster, 1981.

Gerald May. *Will and Spirit.* San Francisco: Harper & Row, 1982.

Rollo May. *My Quest for Beauty.* Dallas: Saybrook, 1985.

Lois Melina. *Raising Adopted Children.* New York: Harper & Row, 1986.

Lois Melina. *Making Sense of Adoption.* New York: Harper & Row, 1989.

Lois Melina and Sharon Roszia-Kaplan. *The Open Adoption Experience.* New York: HarperCollins, 1993.

Thomas Merton. *The Seven Story Mountain.* Garden City, NY: Garden City Books, 1951.

Thomas Merton. *The Wisdom of the Desert.* New York: New Directions Books, 1960.

Thomas Merton. *Contemplation in a World of Action.* New York: Image Books, 1973.

Jane Middelton-Moz. *Shame and Guilt.* Deerfield Beach, FL: Health Communications, 1990.

Tom Morris. *True Success.* New York: Grosset/Putnam, 1994.

Andrew Morrison. *The Culture of Shame.* New York: Ballantine Books, 1996.

Wayne Muller. *Legacy of the Heart.* New York: Fireside, 1993.

Burt Nanus. *The Leader's Edge.* Chicago: Contemporary Books, 1989.

Donald Nathanson (Ed.). *The Many Faces of Shame.* New York: Guilford, 1987.

Donald Nathanson. *Shame and Pride.* New York: W.W. Norton & Company, 1992.

Michael Nichols. *No Place to Hide.* New York: Simon & Schuster, 1991.

Henri Nouwen. *Out of Solitude.* Notre Dame, IN: Ave Marie, 1974.

Henri Nouwen. *The Wounded Healer.* New York: Image, 1979.

Henri Nouwen. *Lifesigns.* New York: Doubleday, 1986.

Henri Nouwen. *Seeds of Hope: A Henri Nouwen Reader.* Robert Durback (Ed.). New York: Bantam, 1989.

Henri Nouwen. *In the Name of Jesus.* New York: Crossroad, 1991.

Henri Nouwen. *The Return of the Prodigal Son.* New York: Doubleday, 1992.

Henri Nouwen. *Life of the Beloved.* New York: Crossroad, 1993.

Henri Nouwen. *Here and Now.* New York: Crossroad, 1994.

Henri Nouwen. *Our Greatest Gift.* New York: HarperCollins, 1994.

Henri Nouwen. *With Burning Hearts.* Maryknoll, NY: Orbis Books, 1994.

M. Scott Peck. *The Road Less Traveled.* New York: Touchstone, 1978.

M. Scott Peck. *The Different Drum.* New York: Simon and Schuster, 1987.

M. Scott Peck. *Further Along the Road Less Traveled.* New York: Simon & Schuster, 1993.

M. Scott Peck. *A World Waiting to Be Born.* New York: Bantam, 1993.

Thomas Peters and Nancy Austin. *A Passion for Excellence.* New York: Warner Books, 1985.

Thomas Peters and Robert Waterman. *In Search of Excellence.* New York: Warner Books, 1982.

Ronald Potter-Efron and Patricia Potter-Efron. *Letting Go of Shame.* New York: Harper/Hazledon, 1989

Mary Jo Rillera and Sharon Kaplan-Roszia. *Cooperative Adoption.* Westminster, CA: Triadoption Publications, 1985.

Elinor Rosenberg. *The Adoption Life Cycle.* New York: The Free Press, 1992.

Carl Schneider. *Shame, Exposure, and Privacy.* New York: W.W. Norton & Company, 1977.

Peter Schwartz. *The Art of the Long View.* New York: Currency, 1991.

Peter Senge. *The Fifth Discipline.* New York: Currency, 1990.

Randolph Severson. *Adoption: Charms and Rituals for Healing.* Dallas: House of Tomorrow, 1991.

Randolph Severson. *A Letter to Parents on Open Adoption.* Dallas: House of Tomorrow, 1991.

Randolph Severson. *Adoption: Philosophy and Experience.* Dallas: House of Tomorrow, 1994

Randolph Severson. *Adoption and Spirituality.* Garland, TX: Aries Center, 1994.

Carolyn Shaffer and Kristen Anundsen. *Creating Community Anywhere.* New York: Tarcher/Perigee, 1993.

Kathleen Silber and Patricia Martinez Dorner. *The Children of Open Adoption.* San Antonio, TX: Corona, 1990.

Kathleen Silber and Phylis Speedlin. *Dear Birthmother.* San Antonio, TX: Corona, 1991.

Marsha Sinetar. *Elegant Choices, Healing Choices.* Mahwah, NJ: Paulist Press, 1988.

Gary Smalley and John Trent. *The Gift of Honor.* New York: Pocket Books, 1987.

Lewis Smedes. *How Can It Be All Right When Everything Is All Wrong?* New York: Harper & Row, 1982.

Lewis Smedes. *Forgive and Forget.* New York: Pocket Books, 1984.

Lewis Smedes. *Choices.* New York: Harper & Row, 1986.

Lewis Smedes. *Caring & Commitment.* New York: Harper & Row, 1989.

Lewis Smedes. *A Pretty Good Person.* New York: Harper & Row, 1990.

Lewis Smedes. *Shame and Grace.* New York: HarperCollins, 1993.

Alexander Solzhenitsyn. *A World Split Apart.* New York: Harper & Row, 1978.

Arthur D.Sororski, Annette Baran, and Reuben Pannor. *The Adoption Triangle.* Second Edition. San Antonio, TX: Corona, 1989.

David Steindl-Rast. *Gratefulness: The Heart of Prayer.* Ramsey, NJ: Paulist Press, 1984.

David Steindl-Rast. *The Listening Heart.* New York: Crossroad, 1994.

Judy Tatelbaum. *The Courage to Grieve: Creative Living, Recovery, and Growth Through Grief.* New York: Harper & Row, 1984.

Judy Tatelbaum. *You Don't Have to Suffer.* New York: Harper & Row, 1989.

Mother Theresa. *One Heart Full of Love.* Ann Arbor: Servant Books, 1984.

Mother Theresa. *Heart of Joy.* Ann Arbor: Sevant Books, 1987.

Paul Tournier. *Secrets.* Richmond, VA: John Knox Press, 1963.

Desmond Tutu. *The Rainbow People of God.* New York: Doubleday, 1994.

Evelyn Underhill. *The Spiritual Life.* Oxford: Oneworld, 1993.

Evelyn Underhill. *The Ways of the Spirit.* New York: Crossroad, 1993.

Carlos Valles. *The Art of Choosing.* New York: Image Books, 1989.

Carlos Valles. *Let Go of Fear.* New York: Triumph Books, 1991.

Jean Vanier. *Community and Growth.* Mahwah, NJ: Paulist Press, 1989.

Nancy Newton Verrier. *The Primal Wound.* Baltimore: Gateway Press, 1993.

David Viscott. *Risking.* New York: Pocket Books, 1977.

Dietrich and Alice Von Hildebrand. *The Art of Living.* Manchester NH: Sophia Institute Press, 1994.

Jim Wallis. *The Soul of Politics.* New York: The New Press, 1994.

Gale D. Webbe. *The Night and Nothing.* New York: Harper & Row, 1964.

Simone Weil. *Waiting for God.* New York: Putnam, 1951.

Charles Whitefield. *Boundaries and Relationships.* Deerfield Beach, FL: Health Communications, 1993.

Claude Whitmyer (Ed.). *In the Company of Others.* New York: Tarcher/Perigee Books, 1993.

Elie Wiesel. *From the Kingdom of Memory.* New York: Summit, 1990.

Viviana Zelizer. *Pricing the Priceless Child.* New York: Basic Books, 1985.

About the Author

James L. Gritter, M.S.W., is a child welfare supervisor and open adoption practitioner with Catholic Human Services, Inc., Traverse City, Michigan. He is the editor of *Adoption Without Fear* (San Antonio, TX: Corona, 1989). He and his wife live in Williamsburg, Michigan, with their three daughters.